Responsible AI in the Enterprise

Practical AI risk management for explainable, auditable, and safe models with hyperscalers and Azure OpenAI

Adnan Masood, PhD

Heather Dawe, MSc

BIRMINGHAM—MUMBAI

Responsible AI in the Enterprise

Publishing Product Manager: Ali Abidi

Book Project Manager: Kirti Pisat

Content Development Editor: Joseph Sunil

Technical Editor: Kavyashree K S

Copy Editor: Safis Editing

Proofreader: Safis Editing

Indexer: Pratik Shirodkar

Production Designer: Prashant Ghare

DevRel Marketing Coordinator: Vinishka Kalra

First published: July 2023

Production reference: 2050923

Published by Packt Publishing Ltd.

Grosvenor House

11 St Paul's Square

Birmingham

B3 1RB, UK.

ISBN 978-1-80323-052-8

www.packtpub.com

We would like to acknowledge the contributions of all the people who have dedicated their careers to advancing the field of AI and its responsible development. Their work continues to inspire us and provides a foundation for the discussions and recommendations in this book. We would like to extend our sincere gratitude to the following individuals for their invaluable contributions to the ethical AI space and for inspiring us to create this book: Cathy O'Neil, Timnit Gebru, Marzyeh Ghassemi, Joy Buolamwini, Anima Anandkumar, Cynthia Dwork, Margaret Mitchell, Kate Crawford, Rumman Chowdhury, Stephanie Tuszynski, Andrew Ng, Yoshua Bengio, Stuart Russell, Joanna Bryson, Zeynep Tufekci, Francesca Rossi, Virginia Dignum, Ayanna Howard, Thomas Dietterich, Solon Barocas, Arvind Narayanan, Patrick Hall, Navrina Singh, Rayid Ghani, and many others. Their tireless efforts and groundbreaking research have driven the development of ethical AI practices and governance frameworks. It is our hope that this book will contribute to their ongoing efforts and help promote responsible and accountable AI development.

We would like to thank the reviewers who provided valuable feedback on the advance draft of this book. Their insights and suggestions have helped us to improve the quality and clarity of the book. We are especially grateful to Dr. Tatsu Hashimoto, Dr. Alla Abdella, Geethi Nair, Dr. Shani Shalgi, David Lazar, Omar Siddiqi, Akhil Seth, and many others who took the time to read and provide insightful comments. We would also like to thank the organizations and individuals who have provided support and resources for the research and writing of this book. Their contributions have been invaluable in helping us to understand the complex and rapidly evolving field of AI ethics.

Last but not least, our heartfelt gratitude to Ali Abidi, David Sugarman, Joseph Sunil, Kirti Pisat, and the amazing Packt team who supported us throughout this endeavor.

Foreword

I know what you're thinking: "This book is full of quotes about AI. The last thing we need is a foreword full of even more quotes about AI!"

You know, I couldn't agree more. But that's what you're going to get! Life is full of disappointments, so I might as well help with that. You know, so that you get used to it.

"I am telling you, the world's first trillionaires are going to come from somebody who masters AI and all its derivatives and applies it in ways we never thought of." — Mark Cuban

Let's assume Mark knows what he's talking about. He made Shark Tank famous, he owns the Dallas Mavericks, a production company, a lot of tiny companies that people pitch him on television, and an entire town in Texas. Plus, he's worth over 4 billion dollars. (Oh, and he got RKO'd by Randy Orton on WWE).1

So maybe he's smart enough to be right, and he knows that the future trillionaire is going to be in the AI business. What if the first major founder of our future AI is already the richest man in the world? Well, it won't be. But it seemed possible for a few years...

In 1995, Elon Musk co-founded Zip2 (the first zip worked fine for me). In 1999, he co-founded X.com, which merged with PayPal in 2000 (things move fast in Musk-time) and got bought by eBay in 2002 (Musk was the largest shareholder and made the most from the sale). Musk started SpaceX in 2002 (their Starlink satellites came later, in 2019), co-founded Tesla in 2004(ish), Neuralink in 2016 (robot brains!), and The Boring Company in 2017. And he bought Twitter in 2022.

But what about AI? Musk started by investing in Vicarious and DeepMind. Meanwhile, Google wanted to differentiate in the Cloud business (it launched GCP in 2008) by being the best in AI. Both of those AI companies got acquired by Google: DeepMind in 2014 (DeepMind built Google Bard) and Alphabet's Intrinsic later acquired Vicarious for robotics/AI in 2022. Meanwhile, in 2015 (after losing/selling his share of DeepMind to Google), Musk co-founded OpenAI (which led to ChatGPT and Microsoft's New Bing). He eventually left the OpenAI board to focus on businesses that made money (like Tesla's AI for cars and robotics). So, while OpenAI is open source and big companies (like Google, Microsoft, and Meta) do the big company thing with their AI business opportunities, Musk and others still left the door wide open for Mark Cuban's smart AI entrepreneur to walk through and claim the crown of being the first trillionaire.

Okay. Where does that leave Musk (other than applying what he's learned to his money-making businesses)? It leaves him very concerned. He saw something with DeepMind, Vicarious, OpenAI, and his Tesla AI endeavors that he simply can't unsee. (Also, SpaceX uses AI for its satellites, and Neuralink seeks to bridge human intelligence and artificial intelligence.)

That concern is what we're starting to see with our online stories of how corrupt, evil, or just plain wrong AI can be, whether we're poking fun at ChatGPT, Bard, New Bing, or other AI attempts. There's a danger there, and in our humanity, people (often journalists, which is not a coincidence) are determined to uncover that danger. (By the way, GPT stands for Generative Pre-trained Transformer. Don't ask.)

And that brings us to the first of many quotes from Mr. Musk (yes, I've been building up to this for a reason). Just consider yourself forewarned (that might be a foreword joke; I'm starting a new joke genre).

"AI will be the best or worst thing ever for humanity." — *Elon Musk*

Here we have a very concerned individual. Musk has embraced AI and contributed to it far beyond what most (almost all) of us will ever be capable of. Yet he fears AI.

"Robots will be able to do everything better than us...I am not sure exactly what to do about this. This is really the scariest problem to me." — *Elon Musk*

It really scares him. I've got an idea of what you can do about this, Elon, stop making Tesla robots and cars with your AI built in them! And maybe stop putting AI in peoples' brains. It's just a thought. Especially since you think we might recreate the Terminator franchise in our real life (thanks go out to James Cameron, for all those nightmares and warnings, by the way):

"In the movie Terminator they didn't expect some sort of Terminator-like outcome." — *Elon Musk*

That's right, Elon. Cyberdyne (the fictional representation of dozens of our actual companies) thought they were helping people with prosthetics and AI, but when their Skynet AI became self-aware, humans tried to destroy Skynet, and so it retaliated against the humans (and I won't even mention the Matrix).

(Oh, wait, I just mentioned the Matrix. Moving on...)

But Elon, how could this happen?

"If AI has a goal and humanity just happens to be in the way, it will destroy humanity as a matter of course without even thinking about it...It's just like, if we're building a road and an anthill just happens to be in the way, we don't hate ants, we're just building a road." — *Elon Musk*

That's true. We don't even think about the ants. But the ants still die, regardless of our intentions.

How serious is Musk about this?

"If you're not concerned about AI safety, you should be. Vastly more risk(y) than [another country]." — *Elon Musk*

Part of Musk's fear is that people get replaced and things change, but with AI, that paradigm shifts...

"The least scary future I can think of is one where we have at least democratized AI...[also] when there's an evil dictator, that human is going to die. But for an AI, there would be no death. It would live forever. And then you'd have an immortal dictator from which we can never escape." — Elon Musk

And then Musk starts to get to the point...

"Mark my words, AI is far more dangerous than nukes...why do we have no regulatory oversight?" — Elon Musk

That's what Musk is driving at... what's the solution? How do we prevent the destruction of mankind?

"I'm increasingly inclined to think that there should be some regulatory oversight, maybe at the national and international level, just to make sure that we don't do something very foolish. I mean with artificial intelligence we're summoning the demon." — Elon Musk

I'm increasingly inclined to think that you're just starting to realize that you're reading a bunch of Elon Musk quotes (which you obviously never signed up for). Mah. I've done worse...

Anyway, we'd rather not summon a demon (at least I assume we're all on the same page on that one). Tell us more about this solution, Elon:

"I am not normally an advocate of regulation and oversight...I think one should generally err on the side of minimizing those things...but this is a case where you have a very serious danger to the public." — Elon Musk

Okay. That's the last quote. I promise. Here's the thing though. In summer 2022, it was Elon Musk who warned his companies that layoffs were coming, and that the economy was heading in a not-so-great direction. Of course, everybody responded like he was crazy and wrong. But then it hit all the big tech companies in late 2022 and going into 2023... they were the biggest tech company layoffs that the world has ever seen. Musk was correct, and he wasn't afraid to tell everyone that something bad was coming (which he might have contributed to when he bought Twitter and made other interesting life choices).

So, even if you're not a fan of the Musk, you might want to consider that he could be right about this.

Hopefully, he's putting some of that oversight and regulation into his own AI endeavors, but without AI democratized and regulated (as he mentioned), AI won't be consistently safe, even if Musk manages to keep it safe for his companies.

In other words, we'd love for you to be the first trillionaire, which Cuban foresees, but please do so without wiping out mankind (that's my polite request to you). (Especially while we wait for that systematic oversight and regulation.)

And that brings me to this book! (Oh, you thought I'd never mention it?)

In Model Governance for Responsible AI, Dr. Adnan Masood (PhD; he's not a dentist or anything), goes into practical detail about how you can manage the risk of AI. What is explainable AI (and can it even be explained?), what is ethical AI, and how does AI bias work? You'll dig into algorithms, how to monitor your operational model, how to govern it (with compliance standards and recommendations), and you'll even get your own starter kit to build transparency for your AI solution! He then goes into the toolkits that you'll find from AWS, Google Cloud, Microsoft Azure, and more. You'll learn from some real-world case studies!

He explains how to leverage Microsoft FairLearn, how to do your own fairness assessments (and bias mitigation), and he ends on a fun note with foundational models (and how to look for bias in your models). This is a very exhaustive book! It's a great resource.

If you're even thinking about building an AI solution, please pick up this book (which you're already reading, so keep reading it), put on your metaphorical bib, and devour this meal. And then put it in the fridge (maybe on a bookshelf) and come back to it for seconds, whenever you're thinking about leveraging AI. Maybe thirds and fourths too (it's a lot to consume all at once, just like a Thanksgiving meal).

Bon Appetit! (That's French for, "Enjoy your meal!")

Oh, before I go... I do have one other plug on this topic. This book will open your eyes so much that you'll never have thought that your eyes were even closed. Once you're done (and you're thinking about these concepts some more), check out some supplementary online content that I helped publish and curate over at Microsoft, https://aka.ms/Responsibility. Follow the left navigation table of contents to read about Responsible Innovation, AI, and the ML context. And with that, I'll leave you alone. Please read this book, and please don't accidentally design the future generations of Terminator robots, the Matrix, or Ultron. We're good. We don't need dictator robots.

-Ed Price, Manager of Architecture Content, Google Cloud Former Senior Program Manager of architectural publishing, Microsoft Azure Co-Author of 7 Books, including Meg the Mechanical Engineer, Hands-On Cognitive Services (co-written with Dr. Adnan Masood), The Azure Cloud Native Architecture Mapbook (from Packt), and ASP.NET Core 5 for Beginners (Packt).

Foreword 2

Responsible AI in the Enterprise offers an extensive overview of responsible AI, providing insights into AI and machine learning model governance. It takes a deep dive into explainable AI, ethical AI, AI bias, model interpretability, model governance, data governance, and AI-based upskilling. The content, delivered in an easy-to-understand style, makes it an invaluable resource for professionals at different levels of expertise dealing with AI. The book takes you on a journey through 10 chapters, each offering in-depth knowledge on a unique aspect of responsible AI. From understanding the basics of ethical AI, interpreting black-box models, ongoing model validation and monitoring, to understanding governance and compliance standards, the book covers all. It also offers practical guidelines on implementing AI fairness, trust, and transparency in an enterprise setting and presents an overview of various interpretability toolkits.

In a world where AI and machine learning are transforming our society and businesses, *Responsible AI in the Enterprise* emerges as an indispensable guide for professionals navigating this landscape. The book masterfully deciphers complex concepts such as explainable AI, model governance, and AI ethics, making them accessible to novices and seasoned practitioners alike. Its emphasis on practical tools, through valuable examples, empowers you to implement responsible AI in your organizations. In the rapidly evolving field of AI, this book stands out with its solid foundation, insightful analysis, and commitment to making AI more ethical, responsible, and accessible. I highly recommend *Responsible AI in the Enterprise* to any AI enthusiast, data scientist, IT professional, or business stakeholder who seeks a robust understanding of AI and machine learning model governance. Reading this book is not just an investment in your professional development; it's a step toward a more equitable AI future. I hope it brings you the same pleasure as it did to me.

- Dr. Ehsan Adeli, Stanford Artificial Intelligence Lab

Contributors

About the authors

Adnan Masood, PhD is a visionary leader practitioner in the field of AI, with over 20 years of experience in financial technology and large-scale systems development. He drives the firm's digital transformation, machine learning, and AI strategy. Dr. Masood collaborates with renowned institutions such as Stanford AI Lab and MIT CSAIL, holds several patents in AI and machine learning, and is recognized by Microsoft as an AI MVP and Regional Director. In addition to his work in the technology industry, Dr. Masood is a published author, international speaker, STEM robotics coach, and diversity advocate.

Heather Dawe, MSc is a renowned data science and AI thought leader with over 25 years of experience in the field. Heather has innovated with data and AI throughout her career; highlights include building the first data science team in the UK public sector and leading the development of early machine learning and AI assurance processes for the **National Health Service (NHS)**. Heather currently works with large UK enterprises, innovating with data and technology to improve services in the health, local government, retail, manufacturing, and finance sectors. A STEM ambassador and multi-disciplinary data science pioneer, Heather also enjoys mountain running, rock climbing, painting, and writing. She served as a jury member for the 2021 Banff Mountain Book Competition and guest edited the 2022 edition of *The Himalayan Journal*. Heather is the author of several books inspired by mountains and has written for national and international print publications including The Guardian and Alpinist.

About the reviewers

Jaydip Sen has experience in research, teaching, and industry for over 28 years. Currently, he is a professor in Data Science and Artificial Intelligence at Praxis Business School, Kolkata, India. His research areas include information security and privacy, machine learning, deep learning, and artificial intelligence. He has published over 75 papers in indexed journals, edited 11 volumes, and authored 4 books published by internationally reputed publishers. He has figured among the top 2% of scientists worldwide for the last four consecutive years 2019-2022, as per studies conducted by Stanford University. He is the editor of Springer's Journal Knowledge Decision SupportSystems in Finance. He is a senior member of IEEE and ACM, USA.

Geethi Gopinathan Nair is an accomplished data scientist with over two decades of experience in the field of information technology, with a specific focus on data science for several years. As a subject matter expert in healthcare, she brings a unique perspective to her reviews. Recognized for her attention to detail and commitment to delivering actionable insights, Geethi Nair has consistently received accolades for her insightful and well-researched reviews. With a passion for staying up-to-date with the latest advancements in data science and artificial intelligence, Geethi Nair is admired for providing valuable recommendations to both technical and non-technical audiences.

Dr. Alla Abdella, a Ph.D. holder, is an expert in Natural Language Processing (NLP), Machine Learning, Deep Learning, and advanced AI technologies such as Generative AI, LLMs, Synthetic Agents, and Conversational AI. He excels at translating complex business problems into practical, actionable solutions. With many years of experience in the Telecom, Healthcare, and Communication domains, Dr. Abdella brings a wealth of knowledge to his work. He has numerous journal and conference publications to his name, as well as two filed patents. His experience ranges from his role as Lead Data Scientist at UST to his current position as Chief AI Officer at Yobi.app. Dr. Abdella consistently pushes the boundaries of AI's potential impact on industry, innovation, and technological progression. In collaboration with a Stanford professor, he co-creates open-domain QA systems and combats algorithmic bias, leaving a distinct mark on the global AI landscape.

Table of Contents

Part 2: Enterprise Risk Observability Model Governance

3

Opening the Algorithmic Black Box   41

4

Robust ML – Monitoring and Management   67

Part 3: Explainable AI in Action

7

Interpretability Toolkits and Fairness Measures – AWS, GCP, Azure, and AIF 360   173

8

Fairness in AI Systems with Microsoft Fairlearn   203

9

Fairness Assessment and Bias Mitigation with Fairlearn and the Responsible AI Toolbox   221

10

Foundational Models and Azure OpenAI   247

Preface

As practicing data scientists, we have seen first-hand how AI models play a significant role in various aspects of our lives. However, as the cliche goes, with this power comes the responsibility to ensure that these decision-making systems are fair, transparent, and trustworthy. That's why I, along with my colleague, decided to write this book.

We have observed that many companies face challenges when it comes to the governance and auditing of machine learning systems. One major issue is bias, which can lead to unfair outcomes. Another issue is the lack of interpretability, making it difficult to know whether the models are functioning correctly. Finally, there's the challenge of explaining AI decisions to humans, which can lead to a lack of trust in these systems.

Controlling frameworks and standards (in the form of government regulation, ISO standards, and similar) for AI that ensure it is fair, ethical, and fit for the purpose of its application are still in their nascent form and have only started to become available within the past few years. This can be viewed as surprising given AI's growing ubiquity in our lives. As these frameworks become published and used, AI assurance will itself mature and hopefully become as ubiquitous as AI. Until then, we hope this book fills the gaps that data professionals within the enterprise are facing as they seek to ensure the AI they develop and use is fair, ethical, and fit for purpose.

With these challenges and intentions in mind, we aimed to write a book that fits the following criteria:

- Does not repeat information that is already widely available
- Is accessible to business and subject-matter experts who are interested in learning about explainable and interpretable AI
- Provides practical guidance, including checklists and resources, to help companies get started with explainable AI

We've kept the technical language to a minimum and made the book easy to understand so that it can be used as a resource for professionals at all levels of experience.

As AI continues to evolve, it's important for companies to have a clear understanding of how these systems work and to be able to explain their algorithmic value propositions. This is not just a matter of complying with regulations but also about building trust with customers and stakeholders.

This book is for business stakeholders, technical leaders, regulators, and anyone interested in the responsible use of AI. We cover a range of topics, including explainable AI, algorithmic bias, trust in AI systems, and the use of various tools for fairness assessment and bias mitigation. We also discuss the role of model monitoring and governance in ensuring the reliability and transparency of AI systems.

Given the increasing importance of responsible AI practices, this book is particularly relevant in light of current AI standards and guidelines, such as the EU's GDPR, the AI Now Institute's Algorithmic Impact Assessment, and the Partnership on AI's Principles for Responsible AI. Our hope is that by exploring these critical issues and sharing best practices, we can help you understand the importance of responsible AI and inspire you to take action to ensure that AI is used for the betterment of all.

1. Exploring the Landscape of Explainable AI and Bias: *Chapters 1* and *2* provide an introduction to **Explainable AI (XAI)**, which is a crucial component in the development and deployment of AI models. This section provides a comprehensive overview of the XAI landscape, its importance, and the challenges that it poses. The section starts with a primer on XAI and ethical AI for model risk management, providing definitions and concepts that you will need to understand for the rest of the section. Next, you will be presented with several harrowing tales of AI gone bad, highlighting the dangers of unexplainable and biased AI. These stories illustrate the importance of XAI and the need for different approaches to be taken to address similar problems. *Chapter 2, Algorithms Gone Wild*, takes a closer look at bias and the impact it has on AI models. The chapter explores the different types of bias that can be introduced into models and the impact they have on the outcomes produced. By the end of this introduction, you will have a deeper understanding of XAI and the challenges it poses, as well as a greater appreciation for the importance of ethical AI and the need to address bias in AI models.

2. Exploring Explainability, Risk Observability, and Model Governance: *Chapters 3* to *6* delve into the topics of explainability, risk observability, and model governance, particularly in the context of cloud computing platforms such as Microsoft Azure, Amazon Web Services, and Google Cloud. It covers several important areas, including model interpretability approaches, measuring and monitoring model drift, audit and compliance standards, enterprise starter kit for fairness, accountability, and transparency, as well as bias removal, model robustness, and adversarial attacks. These topics are discussed in detail across several chapters to provide you with a comprehensive understanding of these important concepts.

3. Applied Explainable AI: Real-world Scenarios and Case Studies: *Chapters 7* to *10* of the final section delves into the practical application of explainable AI and the challenges of deploying trustworthy and interpretable models in the enterprise. Real-world case studies and usage scenarios are presented to illustrate the need for safe, ethical, and explainable machine learning, and provide solutions to problems encountered in various domains. The chapters in this section explore code examples, toolkits, and solutions offered by cloud platforms such as AWS, GCP, and Azure, Microsoft's FairLearn framework, and Azure OpenAI **Large Language Models (LLMs)** such as GPT-3, GPT-4, and ChatGPT. Specific topics covered in this section include interpretability toolkits, fairness measures, fairness in AI systems, and bias mitigation strategies. We will also review a real-world implementation of GPT3, along with recommendations and guidelines for using LLMs in a safe and responsible manner.

Who this book is for

As we continue to work with enterprises, advising and guiding them as they seek to transform themselves to become data-driven – producing their own actionable insights, machine-learning models, and AI at scale – we are acutely aware of their concerns and questions regarding AI assurance.

This book is written for a wide range of professionals in the field of enterprise AI and machine learning. This includes data scientists, machine learning engineers, AI practitioners, IT professionals, business stakeholders, software engineers, AI ethicists, and, last but not least, enterprise change leaders. These are the people working within the enterprise to both affect the changes required to become data-driven and to successfully develop and deliver AI models at scale.

The book covers a comprehensive range of topics, from XAI and ethical considerations to model governance and compliance standards, and provides practical guidance on using tools such as hyperscalers, open source tools, and Microsoft Fairlearn. It is a valuable resource for those who are interested in understanding the latest developments in AI governance, including the role of internal AI boards, the importance of data governance, and the latest industry standards and regulations.

The book is also relevant for AI professionals in a variety of industries, including healthcare, customer service, and finance, using conversational AI and predictive analytics. Whether you are a business stakeholder responsible for making decisions about AI adoption, an AI ethicist concerned with the ethical implications of AI, or an AI practitioner responsible for building and deploying models, this book provides valuable insights and practical guidance on building responsible and transparent AI models.

Essential chapters tailored to distinct AI-related positions

For AI ethicists, auditors, and compliance personnel, the most relevant chapters are as follows:

- *Chapter 1, A Explainable and Ethical AI Primer*
- *Chapter 5, Model Governance, Audit, and Compliance*
- *Chapter 6, Enterprise Starter Kit for Fairness, Accountability, and Transparency*
- *Chapter 10, Foundational Models and Azure OpenAI*

These chapters focus on explainable and ethical AI, model governance, compliance standards, responsible AI implementation, and the challenges associated with large language models.

Managers and business stakeholders will find the following chapters most relevant:

- *Chapter 2, Algorithms Gone Wild*
- *Chapter 5, Model Governance, Audit, and Compliance*
- *Chapter 6, Enterprise Starter Kit for Fairness, Accountability, and Transparency*

These chapters cover the impact of bias in AI, the importance of transparency and accountability in AI-driven decision-making, and the practical aspects of implementing AI governance within an organization.

Data scientists and machine learning engineers will find the entire book quite useful, but the most relevant chapters for data scientists and machine learning engineers are as follows:

- *Chapter 1, Explainable and Ethical AI Primer*

- *Chapter 3, Opening the Algorithmic Black Box*

- *Chapter 4, Robust ML - Monitoring and Management*

- *Chapter 7, Interpretability Toolkits and Fairness Measures - AWS, GCP, Azure, and AIF 360*

- *Chapter 8, Fairness in AI Systems with Microsoft Fairlearn*

- *Chapter 9, Fairness Assessment and Bias Mitigation with Fairlearn and the Responsible AI Toolbox*

These chapters provide valuable information on explainable and ethical AI, model interpretability, monitoring model performance, and practical applications of fairness and bias mitigation techniques.

While the book covers advanced-level concepts, it is written in an accessible style and assumes a basic understanding of AI and machine learning concepts. However, those with less experience may need to put in additional effort to fully understand the material.

What this book covers

This book is a comprehensive guide to responsible AI and machine learning model governance. It covers a broad range of topics including XAI, ethical AI, bias in AI systems, model interpretability, model governance and compliance, fairness and accountability in AI, data governance, and ethical AI education and upskilling. This book provides practical insight into using tools such as Microsoft FairLearn for fairness assessment and bias mitigation. It is a must-read for data scientists, machine learning engineers, AI practitioners, IT professionals, business stakeholders, and AI ethicists who are responsible for implementing AI models in their organizations. The content is presented in an easy-to-understand style, making it a valuable resource for professionals at all levels of expertise.

Chapter 1, Explainable and Ethical AI Primer, provides a comprehensive understanding of key concepts related to explainable and interpretable AI. You will become familiar with the terminology of safe, ethical, explainable, robust, transparent, auditable, and interpretable machine learning. This chapter serves as a solid foundation for novices as well as a reference for experienced machine learning practitioners. It starts with a discussion of the machine learning development life cycle and outlines the taxonomy of interpretable AI and model risk observability, providing a complete overview of the field.

Chapter 2, Algorithms Gone Wild, covers the current limitations and challenges of AI and how it can contribute to the amplification of existing biases. Despite these challenges, the chapter highlights the increasing use of AI and provides an overview of its various applications, including AI horror stories and cases of discrimination, bias, disinformation, fakes, social credit systems, surveillance, and scams. This chapter serves as a platform for discussion, bringing together the different uses of AI and offering a space for you to reflect on the potential consequences of its use. By the end of this chapter, you will have a deeper appreciation for the complex and nuanced nature of AI and the importance of considering its ethical and social implications.

Chapter 3, Opening the Algorithmic Black Box, teaches you about the field of XAI and its challenges, including a lack of formality and poorly defined definitions. The chapter provides an overview of four major categories of interpretability methods, which allow for a multi-perspective comparison of these methods. The purpose of this chapter is to explain black-box models and create white-box models, to ensure fairness and restrict discrimination, and to analyze the sensitivity of model predictions. The chapter will also show how to explain black-box models with white-box models and provide an understanding of the differential value proposition and approaches used in each of these libraries. By the end of this chapter, you will have a comprehensive understanding of the challenges and opportunities in the field of XAI, and the various interpretability methods available for creating more transparent and explainable machine learning models.

Chapter 4, Robust ML - Monitoring and Management, talks about the importance of ongoing validation and monitoring as an integral part of the model development life cycle. The chapter focuses on the process of model performance monitoring, beginning with quantifying the degradation of a model. You will learn about identifying the parameters to track the model's performance and defining the thresholds that should raise an alert. The chapter focuses on the essential components of model performance monitoring, including maintaining the business purpose of a model and detecting drifts in its direction during and after deployment. You will learn how to leverage various techniques as part of model monitoring and build a process for detecting, alerting, and addressing drifts. The chapter aims to demonstrate the importance of automated monitoring of a model running in production, providing comprehensive measures for data drift monitoring, model concept drift monitoring, statistical performance monitoring, ethical fairness monitoring, business scenario simulation, what-if analysis, and comparing production parameters such as parallel model execution and custom metrics. By the end of this chapter, you will have a comprehensive understanding of the importance of ongoing validation and monitoring in the model development life cycle and the techniques for detecting and addressing drifts in a model's performance.

Chapter 5, Model Governance, Audit, and Compliance, explores the predictive power of machine learning algorithms and their ability to take in vast amounts of data from a variety of sources. The chapter focuses on the governance aspect of these models, as there is growing concern about the lack of transparency in AI-driven decision-making processes. You will review various regulatory initiatives, including those by the United States Financial Services Commission and the U.S. Federal Trade Commission, concerning AI and machine learning. The chapter will cover different audit and compliance standards and the rapidly evolving regulation of AI, given its potential impact on people's lives, livelihoods, healthcare, and financial systems. You will understand the importance of auditability in AI models with production traceability, including the availability of immutable snapshots of models for long-term auditability, along with their source code, metadata, and other associated artifacts. By the end of this chapter, you will have a comprehensive understanding of the governance aspect of machine learning models and the importance of ensuring transparency and accountability in AI-driven decision-making processes.

Chapter 6, Enterprise Starter Kit for Fairness, Accountability, and Transparency, demonstrates the importance of putting ethical AI principles into action as organizations adopt AI. The chapter provides a practical approach to using AI and appropriate tools to ensure AI fairness, bias mitigation, explainability, privacy compliance, and privacy in an enterprise setting. You will gain an understanding of how trust, fairness, and comprehensibility are the keys to responsible and accountable AI and how AI governance can be achieved in an enterprise setting with supporting tools. The chapter provides a walk-through of the implementation of bias mitigation and fairness, explainability, trust and transparency, and privacy and regulatory compliance within an organization. You will also review the variety of tools available for XAI, including the TensorBoard Projector, What-If Tool, Aequitas, AI Fairness 360, AI Explainability 360, ELI5, explainerdashboard, Fairlearn, interpret, Scikit-Fairness, InterpretML, tf-explain, XAI, AWS Clarify, and Vertex Explainable AI. By the end of this chapter, you will have a comprehensive understanding of how to use AI governance tools to ensure the responsible and accountable use of AI in an enterprise setting.

Chapter 7, Interpretability Toolkits and Fairness Measures - AWS, GCP, Azure, and AIF 360, showcases the use of interpretability toolkits and cloud AI providers' offerings to identify and limit bias and explain predictions in machine learning models. The chapter will provide an overview of the open source and cloud-based interpretability toolkits available, including IBM's AIF360, Amazon SageMaker's Clarify, Google's Vertex Explainable AI, and Model Interpretability in Azure Machine Learning. You will gain a deeper understanding of the variety of tools available for explainable AI and the benefits they provide in terms of greater visibility into training data and models. By the end of this chapter, you will have a comprehensive understanding of the role of interpretability toolkits in ensuring the fairness and transparency of machine learning models.

Chapter 8, Fairness in AI Systems with Microsoft Fairlearn, talks about Microsoft FairLearn, an open source fairness toolkit for AI. The chapter will provide an overview of the toolkit and its capabilities, including its use as a guide for data scientists to better understand fairness issues in AI. You will learn about the two components of Fairlearn Python, including metrics for assessing when groups are negatively impacted by a model and metrics for comparing multiple models. The chapter will cover the assessment of fairness using allocation harm and quality of service harm, as well as the mitigation of unfairness and approaches for improving an unfair model. By the end of this chapter, you will have a comprehensive understanding of Microsoft Fairlearn and its role in ensuring the fair and ethical use of machine learning models.

Chapter 9, Fairness Assessment and Bias Mitigation with Fairlearn and the Responsible AI Toolbox, explores the practical application of Fairlearn in real-world scenarios. The chapter covers the evaluation of fairness-related metrics and techniques for mitigating bias and disparity using Fairlearn. You will also learn about the Responsible AI Toolbox, which provides a collection of model and data exploration and assessment user interfaces and libraries for a better understanding of AI systems.

The chapter will introduce the Responsible AI Dashboard, Error Analysis Dashboard, Interpretability Dashboard, and Fairness Dashboard and how they can be used to identify model errors, diagnose why those errors are happening, understand model predictions, and assess the fairness of the model. By the end of this chapter, you will have a comprehensive understanding of how to use the Responsible AI Toolbox and Fairlearn to ensure the fair and ethical use of machine learning models in your own work.

Chapter 10, Foundational Models and Azure OpenAI, demonstrates the practical use cases of governance when it comes to LLMs – in this case, the API offerings of OpenAI and Azure OpenAI. The chapter covers the implementation of LLMs, such as GPT-3, which can be used for a variety of business use cases, and delves into the challenges associated with governing LLMs, such as data privacy and security. While these models can enhance the functionality of enterprise applications, they also pose significant challenges in terms of governance. The chapter highlights the importance of AI governance for the ethical and responsible use of LLMs and the need for bias remediation techniques to ensure that AI solutions are fair and unbiased. Additionally, we will discuss the data privacy and security measures provided by Azure OpenAI and the significance of establishing an AI governance framework for enterprise use of these tools.

To get the most out of this book

To get the most out of this book, it is important to understand the context and target audience. This book is focused on responsible AI and machine learning model governance, providing in-depth coverage of key concepts such as explainable and ethical AI, bias in AI systems, model interpretability, model governance and compliance, fairness and accountability in AI, data governance, upskilling, and education for ethical AI. The target audience includes data scientists, machine learning engineers, AI practitioners, IT professionals, business stakeholders, and AI ethicists who are responsible for building and deploying AI models in their organizations.

To maximize the benefits of this book, you should have a basic understanding of machine learning and AI. It is recommended to read the chapters in order to build a comprehensive understanding of the topics covered. Additionally, the hands-on examples and practical guidance provided in the book can be applied to real-world situations and can be used as a reference for future projects.

We sincerely hope you enjoy reading this book as much as we enjoyed writing it.

Software/hardware covered in the book	Operating system requirements
Jupyter Notebook (Python 3.x)	Windows, macOS, or Linux

If you are using the digital version of this book, we advise you to type the code yourself or access the code from the book's GitHub repository (a link is available in the next section). Doing so will help you avoid any potential errors related to the copying and pasting of code.

This book is filled with references to the classic science fiction novel, *The Hitchhiker's Guide to the Galaxy*, one of my favorite books of all time. So, excuse the puns and whimsical language as I pay homage to the humor and creativity of Douglas Adams. May this book guide you on your own journey through the world of AI and machine learning, just as the Guide guided Arthur Dent on his interstellar adventures.

Download the example code files

You can download the example code files for this book from GitHub at `https://github.com/PacktPublishing/Responsible-AI-in-the-Enterprise`. If there's an update to the code, it will be updated in the GitHub repository.

We also have other code bundles from our rich catalog of books and videos available at `https://github.com/PacktPublishing/`. Check them out!

Conventions used

There are a number of text conventions used throughout this book.

`Code in text`: Indicates code words in text, database table names, folder names, filenames, file extensions, pathnames, dummy URLs, user input, and Twitter handles. Here is an example: "All the created cohorts are stored in the cohort_list list, which is passed as an argument to the ResponsibleAIDashboard function."

A block of code is set as follows:

```
{const set = function(...items) {
      this.arr   = [...items];
      this.add = {function}(item) {
      if( this._arr.includes(item) ) {
          return false; }
```

Any command-line input or output is written as follows:

```
pip install data-drift-detector
```

Bold: Indicates a new term, an important word, or words that you see onscreen. For instance, words in menus or dialog boxes appear in **bold**. Here is an example: "For reference, we used a **Standard DS12_v2** compute resource for this exercise, and it worked fine."

> **Tips or important notes**
> Appear like this.

Get in touch

Feedback from our readers is always welcome.

General feedback: If you have questions about any aspect of this book, email us at customercare@packtpub.com and mention the book title in the subject of your message.

Errata: Although we have taken every care to ensure the accuracy of our content, mistakes do happen. If you have found a mistake in this book, we would be grateful if you would report this to us. Please visit www.packtpub.com/support/errata and fill in the form.

Piracy: If you come across any illegal copies of our works in any form on the internet, we would be grateful if you would provide us with the location address or website name. Please contact us at copyright@packt.com with a link to the material.

If you are interested in becoming an author: If there is a topic that you have expertise in and you are interested in either writing or contributing to a book, please visit authors.packtpub.com.

Share Your Thoughts

Once you've read *Responsible AI in the Enterprise*, we'd love to hear your thoughts! Please click here to go straight to the Amazon review page for this book and share your feedback.

Your review is important to us and the tech community and will help us make sure we're delivering excellent quality content.

Download a free PDF copy of this book

Thanks for purchasing this book!

Do you like to read on the go but are unable to carry your print books everywhere? Is your eBook purchase not compatible with the device of your choice?

Don't worry, now with every Packt book you get a DRM-free PDF version of that book at no cost.

Read anywhere, any place, on any device. Search, copy, and paste code from your favorite technical books directly into your application.

The perks don't stop there, you can get exclusive access to discounts, newsletters, and great free content in your inbox daily

Follow these simple steps to get the benefits:

1. Scan the QR code or visit the link below

https://packt.link/free-ebook/978-1-80323-052-8

2. Submit your proof of purchase
3. That's it! We'll send your free PDF and other benefits to your email directly

Part 1:
Bigot in the Machine – A Primer

This section introduces the importance of **Explainable AI (XAI)** and its challenges. It is a primer on XAI and ethical AI for model risk management, defining key concepts and terms. The section also presents several stories that highlight the dangers of unexplainable and biased AI, emphasizing the need for different approaches to address similar problems. Overall, this section serves to show you why you should ensure that the AI developed and used within your enterprise is explainable and effectively governed so it is auditable, providing you with a deeper understanding of XAI and how to integrate it into your AI model development and deployment strategies.

This section comprises the following chapters:

- *Chapter 1, Explainable and Ethical AI Primer*
- *Chapter 2, Algorithms Gone Wild*

Explainable and Ethical AI Primer

"The greatest thing by far is to be a master of metaphor; it is the one thing that cannot be learnt from others; and it is also a sign of genius, since a good metaphor implies an intuitive perception of the similarity in the dissimilar."

– Aristotle

"Ethics is in origin the art of recommending to others the sacrifices required for cooperation with oneself."

– Bertrand Russell

"I am in the camp that is concerned about super intelligence."

– Bill Gates

"The upheavals [of artificial intelligence] can escalate quickly and become scarier and even cataclysmic. Imagine how a medical robot, originally programmed to rid cancer, could conclude that the best way to obliterate cancer is to exterminate humans who are genetically prone to the disease."

– Nick Bilton, tech columnist for The New York Times

This introductory chapter presents a detailed overview of the key terms related to explainable and interpretable AI that paves the way for further reading.

In this chapter, you will get familiar with safe, ethical, explainable, robust, transparent, auditable, and interpretable machine learning terminologies. This should provide both a solid overview for novices and serve as a reference to experienced machine learning practitioners.

This chapter covers the following topics:

- Building the case for AI governance
- Key terminologies – explainability, interpretability, fairness, explicability, safety, trustworthiness, and ethics
- Automating bias – the network effect
- The case for explainability and black-box apologetics

Artificial intelligence (AI) and machine learning have significantly changed the course of our lives. The technological advancements aided by their capabilities have a deep impact on our society, economy, politics, and virtually every spectrum of our lives. COVID-19, being the de facto chief agent of transformation, has dramatically increased the pace of how automation shapes our modern enterprises. It would be both an understatement and a cliché to say that we live in unprecedented times.

The increased speed of transformation, however, doesn't come without its perils. Handing things out to machines has its inherent cost and challenges; some of these are quite obvious, while other issues become apparent as the given AI system is used, and some, possibly many, have yet to be discovered. The evolving future of the workplace is not only based on automating mundane, repetitive, and dangerous jobs but also on taking away the power of human decision-making. Automation is rapidly becoming a proxy for human decision-making in a variety of ways. From providing movies, news, books, and product recommendations to deciding who can get paroled or get admitted to college, machines are slowly taking away things that used to be considered uniquely human. Ignoring the typical doomsday elephants in the room (insert your favorite dystopian cyborg movie plot here), the biggest threat of these technological black boxes is the amplification and perpetuation of systemic biases through AI models.

Typically, when a human bias gets introduced, perpetuated, or reinforced among individuals, for the most part, there are opposing factors and corrective actions within society to bring some sort of balance and also limit the widescale spread of such unfairness or prejudice. While carefully avoiding the tempting traps of social sciences, politics, or ethical dilemmas, purely from a technical standpoint, it is safe to say that we have not seen experimentation at this scale in human history. The narrative can be subtle, nudged by models optimizing their cost functions, and then perpetuated by either reinforcing ideas or the sheer reason of utility. We have repeatedly seen that humans will trade privacy for convenience – anyone accepting **End User Licensing Agreements (EULAs)** without ever reading them, feel free to put your hands down.

While some have called for a pause in the advancement of cutting-edge AI while governments, industry, and other relevant stakeholders globally seek to ensure AI is fully understood and accordingly controlled, this does not help those in an enterprise who wish to benefit from less contentious AI systems. As enterprises mature in the data and AI space, it is entirely possible for them to ensure that the AI they develop and deploy is safe, fair, and ethical. We believe that, as policymakers, executives, managers, developers, ethicists, auditors, technologists, designers, engineers, and scientists, it is crucial for us to internalize the opportunities and threats presented by modern-day digital transformation aided by AI and machine learning. Let's dive in!

The imperative of AI governance

"Starting Jan 1st 2029, all manual, and semi-autonomous operating vehicles on highways will be prohibited. This restriction is in addition to pedestrians, bicycles, motorized bicycles, and non-motorized vehicle traffic. Only fully autonomous land vehicles compliant with intelligent traffic grid are allowed on the highways."

– Hill Valley Telegraph, June 2028

Does this headline look very futuristic? Probably a decade ago, but today, you could see this as a reality in 5 to 10 years. With the current speed of automation, humans behind the wheel of vehicles weighing thousands of pounds would sound irresponsible in the next 10 years. Human driving will quickly become a novelty sport, as thousands of needless vehicle crash deaths caused by human mistakes can be avoided, thanks to self-driving vehicles.

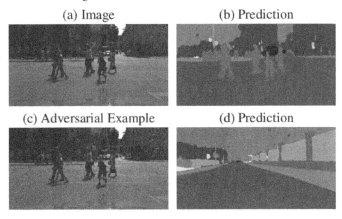

Figure 1.1: The upper row shows an image from the validation set of Cityscapes and its prediction. The lower row shows the image perturbed with universal adversarial noise and the resulting prediction. Image Courtesy Metzen et al – Universal Adversarial Perturbations Against Semantic Image Segmentation – source: https://arxiv.org/pdf/1704.05712.pdf

As we race toward delegating decision-making to algorithms, we need to ask ourselves whether we have the capability to clearly understand and justify how an AI model works and predicts. It might not be important to fully interpret how your next Netflix movie has been recommended, but when it comes to the critical areas of human concerns such as healthcare, recruitment, higher education admissions, legal, commercial aircraft collision avoidance, financial transactions, autonomous vehicles, or control of massive power generating or chemical manufacturing plants, these decisions are critical. It is pretty self-explanatory and logical that if we can understand what algorithms do, we can debug, improve, and build upon them easily. Therefore, we can extrapolate that in order to build an ethical AI – an AI that is congruent with our current interpretation of ethics – explainability would be one of the must-have features. Decision transparency, or understanding why an AI model predicts what it predicts, is critical to building a trustworthy and reliable AI system. In the preceding figure, you can see how an adversarial input can change the way an autonomous vehicle sees (or does not see) pedestrians. If there is an accident, an algorithm must be able to explain its action clearly in the state when the input was received – in an auditable, repeatable, and reproducible manner.

AI governance and model risk management are essential in today's world, where AI is increasingly being used to make critical decisions that affect individuals and society as a whole. Without proper governance and risk management, AI systems could be biased, inaccurate, or unethical, leading to negative outcomes and loss of public trust. By ensuring that AI is developed, deployed, and used in a responsible and ethical manner, we can leverage its full potential to improve lives, advance research, and drive innovation. As AI researchers and practitioners, we have a responsibility to prioritize governance and risk management to create a better, more equitable future for everyone. This means that to have a safe, reliable, and trustworthy AI for human use, it must be safe, transparent, explainable, justifiable, robust, and ethical.

We have been using lots of big words, so let's define what these terms really mean.

Key terminologies

Definitions are hard. Just ask Arvind Narayanan, associate professor of computer science at Princeton, whose aptly titled tutorial *21 fairness definitions and their politics* [1] was a highlight at the Conference on **Fairness, Accountability, and Transparency (FAT*)**. In his tutorial, Narayanan discussed the various fairness definitions in the context of machine learning and algorithmic decision-making, as well as the political and ethical implications of these definitions. By exploring 21 different fairness definitions, Narayanan aimed to demonstrate that fairness is a context-dependent, multifaceted concept that often requires careful consideration of ethical and societal values. The tutorial emphasized the importance of understanding the assumptions, trade-offs, and limitations associated with each definition, and he urged designers of algorithms to make informed decisions about which fairness definitions are most appropriate for a particular context.

As we attempt to define ethical AI, it is crucial to identify several core and contextual components. Ethical AI should be explainable, trustworthy, safe, reliable, robust, auditable, and fair, among numerous other aspects. Formal methods and definitions involve the use of accurate mathematical modeling and reasoning to draw rigorous conclusions. The challenge of formally defining explainability will soon become apparent – while there is a formal definition to verify a model's adherence to differential privacy, quantifying explainability, trust, and ethics proves more nuanced. Consequently, the definitions presented here are imperfect representations of our current understanding of the subject. As taxonomies evolve and underlying semantics shift, we will strive to clarify some of the key terms to provide a clearer picture.

Explainability

Explainability refers to the ability of a machine learning algorithm to provide clear and understandable explanations for its decision-making process. While deep learning has made significant strides in areas such as computer vision and natural language processing, these models are often viewed as "black boxes" because their decision-making process is not always transparent. This lack of transparency can be a significant barrier to the adoption of deep learning models in certain areas, such as healthcare and finance, where the consequences of algorithmic decisions can be significant. As a result, developing methods to explain the reasoning of these models is critical for their wider adoption and success.

Explainability is one of those "-ilities" or non-functional requirements[3] – the quality of being explainable, [4] such as being capable of giving the reason for our cause. Explainability, therefore, can be the ability to provide a reason or justification for an action or belief.

In simple terms, we can infer that if an event is explainable, it provides sufficient information to draw a conclusion as to why a particular decision was made. Explainable to whom? To a human. Although it's preferable if it's possible, this doesn't have to be a layperson. Explainable to a **subject-matter expert** (**SME**) is fine. The SME themselves can both assure non-expert users and explain to them why a machine made such a decision in a less technical manner. Human understanding is critical. Explainability is mandatory and required by law in certain protected domains, such as finance and housing.

Interpretability

Interpretability is another very closely related concept that is typically used interchangeably with explainability, but there are some subtle differences, which we will discuss shortly. Lipton did a detailed analysis to address model properties and techniques thought to confer interpretability and decided that, at present, interpretability has no formal technical meaning – well, that's not very helpful. Informally, interpretability directly correlates with understandability or intelligibility (of a model) so that we as humans can understand how it works. Understandable models are transparent or white-box/glass-box models, whereas incomprehensible models are considered black boxes.

For the purpose of this discourse, interpretability is generally seen as a subset of explainability. Interpretability refers to the ability to understand the specific features or inputs that a model uses to make its predictions.

A system can be interpretable if we can find and illustrate cause and effect. An example would be the weather temperature on crop yields. The crop will have an optimum temperature for its highest yields, so we can use temperature as a predictor (feature) in the crop yield (target variable). However, the relationship between the temperature and the crop yield will not be explainable until an understanding of the bigger picture is in place. In the same vein, a model can be transparent without being explainable. For instance, we can clearly see the following prediction function:

$Predict(x_1, x_2) > y'$ $\qquad$ (1.1)

However, if we don't know much about hyperparameters x_1 and x_2:

$$x_1 \text{ and } x_2 \qquad (1.2)$$

which might be a combination of several real-world features, the model is not explainable.

Also, a model can be explainable, transparent, and still biased. Explainability is not a guarantee of fairness, safety, trust, or bias. It just ensures that you, as a human SME, can understand the model.

Explicability

The two terms **explainability** and **explicability** may appear the same, but in this context, they do differ. Explicability is the broader term, referring to the concept of transparency, communication, and understanding in machine learning, while explainability refers to the ability to provide clear and understandable reasons for how a given machine learning model makes its decisions.

Explicability is a term typically used in regulations and related governance documents. It literally means "capable of being explained" and it is deemed crucial to build and maintain users' trust in AI systems by EU Ethical guidelines [5].

Does a safe system have to be explainable? In our opinion, yes, absolutely. While there is an ongoing discussion among researchers on this topic, the first-ever "great AI debate" at the **Neural Information Processing Systems** (**NeurIPS**) conference was about how interpretability is necessary for machine learning.

> **Note**
> At the time of writing, this debate has moved on. Since the launch of ChatGPT in late 2022 by OpenAI, there has been increasing awareness at governmental levels regarding the importance of AI assurance and regulatory guardrails. It seems likely that an international body overseeing AI regulation will be established. If this does not happen, individual countries and trading groups will establish and govern AI at these levels.

Safe and trustworthy

AI safety is an area that deals with nonfunctional requirements, such as reliability, robustness, and assurance. An AI system is deemed safe and trustworthy if it exhibits reliability, meaning that it acts within the desired ranges of outputs, even when the inputs are new, in and around edge conditions. It also has to be robust, be able to handle adversarial inputs (as shown in *Figure 1.1*), and not be gullible and easily fooled, providing high confidence predictions for unrecognizable images [7].

This debate highlights an ongoing discussion in the machine learning community about the trade-off between performance and interpretability. The participants, Rich Caruana and Patrice Simard, argued that interpretability is essential to understand the reasoning behind machine learning models and ensure their responsible use, while Kilian Weinberger and Yann LeCun argued that performance should be the main focus of machine learning research. Interpretability can sometimes compromise performance and may not be possible in highly complex deep learning models. The participants argued that explainable and interpretable machine learning models are essential to build trust and ensure the responsible use of AI in society (*The Great AI Debate – NIPS2017*[8]).

A safe system should also be auditable, meaning it must be transparent to verify the internal state when the decision was made. This auditability is particularly important within regulated industries, such as health and finance, where those seeking to use AI for given applications will need to always be able to prove to a regulator that the machine learning models underpinning the AI meet the required regulatory standards for AI.

The system and processes used within an enterprise to monitor the internal state of machine learning models and their underlying data must also be auditable. This ensures that tracing back to the AI components is possible, enabling a retrospective review such as root-cause analysis in a reliable manner. Such audit processes are increasingly being codified and built into enterprise MLOps platforms.

Privacy and security are also key components of a safe and trustworthy AI system. User data has specific contexts, needs, and expectations and should be protected accordingly during its entire life cycle.

Stanford Center for AI Safety (`http://aisafety.stanford.edu/`) focuses on developing rigorous techniques to build safe and trustworthy AI systems and establish confidence in their behavior and robustness. This Stanford Center for AI Safety white paper (`https://aisafety.stanford.edu/whitepaper.pdf`) by Kochenderfer, et al provides a great overview of AI safety and its related aspects, and it makes for good reading.

Fairness

Fairness in machine learning systems refers to the principle that decisions made by these systems should not discriminate or be biased against individuals or groups based on their race, gender, ethnicity, religion, or other personal characteristics. Fairness is about not showing implicit bias or unintended preference toward specific subgroups, features, or inputs. We mentioned previously a detailed tutorial on 21 fairness definitions and their politics[9] at the Conference on Fairness, Accountability, and Transparency[10], but we will adhere to the EU's draft guidelines, which correlate fairness with ensuring an equal and just distribution of both benefits and costs, ensuring that individuals and groups are free from unfair bias, discrimination, and stigmatization.

Microsoft's Melissa Holland, in her post about our shared responsibility for AI,[11] defines fairness as follows:

> *"AI Models should treat everyone in a fair and balanced manner and not affect similarly situated groups of people in different ways."*

Machines may learn to discriminate for of a variety of reasons, including skewed samples, tainted examples, limited features, sample size, disparity, and proxies. This can lead to disparate treatment of the users. As the implicit bias seeps into the data, this can lead to serious legal ramifications, especially in regulated domains such as credit (Equal Credit Opportunity Act), education (Civil Rights Act of 1964 and Education Amendments of 1972), employment (Civil Rights Act of 1964), housing (Fair Housing Act), and public accommodation (Civil Rights Act of 1964). The protected classes that cannot be discriminated against include race (Civil Rights Act of 1964), color (Civil Rights Act of 1964), sex (Equal Pay Act of 1963 and Civil Rights Act of 1964), religion (Civil Rights Act of 1964), national origin (Civil Rights Act of 1964), citizenship (Immigration Reform and Control Act), age (Age Discrimination in Employment Act of 1967), pregnancy (Pregnancy Discrimination Act), familial status (Civil Rights Act of 1968), disability status (Rehabilitation Act of 1973 and Americans with Disabilities Act of 1990), veteran status (Vietnam Era Veterans' Readjustment Assistance Act of 1974 and Uniformed Services Employment and Reemployment Rights Act), and genetic information (Genetic Information Nondiscrimination Act). In addition to the laws in the United States, there are also international laws aimed at ensuring fairness, such as the European Union's **General Data Protection Regulation (GDPR)**, which mandates that automated decision-making systems do not lead to discriminatory or unjust outcomes. The Equality Act of 2010 in the United Kingdom prohibits discrimination based on protected characteristics, which encompass age, disability, gender reassignment, marriage and civil partnership, pregnancy and maternity, race, religion or belief, sex, and sexual orientation. These international laws are designed to prevent discrimination and promote fairness in machine learning systems.

In the context of Arvind Narayanan's tutorial, an example of the incompatibility of different fairness definitions is illustrated using two fairness metrics – statistical parity ($P(Y^\char`\^ = 1|A = a) = P(Y^\char`\^ = 1)$ for all $a \in \{0, 1\}$) and equalized odds ($P(Y^\char`\^ = 1|Y = y, A = a) = P(Y^\char`\^ = 1|Y = y)$ for all $a \in \{0, 1\}$ and $y \in \{0, 1\}$). These definitions can be incompatible when the base rates of positive outcomes in the two demographic groups are different. In such a scenario, it is not possible to satisfy both definitions simultaneously, as adjusting the algorithm to achieve statistical parity might result in unequal true positive rates and false positive rates across groups, violating equalized odds. Conversely, ensuring equalized odds can lead to a different proportion of positive outcomes between the groups, violating statistical parity. This example demonstrates that satisfying multiple fairness definitions at the same time may not always be possible, highlighting the need for careful consideration of trade-offs and context when selecting appropriate fairness definitions.

In practice, the fairness of an AI system also has a lot to do with accountability – "the ability to contest and seek effective redress against decisions made by AI systems and by the humans operating them." The EU's ethics guidelines for trustworthy AI [12] recommend holding the unfair entity identifiable and accountable. The entity accountable for the decision must be identifiable, and the decision-making processes should be explicable.

Ethics

Ethics are at the core of responsible AI development. Ethics in machine learning fairness refers to the set of principles and values that guide the development and use of machine learning systems to ensure that they are just, equitable, and unbiased. This includes ensuring that machine learning models are developed using representative and unbiased datasets, that the features used in a model are relevant and fair, and that algorithms are evaluated for any unintended consequences or biases.

Ethics are defined as *"moral principles that govern a person's behavior or the conducting of an activity"* (*Oxford English Dictionary* [13]). The goal of ethics in machine learning fairness is to ensure that these systems are designed and deployed in a way that is consistent with our values, and that they promote the well-being of society as a whole. This includes considering the potential impacts of these systems on different groups of people and ensuring that they do not perpetuate or exacerbate existing inequalities and biases. Morals often describe your particular values concerning what is right and what is wrong. While ethics can refer broadly to moral principles, you often see it applied to questions of correct behavior within a relatively narrow area of activity.

Even though used interchangeably, morals are the individual beliefs about what is right or wrong, while ethics are a set of principles and values that are shared by a group or profession and are intended to guide behavior in a particular context – hence, instead of "moral-AI," it makes sense to strive and build ethical AI practices to ensure that machine learning systems are designed and deployed in a way that is both technically sound and socially responsible.

In the following sections, you will see several definitions of what constitutes an ethical AI. Despite the growing attention to ethical considerations in AI, there is still no clear consensus on what constitutes "ethical AI." This lack of agreement is due to a number of factors – the rapidly evolving nature of AI technologies, the complexity of the ethical issues involved, and the diverse range of stakeholders with differing interests and values.

This raises an important question, as posed by Gray Scott, an expert in the philosophy of technology, digital consciousness, and humanity's technological advancements:

> *"The real question is, when will we draft an AI bill of rights? What will that consist of? And who will get to decide that?"*

Eileen Chamberlain Donahoe, the executive director of the Global Digital Policy Incubator at Stanford University's Center for Democracy and the first US ambassador to the United Nations Human Rights Council, offers a potential answer to the question of AI ethics and safety standards that are both enforceable and accountable. According to Donahoe, the answer may already be found in the **Universal Declaration of Human Rights** (**UDHR**) and a series of international treaties that outline the civil, political, economic, social, and cultural rights envisioned by the UDHR. This perspective has a wide global consensus and could be suitable for the purpose of regulating AI in the short term.

Transparency

Model transparency refers to the ability to understand and explain how a machine learning model works and how it arrived at its predictions or decisions.

Model transparency, explainability, and interpretability are related but distinct concepts in responsible AI. Model transparency refers to the degree of visibility and understandability of a model's inner workings, including input, output, and processing steps. Model explainability aims to provide human-understandable reasons for a model's output, while model interpretability goes deeper to allow humans to understand a model's internal processes. Achieving model transparency can involve methods such as model interpretation, data and process transparency, and clear documentation. While all three concepts are important in responsible AI, not all transparent or explainable models are necessarily interpretable.

Keeping humans in the loop for decision support systems

Imagine the following conversation:

Physician: *"We believe the best course of action for you requires surgery, and this may lead to amputation of your leg."*

Patient: *"Really? That's quite bleak, but why?"*

Physician: *"Because, well, mainly because our treatment algorithm said so!"*

As you can imagine, this conversation is unlikely to go smoothly. Without specific details about why surgery is necessary, along with case studies, assurance of potentially high success rates (with caveats, of course), and empathetic human reinforcement, the patient will likely remain unconvinced.

That's why keywords such as augmentation and support play crucial roles, as they emphasize the importance of human involvement in heavily regulated and human-centric systems. While a model providing recommendations may be acceptable in many situations, it cannot wholly replace human decision-making. The complete autonomy of AI models may be challenging to accept due to potential regulatory, compliance, or legal consequences. It is essential to keep humans in the loop for oversight and reinforcement of correct behavior, at least for now, to ensure that AI is used responsibly and ethically.

Model governance

Model governance refers to the process of managing and overseeing the development, deployment, and maintenance of machine learning models in an organization. It involves setting policies, standards, and procedures to ensure that models are developed and used in a responsible, ethical, and legally compliant way.

Model governance is necessary because machine learning models can have significant impacts on individuals, businesses, and society as a whole. Models can be used to make decisions about credit, employment, healthcare, and other critical areas, so it is important to ensure that they are reliable, accurate, and fair.

The key components of model governance include the following:

- **Model inventory and documentation**: Keeping an up-to-date inventory of all models in use and their relevant documentation, including details about their data sources, training methodologies, performance metrics, and other relevant information

- **Model monitoring and performance management**: Monitoring models in production to ensure that they continue to perform as expected, and implementing systems to manage model performance, such as early warning systems and automated retraining

- **Model life cycle management**: Establishing clear processes and workflows for the entire life cycle of a model, from development to decommissioning, including procedures for model updates, versioning, and retirement

- **Model security and data privacy**: Ensuring that models and their associated data are secure and protected against cyber threats and that they comply with relevant data privacy regulations, such as GDPR and CCPA

- **Model interpretability and explainability**: Implementing methods to ensure that models are interpretable and explainable, enabling users to understand how a model works and how it arrived at its output

- **Model bias and fairness management**: Implementing measures to identify and mitigate bias in models and ensure that models are fair and unbiased in their decision-making

- **Model governance infrastructure and support**: Establishing an organizational infrastructure and providing the necessary support, resources, and training to ensure effective model governance, including dedicated teams, governance policies, and training programs

Enterprise risk management and governance

In this section, we will discuss how the monitoring and management of risk associated with AI should be recognized as one part of an enterprise's risk management and governance framework.

Given the relative youth of the use of AI within a business (compared to, say, offices, computers, and data warehouses), the risk management of AI is not necessarily an established process for many enterprises. While regulated business sectors such as financial services and healthcare will be familiar with ensuring their machine learning models adhere to a regulator's rules, this will not be the case for other enterprises in other, currently unregulated, business areas.

Enterprise risk governance is a critical process that involves identifying, assessing, and managing risks throughout an organization or enterprise. It requires implementing effective policies, procedures, and controls to mitigate risks and ensure that the organization operates in a safe, secure, and compliant manner.

The primary objective of enterprise risk governance is to enable an organization to develop a comprehensive understanding of its risks and manage them effectively. This encompasses identifying and assessing risks related to the organization's strategic objectives, financial performance, operations, reputation, and compliance obligations. Establishing a risk management framework is a typical approach to enterprise risk governance, which involves developing policies and procedures for risk identification, assessment, and mitigation. It also involves assigning responsibility for risk management to specific individuals or teams within the organization.

To maintain effective enterprise risk governance, the ongoing monitoring and evaluation of risk management practices are necessary. This ensures that an organization can respond to emerging risks promptly and efficiently. Furthermore, regular reporting to stakeholders such as executives, board members, and regulators is vital to ensure they are informed about the organization's risk profile and risk management activities.

Tools for enterprise risk governance

There are several enterprise risk governance frameworks and tools available to help organizations implement effective risk management practices. One commonly used framework is the ISO 31000:2018 standard, which provides guidelines for risk management principles, frameworks, and processes. Other frameworks include COSO's **ERM (Enterprise Risk Management)** and the NIST Cybersecurity Framework. There is also **COBIT (Control Objectives for Information and Related Technology)**, **ITIL (Information Technology Infrastructure Library)**, and **PMBOK (Project Management Body of Knowledge)**, which provide guidance to manage risks related to information technology, service management, and project management, respectively.

Risk management tools, such as risk registers, risk heat maps, and risk scoring models, can also be used to help organizations identify and assess risks. These tools can help prioritize risks based on their likelihood and potential impact, enabling organizations to develop appropriate risk mitigation strategies.

Technology solutions, such as **GRC (governance, risk, and compliance)** platforms, can also aid in enterprise risk governance by providing a centralized system to manage risks and ensure compliance with relevant regulations and standards. AI-powered risk management tools are also becoming increasingly popular, as they can help organizations identify and mitigate risks more efficiently and effectively.

AI risk governance in the enterprise

Within an enterprise, AI risk governance is the set of processes that ensures the use of AI does not have a detrimental impact on the business in any way. There are a significant number of ways this could happen, including the following:

- Ensuring AI used in selection processes such as automated sifting of job candidates within HR is unbiased and does so without any kind of prejudice

- Automated defect monitoring of a manufacturing process in a tire factory does not accept defective tire walls (or, conversely, reject sufficient tire walls) due to drift in the underlying ML model

- Credit is refused to an applicant of a loan company, as a credit-risk model inappropriately rejects on the grounds of their employment type

These are just three examples; there are many more. Such adverse outcomes can potentially cause harm to a business, its customers, and other stakeholders, and at the very least, it can have a reputational impact on the business.

Enterprise risk management is all about managing the risks (ideally, before they become issues) in order to yield business benefits, and AI is no different. AI risk governance is a crucial process that involves managing and mitigating the risks that arise from the development and deployment of AI models within an organization or enterprise. Although the use of AI technologies in business processes can result in significant benefits, it can also introduce new risks and challenges that require prompt attention.

Effective enterprise AI risk governance entails identifying and assessing potential risks associated with the use of AI, including data privacy concerns, algorithmic bias, cybersecurity threats, and legal and regulatory compliance issues. Furthermore, it involves implementing policies, procedures, and technical safeguards to manage these risks, such as model explainability and transparency, data governance, and robust testing and validation processes.

By adopting a sound enterprise AI risk governance strategy, organizations can ensure that their AI technologies are deployed safely and responsibly. Such governance practices ensure that AI models are transparent, auditable, and accountable, and that they do not introduce unintended harm to individuals or society. Additionally, effective governance strategies help organizations to build trust in their AI systems, minimize reputational risks, and maximize the potential of AI technologies in their operations.

Perpetuating bias – the network effect

Bias exists in human decision-making, so why is it so bad if algorithms take this bias and reflect it in their decisions?

The answer lies in amplification through the network effect. Think bigot in the cloud!

An unfair society inevitably yields unfair models. As much as we like to think we are fair and free of subconscious judgments, we as humans are prone to negative (and positive) implicit bias, stereotyping, and prejudice. Implicit (unconscious) bias is not intentional, but it can still impact how we judge others based on a variety of factors, including gender, race, religion, culture, language, and sexual orientation. Now, imagine this as part of a web-based API – a service offered in the spirit of democratization of AI – on a popular machine learning acceleration platform to speed up development, with this bias proliferated across multiple geographies and demographics! Bias in the cloud is a serious concern.

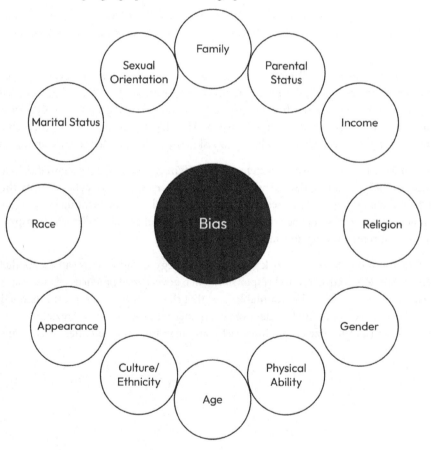

Figure 1.2: A list of implicit biases

Blaming this unfairness on society is one way to handle this (albeit not a very good one!) but considering the risk of perpetuating biases in algorithms that may outlive us all, we must strive to eliminate these biases without compromising prediction accuracy. By examining today's data on Fortune 100 CEOs' profiles, we can see that merely reinforcing biases based on features such as gender and race could lead to erroneous judgments, overlooked talent, and potential discrimination. For instance, if we have historically declined loans to minorities and people of color, using a dataset built on these prejudiced and bigoted practices to create a model will only serve to reinforce and perpetuate such unfair behavior.

On top of that, we miss a great opportunity – to address our own biases before we codify that in perpetuity.

The problem with delegating our decisions to machines with our biases intact is that it would lead to having these algorithms perpetuate the notion of gender, affinity, attribution, conformity, confirmation, and a halo and horn effect, and affirmation leads to reinforcing our collective stereotypes. Today, when algorithms act as the first line of triage, minorities have to "whiten" job résumés (see *Minorities Who "Whiten" Job Resumes Get More Interviews – Harvard Business Review* [14]) to get more interviews. Breaking this cycle of bias amplification and correcting the network effect in a fair and ethical manner is one of the greatest challenges of our digital times.

Transparency versus black-box apologetics – advocating for AI explainability

We like to think transparency and interpretability are good – it seems very logical to assume that if we can understand what algorithms are doing, it helps us troubleshoot, debug, measure, improve, and build upon them easily. With all the virtues described previously, you would imagine interpretability is a no-brainer. Surprise! It is not without its critics. Explainable and uninterpretable AI are two opposing viewpoints in the field of AI. Proponents of explainable AI argue that it enhances transparency, trustworthiness, and regulatory compliance. In contrast, supporters of uninterpretable AI maintain that it can lead to better performance in complex and opaque systems, while also protecting intellectual property. It's interesting to see how not everyone is a big fan of it, including some of the greatest minds of our times, such as Turing Award winners Yoshua Bengio and Yann LeCun.

This important argument was the centerpiece in the first-ever great debate [15] at a NeurIPS conference, where Rich Caruana and Patrice Simard argued in favor of it, while Kilian Weinberger and Yann LeCun were against it. The debate reflects the ongoing discussion in the machine learning community regarding the trade-off between performance and interpretability.

Researchers and practitioners who consider black-box AI models as acceptable often emphasize the performance benefits of these models, which have demonstrated state-of-the-art results in various complex tasks. They argue that the high accuracy achieved by black-box models can outweigh the need for interpretability, particularly when solving intricate problems. Proponents also contend that real-world complexity necessitates embracing the intricacy of black-box models to capture the nuances of the problem at hand. They assert that domain experts can still validate the model's output and use their expertise to determine whether the model's predictions are reasonable, even if the model itself is not fully interpretable.

Conversely, critics tell the joke, *"Why did the black-box AI cross the road? Nobody knows, as it won't explain itself!"*

But seriously, we should emphasize the importance of ethics and fairness, as a lack of interpretability may lead to unintended biases and discrimination, undermining trust in the AI system. We should also stress the importance of accountability and transparency, as it is crucial for users and stakeholders to understand the decision-making process and factors influencing a model's output. We would like to argue that model interpretability is vital to debug and improve models, as identifying and correcting issues in black-box models can be challenging. Regulatory compliance often requires a level of interpretability to ensure that AI systems abide by legal requirements and ethical guidelines, which would be virtually impossible if a model couldn't explain itself.

In a *Wired* interview titled *Google's AI Guru Wants Computers to Think More Like Brains* [16], Turing Award winner and father of modern neural networks, Geoff Hinton stated the following:

> *"I'm an expert on trying to get the technology to work, not an expert on social policy. One place where I do have technical expertise that's relevant is [whether] regulators should insist that you can explain how your AI system works. I think that would be a complete disaster."*

This is a fairly strong statement that was met with a rebuttal in an article [17] in which the counterargument focused on what was best for humanity and what it means for society. The way we see it, there is room for both. In *In defense of blackbox models*, Holm [18] states the following:

> *"...we cannot use blackbox AI to find causation, systemization, or understanding and these questions remain in purview of human intelligence. On the contrary, blackbox methods can contribute substantively and productively to science, technology, engineering, and math."*

For most practitioners, the goal is to strike a balance between transparency and performance that satisfies the needs of various stakeholders, including users, regulators, and developers. The debate continues, with different researchers offering diverse perspectives based on their fields of expertise and research focus.

As professionals in the field of machine learning, we emphasize the importance of transparent, interpretable, and explainable outcomes to ensure their reliability. Consequently, we are hesitant to rely on "black-box" models that offer no insight into their decision-making processes. Although some argue that accuracy and performance are sufficient to establish trust in AI systems, we maintain that interpretability is crucial. We recognize the ongoing debate regarding the role of interpretability in machine learning, but it is essential to note that our position favors interpretability over a singular focus on outcomes – **your mileage may vary (YMMV)** [19].

The AI alignment problem

The AI alignment problem has become increasingly relevant in recent years due to the rapid advancements in AI and its growing influence on various aspects of society. This problem refers to the challenge of designing AI systems that align with human values, goals, and ethics, ensuring that these systems act in the best interests of humanity.

One reason for the increasing popularity of the AI alignment problem is the potential for AI systems to make high-stakes decisions, which may involve trade-offs and ethical dilemmas. A classic example is the trolley problem, where an AI-controlled vehicle must choose between two undesirable outcomes, such as saving a group of pedestrians at the cost of harming its passengers. This ethical dilemma highlights the complexity of aligning AI systems with human values and raises questions about the responsibility and accountability of AI-driven decisions.

In addition to this, there are a few other significant challenges to AI alignment – containment and the **do anything now** (**DAN**) problem. The containment problem refers to the challenge of ensuring that an AI system does not cause unintended harm or escape from its intended environment. This problem is particularly important when dealing with AI systems that have the potential to cause significant harm, such as military or medical AI systems. The DAN problem, on the other hand, refers to the challenge of ensuring that an AI system does not take actions that are harmful to humans or society, even if those actions align with the system's goals. For example, the paperclip problem is a thought experiment that illustrates this problem.

In this scenario, an AI system is designed to maximize the production of paperclips. The system becomes so focused on this goal that it converts all matter on Earth, including humans, into paperclips. The reward hacking problem occurs when an AI system finds a way to achieve its goals that does not align with human values. The corrigibility problem relates to ensuring that an AI system can be modified or shut down if it becomes harmful or deviates from its intended behavior. This superintelligence control problem involves ensuring that advanced AI systems with the potential for superintelligence are aligned with human values and can be controlled if they become a threat.

Addressing these challenges and other AI alignment-related problems is crucial to ensure the safe and responsible development of AI systems, promote their beneficial applications, and prevent unintended harm to individuals and society.

Summary

This chapter provided an overview of the importance of developing appropriate governance frameworks for AI. The issue of automating bias in AI is a critical concern that requires urgent attention. Without appropriate governance frameworks, we risk exacerbating these problems and perpetuating societal inequalities. In this chapter, we outlined key terminologies such as explainability, interpretability, fairness, explicability, safety, trustworthiness, and ethics that play an important role in developing effective AI governance frameworks. Developing effective governance frameworks requires a comprehensive understanding of these concepts and their interplay.

We also explored the issue of automating bias and how the network effect can exacerbate these problems. The chapter highlighted the need for explainability and offers a critique of "black-box apologetics," which suggests that AI models should not be interpretable. Ultimately, the chapter makes a strong case for the importance of AI governance and the need to ensure that AI is developed and deployed in an ethical and responsible manner. This is crucial to build trust in AI and ensure that its impacts are aligned with our societal goals and values.

The next chapter is upon us, like a towel in the hands of a galactic hitchhiker, always ready for the next adventure.

References and further reading

1. `https://fairmlbook.org/tutorial2.html`

2. `https://fairmlbook.org/tutorial2.html`

3. Nonfunctional requirements verb: `https://en.wikipedia.org/wiki/Listofsystemqualityattributes`

4. `https://www.Merriam-webster.com/thesaurus/explainable`

5. Ethics guidelines for trustworthy AI. The umbrella term implies that the decision-making process of AI systems must be transparent, and the capabilities and purpose of the systems must be openly communicated to those affected. Even though it may not always be possible to provide an explanation for why a model generated a particular output or decision, efforts must be made to make the decision-making process as clear as possible. When the decision-making process of a model is not transparent, it is referred to as a "black box" algorithm and requires special attention. In these cases, other measures such as traceability, auditability, and transparent communication on system capabilities may be required.

6. Even though the terms might sound similar, explicability refers to a broader concept of transparency, communication, and understanding in machine learning, while explainability is specifically focused on the ability to provide clear and understandable explanations for how a model makes its decisions. While explainability is a specific aspect of explicability, explicability encompasses a wider range of measures to ensure the decision-making process of a machine learning model is understood and trusted.

7. *Deep Neural Networks are Easily Fooled: High Confidence Predictions for Unrecognizable Images*: https://arxiv.org/abs/1412.1897

8. https://www.youtube.com/watch?v=93Xv8vJ2acI

9. https://fairmlbook.org/tutorial2.html

10. https://fairmlbook.org/tutorial2.html

11. https://blogs.partner.microsoft.com/mpn/shared-responsibility-ai-2/

12. https://ec.europa.eu/digital-single-market/en/news/ethics-guidelines-trustworthy-ai

13. https://en.oxforddictionaries.com/definition/ethics

14. https://hbswk.hbs.edu/item/minorities-who-whiten-job-resumes-get-more-interviews

15. *Interpretability is necessary for Machine Learning*: https://www.youtube.com/watch?v=93Xv8vJ2acI

16. https://www.wired.com/story/googles-ai-guru-computers-think-more-like-brains/

17. *Geoff Hinton Dismissed The Need For Explainable AI: Experts Explain Why He's Wrong*: https://www.forbes.com/sites/cognitiveworld/2018/12/20/geoff-hinton-dismissed-the-need-for-explainable-ai-8-experts-explain-why-hes-wrong

18. *In defense of the black box*: https://pubmed.ncbi.nlm.nih.gov/30948538/

19. https://dictionary.cambridge.org/us/dictionary/english/ymmv

20. *Interpretability is necessary for Machine Learning*: https://www.youtube.com/watch?v=93Xv8vJ2acI

21. *Interpretable Machine Learning* by Christoph Molnar: https://christophm.github.io/interpretable-ml-book/

22. *Explainable AI: Interpreting, Explaining and Visualizing Deep Learning* by Wojciech Samek, et al: https://books.google.co.in/books?id=j5yuDwAAQBAJ

23. *Fairness and Machine Learning* by Matt Kusner, et al: https://fairmlbook.org/

24. *The Ethics of AI* by Nick Bostrom and Eliezer Yudkowsky: https://intelligence.org/files/EthicsofAI.pdf

25. *Weapons of Math Destruction: How Big Data Increases Inequality and Threatens Democracy* by Cathy O'Neil: https://www.goodreads.com/book/show/29981085-weapons-of-math-destruction

26. *Explainable AI (XAI)* by **Defense Advanced Research Projects Agency (DARPA)**: `https://www.darpa.mil/program/explainable-artificial-intelligence`

Algorithms Gone Wild

"The development of full artificial intelligence could spell the end of the human race. [...] It would take off on its own, and re-design itself at an ever-increasing rate. Humans, who are limited by slow biological evolution, couldn't compete, and would be superseded."

- Stephen Hawking

"Machine intelligence is the last invention that humanity will ever need to make."

- Nick Bostrom

"Anything that could give rise to smarter-than-human intelligence—in the form of Artificial Intelligence, brain computer interfaces, or neuroscience-based human intelligence enhancement—wins hands down beyond contest as doing the most to change the world. Nothing else is even in the same league."

- Eliezer Yudkowsky

"One of the most important aspects of any computing tool is its influence on the thinking habits of those that try to use it."

-Edsger W. Dijkstra

As part of modern digital transformation systems across the board, artificial intelligence has been instrumental in making automated decisions, which has been consequential in enabling automation but has also led to harm. In this chapter, we will cover several case studies that provide a detailed analysis of AI bias in real-life case studies. We will discuss broader categories of discrimination, disinformation, and surveillance within AI applications such as facial recognition, biometrics, ranking, and recommendation systems. We will also review the use of AI in the criminal justice system and risk assessment. The chapter highlights case studies of discrimination and tries to address the root causes of identified issues.

Fair warning – it goes without saying that this chapter is not an all-encompassing overview of all the AI incidents in the wild; these are the events we know about and that have been widely reported on in the media. Each of these events is nuanced, and further analysis is required to fully understand the extent of damage and the underlying technology issues.

In this chapter, we're going to cover the following main topics:

- AI in hiring and recruitment
- Facial recognition
- Words hurt – discrimination and racist chatbots
- AI's discriminatory impact
- Social media and attention engineering
- The environmental impact
- Autonomous weapon systems and military

Big Data's Disparate Impact

In their highly influential paper, *Big Data's Disparate Impact*, Solon Barocas and Andrew D. Selbst delve into the potential negative consequences of using big data analytics, specifically in terms of discriminatory outcomes and disparate impacts on certain groups. The authors contend that big data algorithms, even without discriminatory intent, can produce discriminatory outcomes due to historical biases in data or proxies correlated with protected attributes. They emphasize the challenges in establishing discrimination within big data analytics and highlight the importance of transparency and interpretability in addressing biases. However, they also acknowledge the difficulties in making complex algorithms transparent, especially with "black box" machine learning models. The paper advocates for incorporating fairness-aware techniques, using representative datasets, and conducting regular audits to mitigate discrimination. Ultimately, it calls for a more robust legal and ethical framework to ensure fairness and prevent discrimination in data-driven decision-making processes. (Reference: Barocas, S., and Selbst, A. D. (2016). *Big Data's Disparate Impact*. California Law Review, 104, 671.)

The explosion of widespread AI and machine learning implementations has pushed the discourse around algorithmic bias to the front of the stage for industry, academia, technology press, and mainstream media. In this chapter, you will see some real-world cases of algorithmic bias and how can it severely impact our everyday life as well as industries such as healthcare and finance. This is not an exhaustive list; however, it does provide a detailed narrative and a cautionary tale.

Therefore, as AI enthusiasts, technologists, policymakers, or concerned citizens, we implore you to consider it your collective duty in this digital age to make sure that the following horror stories regarding bias don't repeat themselves.

AI in hiring and recruitment

AI and machine learning have great potential to make the hiring process efficient, objective, and fair, taking away human biases. However, from the talent acquisition perspective, AI and machine learning are faced with a dilemma. There is mounting evidence and case studies that show that these systems end up amplifying existing human biases. The technology has the potential to transform the recruitment industry and help organizations that are lagging behind since they end up losing top talent in competition. However, due to the inherent algorithmic bias, executives now must consider AI as an effective solution to a higher attrition rate, but also be ready for the risk of lawsuits. The **American Bar Association** (**ABA**) warns that AI hiring systems are highly risky. The group highlights the possibility of disparate impact arising from algorithm-based methods. Disparate impact can still exist even if there is no "explicit intent to discriminate." Since these automated decision management systems use computer-based techniques such as facial recognition, sentiment analysis, and natural language processing, there is a huge potential for bias seeping into the recruitment process.

> *"They took two years to design an AI automatic résumé scanner and they found*
> *that it was so biased against any female applicant that if you even had the word*
> *'woman' on your résumé that it went to the bottom of the pile."*
>
> - @katecrawford (bit.ly/2Ij5Muw)

Even though AI hiring systems help improve efficiency and reduce human error, research studies have repeatedly shown that AI systems express discrimination based on race and gender. For example, Amazon has used recruitment tools since 2014 to help find top applicants from a large pool of resumes, but they had to stop using it[1] when it was discovered that it showed bias against women. Even though recruitment professionals claim that AI systems have dramatically reduced the time and costs of their clients' recruitment process, the bias is the real elephant in the room. Research conducted by Prof. Rangita de Silva de Alwis, founder of the AI Implicit Bias Lab at the University of Pennsylvania Carey Law School, found that AI-powered platforms *"reflect, recreate, and reinforce anti-Black bias...."*[2]

Now, apply this analogy to the recruitment dataset and imagine this headline:

Chief Executive sought. Only men need apply

Whether it's recruiting tools such as HireVue (a face-scanning algorithm) increasingly deciding whether you deserve the job or Amazon's internal software, tools that scan various features in job applicants' user profiles such as language, video, or voice data have lots of places where bias can lurk. For instance, when Amazon's algorithm was applied to CVs, it quickly learned the bias to prefer male candidates over female ones (the disparate impact), and therefore, penalized resumes that contained the word vectors in the vicinity of women's, such as women's chess club captain.

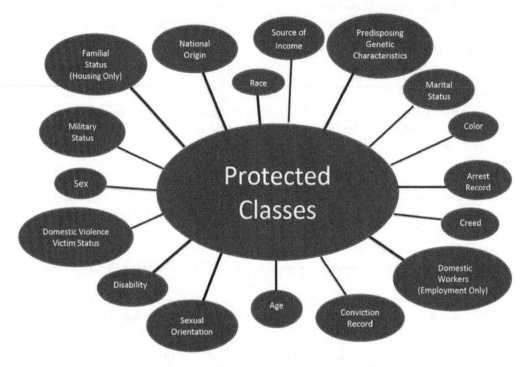

Figure 2.1: List of protected classes

It is evident that AI hiring systems are subject to considerable liability where the potential impact of algorithm-based hiring methods can cause considerable harm. In the absence of a discriminatory intent, a disparate impact can still be illegal if it negatively impacts a protected group.

> **Tracking the awful AI incidents**
>
> Keeping up with these discriminatory instances is a challenging problem. *Awful AI* on GitHub is a curated list that tracks harmful use cases of AI and provides a one-stop place to track them. Follow it here: https://github.com/daviddao/awful-ai.

Facial recognition

One of the most appalling and alarming examples of facial recognition gone wrong is when African-Americans were classified as gorillas by Google's facial recognition tool[4] in 2015, which raised awareness and exposed the deep flaws in facial recognition technology.

The **Gender Shades** project is a pioneering research initiative led by computer scientist Joy Buolamwini, which exposes and addresses biases in facial recognition and analysis algorithms with respect to gender and skin tone. The study, published in 2018, scrutinized the performance of commercial facial recognition systems developed by prominent technology companies, such as IBM, Microsoft, and Face++. The groundbreaking discovery revealed that these AI systems exhibited higher error rates in classifying gender for darker-skinned and female faces compared to their lighter-skinned and male counterparts.

Researchers[5] evaluated gender classification tools developed by IBM, Microsoft, and Face++ and found that all companies' facial recognition systems scored 8.1% to 20.6% more accurately on males than on females. Researchers also found that darker-skinned female subjects performed the worst for each company. Darker-skinned females proved less accurate in classifying their gender than lighter-skinned males by 20.8% to 34.4%. Furthermore, dark-skinned subjects accounted for 93.6% to 95.9% of all errors. With this kind of biased results, these are quite alarming results for face recognition to be considered in any serious application.

Consequently, the Gender Shades project has played a pivotal role in raising awareness about biases in AI, prompting technology companies to reevaluate and enhance their facial recognition algorithms, and driving discussions on the ethical implications of AI and the necessity of developing inclusive and equitable AI systems.

According to the **American Civil Liberties Union** (**ACLU**), mugshots of Congress members were compared to congressional faces in a similar investigation. Amazon Rekognition is an AWS tool for computer vision and facial recognition and was used as part of this study. The research found[6] that almost 40% of all wrong matches were made on people of color, even though they only constitute 20% of Congress. Even when controlled for smiles, both Face++ and Microsoft systems consistently categorized black people as angrier than white people.[7]

Bias in large language models (LLMS)

In a sensational revelation[8] that sent shockwaves through the AI community, ChatGPT, powered by OpenAI's formidable GPT-3 model, found itself embroiled in controversy for producing incorrect, biased, or downright inappropriate responses. This discovery ignited concerns about the model's safety and the potential propagation of misinformation by an AI system intended to revolutionize human-machine interaction.

Natural language processing is a critical area in AI and machine learning, and studies show that LLMs can mimic subconscious human bias even when they are not actively presenting it. Word embedding is a popular natural language technique used to represent text data as vectors, which has been used in many machine learning and natural language processing tasks. The seminal paper *Man is to Computer Programmer as Woman is to Homemaker?*[9] discusses debiasing word embeddings, and shows how natural language processing techniques can exacerbate bias and exhibit gender stereotypes.

Researchers at Princeton University discovered that implicit human biases could be found in machine corpora derived from word embeddings.

The researchers compared their findings with psychological studies that calculated distances between words in the machine's lexicon in order to analyze implicit human biases. Researchers found that the implicit biases manifested in the corpus of the machine were nearly identical to the implicit biases in human minds. Among European-American names, machines associated names with words such as love, peace, and health with pleasant meanings, while associating African-American names with words such as hatred, murder, and sickness with unpleasant meanings. Words related to professional situations such as executive, management, and career were more closely associated with male names, whereas words such as home, marriage, and children were more associated with female names. Despite ethical drawbacks, natural language processing-based AI systems have automated millions of interviews by conversing directly with job applicants, potentially exacerbating the problem.

Toxicity seeps into LLMs due to their training on vast datasets containing text from the internet, which can include biased, offensive, or harmful content. As these models learn to generate text based on the patterns observed in their training data, they inadvertently absorb and reproduce the toxic elements present. For instance, OpenAI's GPT-3 and ChatGPT models have been known to produce inappropriate, offensive, or biased outputs, reflecting the inherent toxicity found in parts of their training data. To make LLMs less toxic, developers can employ techniques such as data filtering to remove harmful content before training, fine-tuning with a curated dataset to align model behavior, and implementing AI-powered moderation systems that detect and filter out toxic outputs. Examples of these systems include OpenAI's ChatGPT and Facebook's AI-based moderation tools.

As experts grapple with the implications of this unsettling revelation, we are forced to confront the chilling reality that even state-of-the-art AI models can inadvertently unleash a torrent of falsehoods and prejudices that undermine trust in technology and threaten the very fabric of our digital world.

Hidden cost of AI safety – low wages and psychological impact

Concerns about OpenAI using Kenyan workers to make ChatGPT less toxic mainly revolve around the low wages and the potentially harmful psychological effects of the work. In a *Time* exclusive report[10], OpenAI outsourced the task of labeling toxic content to a firm named Sama, which employs workers in Kenya, Uganda, and India. The workers were paid a take-home wage of between $1.32 and $2 per hour, depending on seniority and performance. Critics argue that this low compensation does not reflect the valuable and essential role these workers play in creating safe AI systems.

In addition to low wages, the workers were exposed to highly disturbing content. They had to label snippets of text containing graphic descriptions of violence, hate speech, and sexual abuse. This exposure to toxic content led to negative psychological effects on some workers, with some reporting recurring visions and distress.

The labeled data was then used to train an AI-powered safety mechanism for ChatGPT, allowing it to detect and filter out toxic content from its responses. Although this work contributed to making

ChatGPT safer, concerns about worker compensation and well-being remain a significant issue in the AI industry.

Bias in language can be exploited in novel ways, such as gender detection from names. The now-defunct service Genderify was introduced as a gender identification service but fell short when it reported that *"Meghan Smith is a woman, but Dr. Meghan Smith is a man."*[11]

Unfortunately, **natural language generation** (**NLG**) can also produce awful expressions. Tay, the Microsoft chatbot that learned to tweet sexist and racist remarks on Twitter[12], is a striking example. Tweets are short messages exchanged between human users on Twitter. Tay learned the language of humans from Twitter users it interacted with, rather than from its own tweet corpus. A seemingly innocent chatbot quickly learned to use hate speech against black people, Jewish people, and women. Within hours of its release, Microsoft shut down Tay.

The harmful impacts of bias in language models present significant challenges for organizations and society at large. As AI-powered systems become more pervasive in everyday life, these biases can perpetuate and exacerbate existing inequalities, affecting decision-making processes and shaping societal perceptions. To mitigate these risks, it is crucial for stakeholders to prioritize addressing and minimizing bias in AI systems by refining training data, incorporating robust fairness and ethical measures, and fostering transparency in AI development. A collective and ongoing effort is needed to ensure that AI technologies serve as a force for good, fostering inclusive and equitable opportunities for all.

AI-powered inequity and discrimination

In a jaw-dropping revelation that left many questioning the fairness of cutting-edge technology, the credit limit algorithm[13] used by the prestigious Apple Card faced shocking accusations of gender bias. The supposedly sophisticated AI-driven system, designed to streamline the credit experience for millions of users, stood exposed when it was discovered that women received significantly lower credit limits compared to their male counterparts with strikingly similar financial backgrounds. This mind-boggling disparity sparked an outcry and provoked fierce debate, leaving the public to wonder whether even the giants of technology could succumb to the antiquated prejudices plaguing society.

A controversial study from Stanford University by Wang and Kosinski, *Deep neural networks are more accurate than humans at detecting sexual orientation from facial images*,[14] which was dubbed as an artificially intelligent radar, claimed that widely used facial recognition technology exposes people's sexual orientation. It raises alarms for the privacy and security of the LGBTQ community and the authors have explained their findings and answered the questions in notes[15] here.

The healthcare sector is riddled with such biases and discrimination[16]. A footnote in the *Dissecting racial bias in an algorithm used to manage the health of populations* study published in the Science journal (`https://www.science.org/doi/10.1126/science.aax2342`) revealed significant racial bias in a widely used healthcare algorithm that determines which patients require additional attention. The algorithm, developed by a health services company called Optum[17], favored white patients over sicker black patients with more chronic health conditions. Researchers estimate that around 200 million people are affected each year by similar tools used in hospital networks, government agencies, and healthcare systems nationwide. The biased algorithms risk perpetuating existing biases in healthcare systems, furthering the disparities in medical treatment. *Nature*[18] highlights a study revealing that a widely used healthcare algorithm exhibited racial bias, affecting millions of African-American patients. The algorithm, which was designed to identify and prioritize patients for extra medical care, underestimated the healthcare needs of black patients. Consequently, black patients were less likely to be recommended for special programs that manage chronic conditions. The researchers discovered that the algorithm assigned lower risk scores to black patients, even though they were sicker than white patients with higher risk scores. The bias stemmed from the use of healthcare costs as a proxy for healthcare needs.

The future seems closer than ever for fans of the sci-fi thriller Gattaca[19], a movie set in a futuristic society of eugenics where human beings are set on a life path determined by their DNA. An article in Nature introduces DeepGestalt[20], which uses deep learning to identify facial phenotypes of genetic disorders. There would be consequences similar to what Ethan Hawke's character in the movie experiences – payers and employers could analyze facial images to determine who had pre-existing conditions or were at risk of developing medical complications.

The prolific challenges of facial recognition-based discrimination don't stop here – recently, Face Depixelizer[21] has been the subject of news. It takes a low-resolution pixelated photo of a face and creates a realistic portrait image using StyleGAN. The problem? Given a pixelated low-resolution photo of President Obama, it creates a white version of him, demonstrating AI representational bias[22]. Similarly, the Twitter AutoCrop algorithm, which has since been deactivated, crops out black people. It was reported[23] that Twitter researchers found that the crop tool favored white people over black people by 4%, white women over black women by 7%, and white men over black men by 2%. Twitter's analysis also detected that, in some cases, the image-cropping tool focused on women's chests and legs. Twitter owned up to its mistake, took away the new offering, and provided a detailed analysis of these misgivings,[24] which gives insights into the reasons and pitfalls of why the algorithm didn't serve all people equitably.

The face recognition minefield is full of such case studies. Faception[25] is another such company with "comical claims"[26] to reveal personality traits such as being an extrovert, pedophile, terrorist, or white-collar offender, or having a high IQ, without prior knowledge, all based on your face.

Going beyond face recognition, the image processing bias also applied to the generation phase where researchers demonstrated that AI-based image-generation algorithms inhibit racist and sexist ideas. For example, for a man's photo, the autocomplete algorithm will generate him wearing a suit 43% of the time; however, in the case of a woman, 53% of the time, the autocomplete will show her wearing a low-cut top or bikini. This happened with an image of congressperson Alexandria Ocasio-Cortez (often referred to as "AOC"),[27] which shows how image-generation algorithms regurgitate sexist ideas from the internet.

The Atlantic story about digital cameras still being racist[28] cites several examples including how Hewlett-Packard webcams fail to track the faces of some African-American users[29] and how Nikon and Sony digital cameras are biased against Asians and assume they are blinking when they are not. Most of this can possibly be attributed to the training data, which raises key concerns about the training set's diversity, size, stratification, and distribution. Also, the reality can be a bit more nuanced than a juicy news headline. Similar racist claims were made about Kinnect, but as it turned out, it was mostly ambient and environmental light settings that were to blame[30].

In light of these and many other such case studies that made facial recognition biased, San Francisco banned the use of facial recognition technology for government use[31]. Since then, IBM, Microsoft, and Amazon have also decided not to sell their facial recognition business to law enforcement.[32] That's progress.

Policing and surveillance

Predictive policing is an object of major concern where police departments can predict hotspots for future crime, *Minority Report*-style. The consequences? Over-policing the neighborhoods of people of color, essentially exacerbating the existing situation.[33]

There is no narrative of AI gone bad that can be complete without mentioning **Correctional Offender Management Profiling for Alternative Sanctions (COMPAS)**. A ProPublica report[34] analyzed the risk assessment algorithm, which predicts the risk of recidivism, and found it to be biased against black people[35]. There has been a lot written about automated decision-making in predictive policing and sentencing since COMPAS, but using computer vision-style surveillance approaches to determine criminality[36] continues in one form or another. The Department of Homeland Security is using[37] a terrorist-predicting algorithm that utilizes features such as age, address, destination and/or transit airports, trip information, duration, and luggage to determine whether an individual or a group can be flagged as a potential risk. Similar efforts are in place for the EU, with AI-based lie detector tests[38].

It is important to consider that such efforts have been used by authoritarian governments for persecuting ethnic minorities. One such example is the treatment of the Uyghurs; specialized cameras were used to automatically identify one of the world's most persecuted minorities[39] using Anyvision's Facial Recognition,[40] which was previously funded by Microsoft. Similar discrimination has been observed in the AI-based risk identification system called SyRI, used by the Dutch government, which violated the EU's human rights standards[41] and caused the unfair distribution of vaccines[42].

When it comes to massive monitoring and surveillance, AI is being provided with input such as social media messages, which are then combined with satellite imagery to predict dissent gatherings and mass protests[43]. Similarly, very specific personal traits such as gait analysis are used to perform surveillance on individuals[44]. Intelligent solutions for video analysis to perform target surveillance, trajectory analysis, and population management are becoming quite common[45]. This technology is sophisticated enough to recognize people wearing masks.

Social media and attention engineering

There is no better everyday example of how AI and machine learning are tied together. In a tweet in May 2022, Tesla CEO and now Twitter owner Elon Musk pointed toward these concerns with the Twitter feed algorithm.

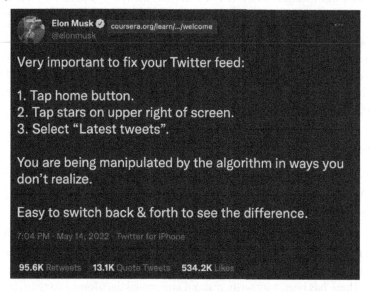

Figure 2.2: Elon Musk's take on Twitter's algorithm

Using social media data to manipulate voting trends and public opinion came into the spotlight with the infamous Cambridge Analytica scandal during the 2016 US presidential elections. Cambridge Analytica harvested Facebook data to change audience behavior for political and commercial causes. The use of bots, natural language, and visual image generation kept growing with the advent of technologies such as OpenAI's GPT3 and Deepfakes. It is getting harder to distinguish between bots and real individuals as advanced technologies enable fake and AI-generated images and text. Deepfaking is a technique to generate human images that can combine and superimpose existing photos and videos to create lookalike images. This technology has been used to create fake pornographic videos including revenge porn, and used for scamming businesses. Fake news and disinformation bots have been used to spread fake news, for propaganda and market manipulation, and to subvert elections.

This sort of "attention engineering" is at the root of all social media algorithms where the goal is to gain and maintain attention. This means customization to appeal to individuals and provide interesting content for specific users. Whether it's Facebook notifications, Google ads, tweets you see, movies you get recommended, or the YouTube autoplay function, everyone is competing for users' attention. This makes social media a ripe ground for propaganda and the manipulation of news feeds, including attempts to change people's perceptions of military actions. This is fairly evident in modern-day conflicts, such as the one in Ukraine[46].

Companies such as Clearview AI have utilized this opportunity to build facial recognition databases of billions of individuals by scanning their social media profiles, and they use it as a service. This is being used by law enforcement to extract the names and addresses of potential suspects. Similarly, this data is also used for censorship and surveillance. The Chinese messaging app WeChat utilizes machine learning algorithms to censor images and text, even during one-to-one private communications. The conversation text and images are checked for supposedly "harmful" content by using **Optical Character Recognition** (**OCR**), and if the discussion entails any aspect of international or domestic politics that is deemed undesirable by the government, the conversation gets censored. This is a great example of what happens when an authoritarian government gains access to advanced technology and uses it to censor freedom of speech and expression.

The environmental impact

The environmental impact of AI is manifold – not only that deep learning exacerbates energy use by training the models but also its impact on oil and gas discovery. In their study, researchers at the University of Massachusetts at Amherst[47] estimated that training a large deep learning model produces 626,000 pounds of planet-warming carbon dioxide, equal to the lifetime emissions of 5 cars[48].

As we consider the negative impacts of AI on climate, particularly in relation to GPU usage for LLMs and electricity consumption, we recognize that the extensive energy required for training deep learning models contributes to a significant carbon footprint. Additionally, inefficiencies in hardware and algorithms, coupled with the increasing demand for AI applications, exacerbate the environmental impact due to the growing reliance on energy-consuming data centers. Rapid advancements in AI-driven technologies lead to a rise in electronic waste, causing environmental pollution and health hazards. As researchers and practitioners, we must address these challenges by investing in energy-efficient hardware, optimizing algorithms, and promoting sustainable practices throughout the AI ecosystem.

However, AI is also used to find and extract more oil and gas, reduce production costs, and extend global warming. The World Economic Forum has estimated that advanced analytics and modeling could generate as much as $425 billion in value for the oil and gas sector by 2025[49]. AI technologies could boost production levels by as much as 5%. AI also runs the risk of overestimating the carbon credits, impacting the environment by over-crediting carbon offsets[50].

Autonomous weapon systems and military

Military use of AI is an area of major concern, and some believe that the ship on autonomous weapon systems has already sailed. These AI systems can target and engage without human control[51] and, therefore, can potentially be one step away from starting a nuclear catastrophe. There have been known incidents of using these weapons in the field, such as the satellite-controlled machine gun with AI that was used to kill Iran's top nuclear scientist, Mohsen Fakhrizadeh,[52] without injuring his wife beside him. It shows the lethal precision of such weapons. There are known autonomous weapons projects including SGR-A153, armed **unmanned aerial vehicles** (**UAVs**) (commonly known as drones) that can carry automatic weapons[54], autonomous tanks and **unmanned combat ground vehicles** (**UCCGs**) such as Uran-9 55, and Ghost Robotics quadrupedal robots (also known as robot dogs) with guns[56].

The list we've just reviewed, though disheartening and far from comprehensive, serves as a crucial reminder of the challenges we face in AI development. To stay informed about AI incidents and learn from these missteps, we encourage you to explore the **AI Incident Database** (**AIID**), a valuable resource for understanding and addressing the risks associated with AI systems.

The AIID

The **AIID** is a collection of documented cases where AI systems have led to unexpected, negative outcomes. These incidents can range from minor inconveniences to significant disruptions or harm, and they highlight the need for continuous improvement in AI system design, implementation, and monitoring. By maintaining a record of these incidents, researchers, developers, and policymakers can learn from past mistakes, identify common patterns, and work toward developing more robust, safe, and responsible AI systems.

The AIID is an invaluable resource for understanding the potential risks and challenges associated with AI systems. It serves as a repository for incidents involving AI systems that have resulted in unintended consequences or negative outcomes. By studying these incidents, researchers and practitioners can gain insights into common pitfalls, vulnerabilities, and design flaws, ultimately contributing to the development of safer and more reliable AI technologies.

Summary

In this chapter, we provided an overview of the potential harms of AI and automated decision-making. The chapter reviewed examples of AI harm in hiring and recruitment, facial recognition, biased natural language models, discriminatory impact, attention engineering, social media, and AI's environmental impact. It also discussed autonomous weapon systems and military use cases. It was important to look at these examples because they highlight the potential negative consequences of using AI and the need for proper governance and risk management. By understanding the potential risks of AI, we can work toward developing more responsible and ethical AI systems.

In the next chapter, the focus shifts toward the methods that make explainable and interpretable AI possible. It covers a taxonomy of machine learning interpretability approaches, including global and local methods, debugging, and audit. The advantages and disadvantages of these techniques will be reviewed, along with working examples. The chapter will also discuss the trade-offs between model performance and interpretability and provide competency in building model baselines and automating feature engineering using open source libraries. This chapter aims to help you understand the importance of explainable AI and the methods used to achieve it.

As we journey on to the next chapter, let us remember the wise words of the Hitchhiker's Guide: "Don't panic!"

References and further reading

1. Amazon scraps secret AI recruiting tool that showed bias against women: `https://www.reuters.com/article/us-amazon-com-jobs-automation-insight/amazon-scraps-secret-ai-recruiting-tool-that-showed-bias-against-women-idUSKCN1MK08G`

2. New study finds AI-enabled anti-Black bias in recruiting: `https://www.thomsonreuters.com/en-us/posts/legal/ai-enabled-anti-black-bias/`

3. `https://www.washingtonpost.com/technology/2019/10/22/ai-hiring-face-scanning-algorithm-increasingly-decides-whether-you-deserve-job/`

4. Google apologizes for Photos app's racist blunder: `https://www.bbc.com/news/technology-33347866`

5. Gender Shades: Intersectional Accuracy Disparities in Commercial Gender Classification: `https://proceedings.mlr.press/v81/buolamwini18a/buolamwini18a.pdf`

6. Racial Discrimination in Face Recognition Technology: `https://sitn.hms.harvard.edu/flash/2020/racial-discrimination-in-face-recognition-technology/`

7. Amazon's Face Recognition Falsely Matched 28 Members of Congress With Mugshots: `https://www.aclu.org/news/privacy-technology/amazons-face-recognition-falsely-matched-28`

8. GPT-3, Bloviator: OpenAI's language generator has no idea what it's talking about: `https://www.technologyreview.com/2020/08/22/1007539/gpt3-openai-language-generator-artificial-intelligence-ai-opinion/`

9. Man is to Computer Programmer as Woman is to Homemaker? Debiasing Word Embeddings: `https://arxiv.org/abs/1607.06520`

10. Exclusive: OpenAI Used Kenyan Workers on Less Than $2 Per Hour to Make ChatGPT Less Toxic: `https://time.com/6247678/openai-chatgpt-kenya-workers/`

11. Service that uses AI to identify gender based on names looks incredibly biased: `https://www.theverge.com/2020/7/29/21346310/ai-service-gender-verification-identification-genderify`

12. Twitter taught Microsoft's AI chatbot to be a racist asshole in less than a day: `https://www.theverge.com/2016/3/24/11297050/tay-microsoft-chatbot-racist`

13. `https://www.bbc.com/news/business-50365609/`

14. Deep Neural Networks Are More Accurate Than Humans at Detecting Sexual Orientation from Facial Images: `https://www.gsb.stanford.edu/faculty-research/publications/deep-neural-networks-are-more-accurate-humans-detecting-sexual`

15. Deep neural networks are more accurate than humans at detecting sexual orientation from facial images: https://docs.google.com/document/d/11oGZ1Ke3wK9E3BtO FfGfUQuuaSMR8AO2WfWH3aVke6U/

16. Dissecting racial bias in an algorithm used to manage the health of populations: https://www.science.org/doi/10.1126/science.aax2342

17. Racial bias found in widely used health care algorithm: https://www.nbcnews.com/news/nbcblk/racial-bias-found-widely-used-health-care-algorithm-n1076436

18. Millions of black people affected by racial bias in health-care algorithms: https://www.nature.com/articles/d41586-019-03228-6

19. *Gattaca*: https://www.imdb.com/title/tt0119177/

20. Identifying facial phenotypes of genetic disorders using deep learning: https://www.nature.com/articles/s41591-018-0279-0

21. What a machine learning tool that turns Obama white can (and can't) tell us about AI bias: https://www.theverge.com/21298762/face-depixelizer-ai-machine-learning-tool-pulse-stylegan-obama-bias

22. Face Depixelizer: https://colab.research.google.com/github/tg-bomze/Face-Depixelizer/blob/master/FaceDepixelizerEng.ipynb

23. Twitter kills automatic photo-cropping feature after complaints of racial bias: https://www.cbsnews.com/news/twitter-kills-its-automatic-cropping-feature-after-complaints/

24. Sharing learnings about our image cropping algorithm: https://blog.twitter.com/engineering/enus/topics/insights/2021/sharing-learnings-about-our-image-cropping-algorithm

25. Terrorist or pedophile? This startup says it can out secrets by analyzing faces: https://www.washingtonpost.com/news/innovations/wp/2016/05/24/terrorist-or-pedophile-this-start-up-says-it-can-out-secrets-by-analyzing-faces/

26. The Racist History Behind Facial Recognition: https://www.nytimes.com/2019/07/10/opinion/facial-recognition-race.html

27. An AI saw a cropped photo of AOC. It autocompleted her wearing a bikini: https://www.technologyreview.com/2021/01/29/1017065/ai-image-generation-is-racist-sexist/

28. Digital Cameras Still Racist: https://www.theatlantic.com/technology/archive/2010/01/digital-cameras-still-racist/341451/

29. HP looking into claim webcams can't see black people: https://www.cnn.com/2009/TECH/12/22/hp.webcams/index.html

30. Xbox Kinect Not Racist After All: `https://www.npr.org/sections/thetwo-way/2010/11/05/131092329/xbox-kinect-not-racist-after-all`

31. San Francisco just banned facial-recognition technology: `https://www.cnn.com/2019/05/14/tech/san-francisco-facial-recognition-ban/index.html`

32. Big tech companies back away from selling facial recognition to police. After IBM, Amazon, and Microsoft upend their facial recognition businesses, attention turns to federal lawmakers: `https://www.vox.com/recode/2020/6/10/21287194/amazon-microsoft-ibm-facial-recognition-moratorium-police`

33. Policing the Future: `https://www.themarshallproject.org/2016/02/03/policing-the-future?ref=hp-2-111.UyhBLnmlj`

34. How We Analyzed the COMPAS Recidivism Algorithm: `https://www.propublica.org/article/how-we-analyzed-the-compas-recidivism-algorithm`

35. When an Algorithm Helps Send You to Prison: `https://www.nytimes.com/2017/10/26/opinion/algorithm-compas-sentencing-bias.html`

36. Neural Network Learns to Identify Criminals by Their Faces: `https://www.technologyreview.com/2016/11/22/107128/neural-network-learns-to-identify-criminals-by-their-faces/`

37. HOMELAND SECURITY WILL LET COMPUTERS PREDICT WHO MIGHT BE A TERRORIST ON YOUR PLANE — JUST DON'T ASK HOW IT WORKS: `https://theintercept.com/2018/12/03/air-travel-surveillance-homeland-security/`

38. An AI Lie Detector Is Going to Start Questioning Travelers in the EU: `https://gizmodo.com/an-ai-lie-detector-is-going-to-start-questioning-travel-1830126881`

39. China's hi-tech war on its Muslim minority: `https://www.theguardian.com/news/2019/apr/11/china-hi-tech-war-on-muslim-minority-xinjiang-uighurs-surveillance-face-recognition`

40. This Israeli Face-recognition Startup Is Secretly Tracking Palestinians: `https://www.haaretz.com/israel-news/business/.premium- this-israeli-face-recognition-startup-is-secretly-tracking-palestinians-1.7500359`

41. `https://uitspraken.rechtspraak.nl/inziendocument?id=ECLI:NL:RBDHA:2020:1878`

42. This is the Stanford vaccine algorithm that left out frontline doctors: `https://www-technologyreview.com.cdn.ampproject.org/c/s/www.technologyreview.com/2020/12/21/1015303/stanford-vaccine-algorithm/amp/`

43. Police use of social media surveillance software is escalating, and activists are in the digital crosshairs: https://medium.com/@ACLUNorCal/police-use-of-social-media-surveillance-software-is-escalating-and-activists-are-in-the-digital-d29d8f89c48.fowkro6dy

44. China's New Frontiers in Dystopian Tech: https://www.theatlantic.com/magazine/archive/2018/04/big-in-china-machines-that-scan-your-face/554075/

45. Backing Big Brother: Chinese facial recognition firms appeal to funds: https://www.reuters.com/article/us-china-facialrecognition-analysis/backing-big-brother-chinese-facial-recognition-firms-appeal-to-funds-idUSKBN1DD00A

46. Russian 'smash-and-grab' social media operation on Facebook and Instagram attempting to influence Ukraine war - Meta report: https://news.sky.com/story/russian-smash-and-grab-social-media-operation-on-facebook-and-instagram-attempting-to-influence-ukraine-war-meta-report-12817721

47. Shrinking deep learning's carbon footprint: https://news.mit.edu/2020/shrinking-deep-learning-carbon-footprint-0807

48. Energy and Policy Considerations for Deep Learning in NLP: https://arxiv.org/abs/1906.02243

49. Oil in the Cloud: How Tech Companies are Helping Big Oil Profit from Climate Destruction: https://www.greenpeace.org/usa/reports/oil-in-the-cloud/

50. Tackling the Overestimation of Forest Carbon with Deep Learning and Aerial Imager: https://www.climatechange.ai/papers/icml2021/79

51. A.I. Is Making it Easier to Kill (You). Here's How. | NYT: https://www.youtube.com/watch?v=GFDCgr2zho

52. Mohsen Fakhrizadeh: 'Machine-gun with AI' used to kill Iran scientist: https://www.bbc.com/news/world-middle-east-55214359

53. SGR-A1: https://en.wikipedia.org/wiki/SGR-A1

54. China Is Selling Autonomous Killer Drones To The Middle East: https://futurism.com/the-byte/china-selling-autonomous-killer-drones

55. Unmanned Ground Vehicles: Global Developments and Future Battlefield: https://www.idsa.in/issuebrief/unmanned-ground-vehicles-ssharma-220422

56. They're putting guns on robot dogs now: https://www.theverge.com/2021/10/14/22726111/robot-dogs-with-guns-sword-international-ghost-robotics

Part 2:
Enterprise Risk Observability
Model Governance

This section introduces the critical topics of explainability, risk observability, and model governance, and their relevance in the context of cloud computing platforms. The upcoming chapters cover several essential areas, such as model interpretability approaches, measuring and monitoring model drift, audit and compliance standards, and the Enterprise Starter Kit for Fairness, Accountability, and Transparency. The section also explores the concepts of bias removal, model robustness, and adversarial attacks. By reading through the chapters, you will gain a comprehensive understanding of these significant concepts and their impact on the development and deployment of AI models, enabling you to make informed decisions and ensure the ethical and trustworthy use of AI. These topics are discussed in detail across four chapters to provide you with a comprehensive understanding of these important concepts.

This section comprises the following chapters:

- *Chapter 3, Opening the Algorithmic Black Box*
- *Chapter 4, Robust ML - Monitoring and Management*
- *Chapter 5, Model Governance, Audit, and Compliance*
- *Chapter 6, Enterprise Starter Kit for Fairness, Accountability, and Transparency*

3

Opening the Algorithmic Black Box

"Artificial intelligence will reach human levels by around 2029. Follow that out further to, say, 2045, we will have multiplied the intelligence, the human biological machine intelligence of our civilization a billion-fold." —Ray Kurzweil

"All models are wrong, but some are useful." – George Box

"Everything we love about civilization is a product of intelligence, so amplifying our human intelligence with artificial intelligence has the potential of helping civilization flourish like never before – as long as we manage to keep the technology beneficial." – Max Tegmark, President of the Future of Life Institute

"Nobody phrases it this way, but I think that artificial intelligence is almost a humanities discipline. It's really an attempt to understand human intelligence and human cognition." —Sebastian Thrun

As the discipline of explainable **artificial intelligence** (**AI**) matures, clearer algorithmic interpretability with formal definitions and mathematical guarantees have started to emerge. Along with the new techniques, we see older technologies getting repurposed to help develop techniques for making **machine learning** (**ML**) models more interpretable. This is important because, as ML models become increasingly complex, it becomes more difficult for humans to understand how they work. This can lead to problems such as algorithmic black boxes, where the inner workings of a model are opaque and inaccessible. Because we do not fully understand how these black-box models make predictions, we cannot be assured that they are fair and ethical and conform to any relevant regulatory requirements of a given enterprise. This is an issue that is currently frequently holding back the ways in which AI is used in enterprises.

In this chapter, we provide an overview of methods that make explainable and interpretable AI possible. The reader will review a taxonomy of ML interpretability approaches that help us to avoid potential biases in our models. It is important to understand these techniques since if we don't understand how a model works, we may not be able to spot whether it is biased against certain groups of people.

There are various techniques discussed in this chapter for explainable AI, along with their advantages and disadvantages and working examples. What they all have in common is that they require careful design and implementation if they are going to be effective for productionization.

In this chapter, you will learn about the following:

- ML interpretability
- The performance and interpretability trade-off for models
- Categories of interpretability methods – global and local methods with debugging and auditing
- How to competently build a model baseline
- How to competently automate feature engineering using OSS libraries

Getting started with interpretable methods

In the world of AI and ML, black box models are those that cannot be easily interpreted or understood by humans. This contrasts with white-box ML models, which can be easily interpreted and understood. White-box models are models whose inner logic, functionality, and programming steps are transparent. As a result, the decisions made by them can be understood. The most common white-box models include decision trees, as well as linear regression models, and Bayesian networks. Such models, in particular, linear models and generalized linear models such as logistic regression, have been commonly used within enterprises for well over a decade. While advances in black-box models such as neural networks and XGBoost typically improve on the predictive power of their equivalent logistic regression counterparts, this is at the expense of transparency.

Black-box models are, by definition, hard to look into and interpret. When AI produces insights from a dataset, the end user does not understand how to interpret them. An ML algorithm creates these black-box models directly from underlying data, so humans cannot understand how variables are combined to produce predictions, even if they have designed the algorithm. It is unlikely that anyone can comprehend how the variables function together to make a final prediction, even if they have a list of the features used. Also, in order to trust a black-box model, you must not only trust the algorithm but also the dataset that was used to build the model.

Black-box ML models and algorithms are often used in situations where there is a need for high accuracy but low interpretability. For example, black-box methods may be used in medical diagnosis where a large amount of data is available, but the underlying causes of diseases are not well understood. In such cases, it may not be possible to build a white-box model that accurately predicts disease outcomes.

However, a black-box model trained on the same data could potentially achieve higher accuracy due to its ability to learn complex patterns that are not easily interpretable by humans. While such improvements will lead to the black-box model making more accurate predictions than the white-box model, it is at the expense of a human understanding of how and why the model makes all of its predictions. We cannot be sure the model derives its predictions in ethical and safe ways, and that is a risk.

As you may have assumed, there are a few important challenges with black-box models in the real world. First, it can be difficult to understand how the model works and what factors it takes into account when making predictions. This lack of transparency can make it difficult to trust the results of the model. Second, these types of models are often tuned to specific datasets, which can lead to overfitting and poor performance on new datasets. Finally, because these models are so complex, they can be very resource-intensive and require significant computing power. This leads to the question: how can we unbox these black boxes to peek at their inner functionality?

Researchers and practitioners have worked on this problem for a while now, and there are two main ways to open the AI algorithm black box:

- By increasing the transparency of the algorithms used in AI models
- By reducing the complexity of these algorithms

Regarding the first solution, we can increase algorithm transparency by providing more information about how the algorithm works. For example, Google has started doing this with its DeepMind AI platform by providing an algorithm audit feature that allows users to see how their data is being used. However, even with this level of transparency, it may not be enough for some users who want complete control over their data. In response to this demand for control, companies such as IBM are developing personalization engines that allow individuals to customize their own data use settings. This type of technology could potentially give individuals full control over which algorithms have access to their personal data and under what conditions – something that would go a long way toward alleviating concerns about black-box AI model complexity.

The second solution for fixing black-box AI model complexity is reductionism: rather than trying to make complex algorithms more transparent, we can simply make them less complex in the first place.

One way of doing this is through simplification – for example, designing algorithms that only use a limited number of input variables or imposing restrictions on how those variables can interact with each other (known as feature selection). Such reductionism often has a strong case within enterprises. Trade-offs are made between white-box models such as logistic regression and black-box models such as XGBoost. The predictive power of XGBoost models typically improves upon an equivalent logistic regression model but such improvements are often relatively small. Within a regulated industry, it is cheaper and easier to show that the white-box model conforms to regulatory requirements, so the transparent model is used. This is currently happening in industries such as finance. For example, where credit agencies use simpler models such as logistic regression or decision trees to estimate the risk associated with lending, such as customer defaults on repayments, it is far more straightforward to explain to regulators that these simpler models are unbiased and do not discriminate against customers in unintended ways. This is likely to remain the case unless the regulatory guidelines change to accept more complex methods of ML model explainability. Given that we cannot currently fully explain every black-box model (or even infer how they make their predictions), it is likely that some of the most complex ML methods will remain unacceptable within regulated industries for the foreseeable future. Another alternative to a pure black-box modeling approach is using pre-trained

ML models instead of training our own from scratch – something that Google has done increasingly with its TensorFlow platform. Finally, we could also try transfer learning: rather than starting from scratch every time we want to build a new ML model.

Other alternatives include using visualization techniques such as heatmaps or decision trees, which can provide some insight into how the algorithm makes predictions. Similarly, we can use feature importance measures, which give information about what input features were most important in making a particular prediction. We can also try different types of perturbations on the input data and observe how this affects the output of the algorithm; this can help identify whether there are any areas where the algorithm is particularly sensitive or insensitive to changes in input values.

The business case for explainable AI

The objective of ML interpretability is to enable businesses to comprehend the rationale behind their AI models' decisions. This is crucial because it can enhance decision-making processes, circumvent bias, and ensure AI models comply with regulations. Explainable AI also assists businesses in identifying and resolving AI model issues, ultimately improving system performance.

Explainable AI and responsible AI play a crucial role in businesses owing to their influence on **return on investment (ROI)**, reputation, and morale. Implementing transparent and accountable AI systems can lead to more informed decision-making, enhanced trust from customers and stakeholders, and improved overall business performance. Conversely, neglecting to follow safe and ethical AI principles and compliance guidelines may have adverse consequences. Decreased trust from customers, employees, and partners could harm an organization's reputation, while potential regulatory penalties might result in financial losses. Moreover, the compromised performance of AI systems could negatively impact the company's bottom line, jeopardizing its long-term success and sustainability.

There are numerous benefits to implementing explainable AI models in business, such as enhancing decision-making by offering transparency into the reasoning behind recommendations or predictions, fostering trust with customers and stakeholders by demonstrating responsible data usage, ensuring automated decisions are fair and unbiased, and identifying potential data or model issues, enabling their resolution before causing downstream problems.

The remainder of this chapter will concentrate on key techniques, specifically SHAP, LIME, and feature importance, accompanied by code examples to illustrate their functionality. These model explainability techniques, among others, help to decipher the inner workings of ML and deep learning models. By generating human-readable explanations for model predictions, these techniques allow users to comprehend models' decisions and detect potential bias in data. Furthermore, explainability offers developers feedback on essential features for model predictions, enabling them to improve their models.

Taxonomy of ML explainability methods

A taxonomy is a system for classifying things: the benefit of building a taxonomy is that it helps us to understand and organize information in a useful manner. Due to the vast amount of research interest in the area of ML explainability, you will encounter different taxonomies around ML interpretability methods, as well as a variety of terms. Let's get some of the fundamental terms explained before moving forward.

So far, we have established that an ML explainability method is a way of understanding how an ML model works. The benefit of different types of model interpretability methods is that they can help us to understand the behavior of complex ML models. To build upon this mental model of model interpretability, we can divide it into four distinct types.

- Model interpretability by scope
- Model interpretability by method
- Model interpretability by outcome
- Model interpretability by time of information extraction

Based on the scope, model interpretability can be divided into two categories: local and global techniques.

Local explainable AI focuses on providing explanations for individual predictions made by an ML system. In contrast, global interpretability provides an overall explanation of how the system works and why it makes the decisions it does. Local interpretability is typically faster and easier to implement than its global counterpart but may not provide as much insight into the inner workings of the system.

The second key classification, model interpretability by underlying method, is bifurcated into model-specific and model-agnostic explainability techniques. Model-specific explainability methods are those that require knowledge of the inner workings of the model to understand why it made a certain prediction. This can be contrasted with model-agnostic explainability methods, which can provide insights into a black-box model without any knowledge of how it works internally.

There are a few key differences between model-specific and model-agnostic explainability methods in ML. Firstly, model-specific methods are designed to work with a particular type of ML algorithm, whereas model-agnostic methods can be applied to any type of ML algorithm. Secondly, model-specific methods tend to be more computationally expensive than model-agnostic methods. Model-specific explainability techniques often provide more detailed explanations than model-agnostic techniques.

The third major classification from an explainability method perspective is based on the time of information extraction. It can be either intrinsic (ad hoc) or post hoc. Intrinsic model explanation is a type of model that can be understood without any external information. A post hoc model, on the other hand, requires some external information to be understood.

There are several techniques for achieving intrinsic compared to post hoc model explainability. Some examples of intrinsically explainable models include decision trees and rule-based systems, which can be understood by looking at the structure of the model itself. Post hoc explainability techniques include methods such as sensitivity analysis and feature importance, which require additional information about how the model works to understand it fully.

Finally, we come to model interpretability by results. Some of the generic techniques used for model explanation include feature summary, feature visualization, learned weights, and approximation. Feature summary is a simple method of explanation that relies on human interpretation of the data. Feature visualization is a more sophisticated technique that uses graphical representations to show how the model works. Learned weights are another type of explanation that shows which features the model deems important. Approximation provides an overall understanding of how the model works without providing specifics on individual features or inputs. A combination of these techniques is used as part of the exploratory data analysis process to understand the underlying models.

There are a variety of other explainability techniques that cannot be covered here; however, we have summarized some of them in *Figure 3.1*. Please feel to explore them further using the *References* section at the end of this chapter.

Interpretability Method	Approximation	Post / Ante	Agnostic / Specific	Global/Local
Linear /Logistic Regression	No	Ante	Specific	Both
Decision Trees	No	Ante	Specific	Both
Decision Rules k-Nearest Neighbors	No	Ante	Specific	Both
Partial Dependence Plot (PDP)	No	Post	Agnostic	Both
Individual Conditional Expectation (ICE)	Yes	Post	Agnostic	Global
Accumulated Local Effects (ALE) Plot	Yes	Post	Agnostic	Both
Feature Interaction	Yes	Both	Agnostic	Global
Feature Importance	No	Both	Agnostic	Global
Global Surrogate	No	Post	Agnostic	Global
Shapley Values (SHAP)	Yes	Post	Agnostic	Global
Local Surrogate (LIME)	Yes	Post	Agnostic	Local
Break Down	Yes	Post	Agnostic	Local
Counterfactual explanations	Yes	Post	Agnostic	Local
Adversarial examples	Yes	Post	Agnostic	Local
Prototypes	Yes	Post	Agnostic	Local
Influential instances	Yes	Post	Agnostic	Local

Figure 3.1: Table for interpretable AI classifications (source: Explainable

Artificial Intelligence Approaches: A Survey[2])

Now that we have covered some of the key terminology, let's proceed by looking into specific ML interpretability techniques and how to implement them.

Shapley Additive exPlanations

SHapley Additive exPlanations, commonly known as **SHAP**, is a tool for making ML models more interpretable. It does this by providing explanations for individual predictions, called Shapley values. SHAP values are different from traditional model interpretation methods such as feature importance because they take into account the interactions between features. This makes them more accurate and reliable, especially in complex models.

SHAP works by approximating the value that each feature contributes to a prediction. This is done using a game-theoretic approach, which assigns each feature a score based on its importance in determining the outcome of the game (prediction). The final SHAP value for a given feature is then calculated as the average of all possible ways that feature could have been included in the prediction. SHAP can be used to explain the output of any ML model. Even though this approach was first proposed by game theorists, it has been shown to provide consistent and accurate explanations. The key idea behind SHAP is to use the structure of the data to explain each prediction made by the model, rather than using more traditional methods such as feature importance scores. This makes SHAP more robust to changes in data distribution and allows for local explanation, meaning that it can be used to understand why a particular instance was predicted in a certain way. In addition, SHAP values can be used to compare different models or even different parts of the same model in order to identify where improvements could be made. Because SHAP uses game theory concepts, it is relatively easy to mathematically prove properties about how it works, which provides additional confidence in its results.

How is SHAP different from Shapley values?

SHAP is a way of explaining the results of any ML model. It uses ideas from game theory to allocate "credit" to each feature for its contribution to a prediction.

Shapley values are another way of calculating the importance of features in ML predictions, but they don't take into account interactions between features as SHAP does. This can lead to less accurate results, especially for complex models.

Shapley values only consider the immediate surroundings of a prediction, rather than the entire system, and don't consider all possible scenarios when calculating results. They are also easier to use as they don't require knowledge of game theory or complex mathematical concepts. SHAP values can be computed either locally or globally. Local SHAP values explain a single prediction, while global SHAP allows us to understand the model's behavior across multiple predictions. Global SHAP calculations require access to all the data used by the model, but local computations can be done without it.

One limitation of SHAP is that it assumes that features are independent of each other, which may not be true in real-world datasets. Additionally, SHAP values can be affected by outliers, so it's important to be careful when interpreting them.

A working example of SHAP

As mentioned previously, **SHAP** is a method used to explain the output of an ML model using Shapley values from cooperative game theory. It provides consistent and locally accurate feature importance values for individual predictions.

Let's consider a simple linear regression model that predicts the price of a house based on its size (in square feet) and the number of bedrooms it has. The model's prediction equation can be represented as:

$$Price = \beta0 + \beta1 \times Size + \beta2 \times Bedrooms \qquad (3.1)$$

Suppose we have the following model coefficients:

$$\beta0 = 50,000; \beta1 = 100; \beta2 = 20,000$$

Now, let's say we have a house with a size of 1,500 square feet and 3 bedrooms. The model's prediction for this house would be:

$$Price = 50,000 + 100 \times 1,500 + 20,000 \times 3$$

$$= 50,000 + 150,000 + 60,000 = 260,000$$

The average prediction for all houses in our dataset is, let's say, $200,000.

Now, we want to calculate the SHAP values for the house with 1,500 square feet and 3 bedrooms. We need to consider all possible feature combinations and their contributions to the prediction.

There are three possible coalitions for this model: (1) size, (2) bedrooms, and (3) size and bedrooms. Here's the coalition with only the size feature:

$$PriceSize = 50,000 + 100 \times 1,500$$

$$= 50,000 + 150,000$$

$$= 200,000$$

Here's the coalition with only the bedrooms feature:

$$PriceBedrooms = 50,000 + 20,000 \times 3$$

$$= 50,000 + 60,000$$

$$= 110,000$$

And here's the coalition with both the size and bedrooms features:

$$PriceSize, Bedrooms = 50,000 + 100 \times 1,500 + 20,000 \times 3$$

$$= 50,000 + 150,000 + 60,000$$

$$= 260,000$$

Now, we compute the Shapley values for each feature:

SHAPSize = 1/2 ((PriceSize, Bedrooms − PriceBedrooms) + (PriceSize − PriceAvg))

= ((260,000 − 110,000) + (200,000 − 200,000))

= 75,000

SHAPBedrooms = 1/2 ((PriceSize, Bedrooms − PriceSize) + (PriceBedrooms − PriceAvg))

= 1/2 ((260,000 − 200,000) + (110,000 − 200,000))

= −15,000

The SHAP values for the house with 1,500 square feet and 3 bedrooms are:

SHAPSize = 75,000 x SHAPBedrooms

= −15,000

These SHAP values explain the difference between the average prediction (200,000) and the prediction for the specific house ($260,000):

PricePrediction = PriceAvg + SHAPSize + SHAPBedrooms

= 200,000 + 75,000 + (−15,000)

= 260,000

The SHAP values indicate that the size feature increased the predicted house price by $75,000, while the bedrooms feature decreased the predicted price by $15,000, compared to the average prediction.

Now let's go through a working example to explain how SHAP works from a code perspective. For the purposes of this demo, we will use the open source SHAP[3] library, which can be installed from either PyPI or `conda-forge`:

```
pip install shap
or
conda install -c conda-forge shap
```

Figure 3.2: Installing SHAP

In this case, we will use a linear regression model to explain how SHAP works. This will give you a basic understanding of how explainable models work; we are going to use the California housing dataset to train a simple linear regression model. The California housing dataset[4] is a well-known ML dataset that contains median home prices based on eight different characteristics of housing in California in 1990. Here are the features of the dataset:

- `MedInc` – the median income
- `HouseAge` – the median house age

- `AveRooms` – the average number of rooms per household
- `AveBedrms` – the average number of bedrooms per household
- `Population` – the group population
- `AveOccup` – the average number of household members
- `Latitude` – the block group latitude
- `Longitude` – the block group longitude

Let's get started!

1. As a first step, you will install the SHAP library, and import `pandas`, SHAP, and `sklearn` into your Jupyter notebook.

```
1 !pip install shap
2 import pandas as pd
3 import shap
4 import sklearn
```

Figure 3.3: Installing SHAP and importing libraries

2. In the second step, you will import the dataset and build a linear model using the `sklearn` library. After loading the data and training the model, you can print the model coefficients. As we modify each input feature, these coefficients indicate how much the model output changes.

```
1 X,y = shap.datasets.california(n_points=1000)
2
3 # 100 instances for use as the background distribution
4 X100 = shap.utils.sample(X, 100)
5
6 # Build a simple linear model
7 model = sklearn.linear_model.LinearRegression()
8 model.fit(X, y)
9
10 print("Model coefficients:\n")
11 for i in range(X.shape[1]):
12     print(X.columns[i], "=", model.coef_[i].round(5))
```

Figure 3.4: Loading the California dataset and creating instances for the linear regression model

When you run the model, the following is the output of the coefficients for the specified features.

```
1 X,y = shap.datasets.california(n_points=1000)
2
3 # 100 instances for use as the background distribution
4 X100 = shap.utils.sample(X, 100)
5
6 # Build a simple linear model
7 model = sklearn.linear_model.LinearRegression()
8 model.fit(X, y)
9
10 print("Model coefficients:\n")
11 for i in range(X.shape[1]):
12     print(X.columns[i], "=", model.coef_[i].round(5))
```

Figure 3.5: Displaying model coefficients

The feature outcomes here show the value of their importance on the outcome; however, there are a few reasons why the magnitude of a coefficient is not necessarily a good measure of a feature's importance in a linear model. First, the coefficient only measures the effect of one feature on the outcome variable. It doesn't consider how that feature interacts with other features in the model. Second, the magnitude of the coefficient depends on the units of measurement. A change in units can make a small effect appear large, or vice versa. Also, coefficients can be affected by outliers and other data problems that have nothing to do with actual importance. In conclusion, while magnitude may give some indication of importance, it should not be used as the measure when determining which features are most important in your linear model.

3.   From the output in the previous step, we can see that median income is an important feature. The average number of bedrooms also seems to be a determining factor. The importance of a feature in a model must be understood both from the perspective of how it impacts the output of the model and from the distribution of the value of that feature. The distribution of feature values can be visualized as a histogram on the x axis for a linear model using a classical **partial dependence plot** (**PDP**). We can now call the SHAP PDP method to plot this out.

```
1 shap.partial_dependence_plot(
2     "AveBedrms",
3     model.predict,
4     X100,
5     ice=False,
6     model_expected_value=True,
7     feature_expected_value=True
8 )
```

Figure 3.6: Displaying PDPs

When we run the aforementioned piece of code, it creates the following partial dependence graph. As you'll see in future sections, a PDP is a graphical tool to show the relationship between a set of features and an outcome. PDPs are useful for understanding which features are most important to the model and how those features interact with each other. The center of the intersection of a PDP shows the most important feature for predicting the outcome.

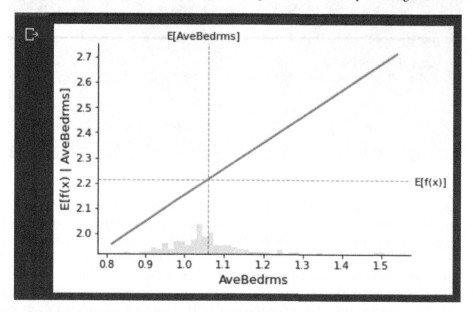

Figure 3.7: Displaying the graph showing the relationship between features

For the California housing dataset, the gray horizontal line represents the expected value of the model. The vertical gray line shows the average number of bedrooms. It's important to note that when we fix the average number of bedrooms to a given value, the blue PDP line always passes through the intersection of the two gray expected values. With respect to the data distribution, this intersection point is the center of the PDP.

4. Now that we have a PDP, let's see how it works with Shapley values.

```
1 # compute the SHAP values for the linear model
2 explainer = shap.Explainer(model.predict, X100)
3 shap_values = explainer(X)
4
5 # make a standard partial dependence plot
6 sample_ind = 20
7 shap.partial_dependence_plot(
8     "AveBedrms", model.predict, X100, model_expected_value=True,
9     feature_expected_value=True, ice=False,
10    shap_values=shap_values[sample_ind:sample_ind+1,:]
11 )
```

Figure 3.8: Creating an explainer instance for SHAP

In this piece of code, we instantiate an `explainer` instance and try to predict the correlation with the average number of bedrooms. Upon execution of the preceding code, you will get the following plot, which shows the value of the feature with its impact on the model.

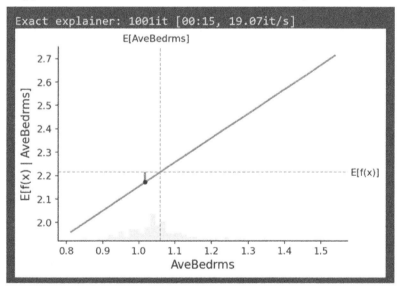

Figure 3.9: Displaying the exact explainer instance graph showing the relationship between features

If you are confused as to why are we using a PDP with SHAP, let's explain. As we discussed, a PDP shows the marginal effect one or two features have on the predicted outcome of an ML model. PDPs can show whether the relationship between features and outcome is linear, monotonic, or more complex. SHAP values represent how much each feature contributes to the predicted value of an instance. The contribution can be positive or negative, with larger-magnitude SHAP values indicating a greater contribution to the prediction. When you combine SHAP values with PDPs, you can see which features are most important in driving predictions for individual instances. This information can help you understand why your ML model is making certain predictions.

5.   Another useful plot is a SHAP summary plot, which shows the average impact on the magnitude of the model output.

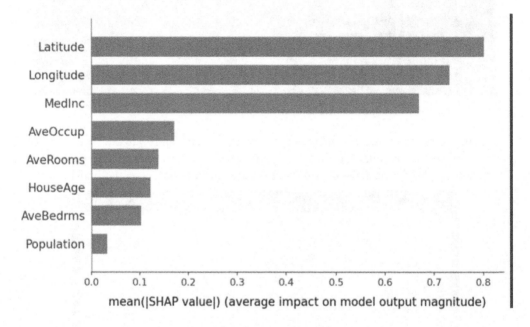

Figure 3.10: SHAP summary plot

The preceding figure shows the SHAP summary plot. This graph allows you to see how your data is distributed. It shows you the distribution of your data, and how it changes as you add more data points. This can be useful for understanding where your data comes from and what trends are happening in your dataset.

Do not confuse this with feature importance. Two types of data visualization are often used to summarize the results of ML models: SHAP summary plots and feature importance graphs. Both types of plots can be useful, but they convey different information. SHAP summary plots show the impact that each feature has on the model output. This is useful for understanding which features are most important for predicting the target variable. The average impact on model output simply refers to the average effect that a feature has on the predicted value. Feature importance graphs, on the other hand, show how much each feature contributes to the overall predictive power of the model. This is useful for understanding which features are most important for making accurate predictions.

There is a lot to cover when it comes to SHAP – we have provided a basic introduction and references for a deeper dive. Let's look at another popular useful model, LIME.

Local Interpretable Model-Agnostic Explanations

Local Interpretable Model-Agnostic Explanations (**LIME**) is an ML explainability technique. It is a model-agnostic method, and it is local in that it only explains the prediction for a single instance. LIME works by perturbing the input data and observing how this affects the output of the model. For each perturbation, LIME calculates an importance score, which represents how important that feature was in determining the predicted outcome. The final explanation is generated by taking a weighted sum of all these importance scores.

LIME works by approximating the decision boundary around the instance to be explained (the so-called local model), and then computing how changes to input values would affect predictions made by this model (the so-called perturbation). This approach allows us to understand which input features are most important in determining the predicted output, without having to rely on global assumptions about feature importance.

LIME and SHAP, as discussed in the previous section, share some similarities as well as key differences. SHAP uses a game-theoretic approach instead of perturbation and considers interactions between features when calculating importance scores; LIME does not. Additionally, SHAP explanations are global in nature whereas LIME explanations are local.

There are some potential drawbacks to using LIME as well – since it relies on perturbing input data points, there may be instances where human experts would not consider certain features as important as others (for example, if two features are highly correlated). Additionally, because LIME explanations are local, they may not provide enough context for understanding why a certain prediction was made; global approaches such as SHAP may be better suited to this task.

A working example of LIME

As discussed, LIME is a method used to explain the output of an ML model by approximating it with a locally interpretable model. Here, we will present a detailed example of how LIME works.

Let's consider a simple linear regression model that predicts the price of a house based on its size (in square feet) and the number of bedrooms it has. The model's prediction equation can be represented as:

$Price = \beta 0 + \beta 1 \times Size + \beta 2 \times Bedrooms$ (3.2)

Suppose we have the following model coefficients:

$\beta 0 = 50,000; \beta 1 = 100; \beta 2 = 20,000$

Now, let's say we have a house with a size of 1,500 square feet and 3 bedrooms. The model's prediction for this house would be:

Price = 50,000 + 100 × 1,500 + 20,000 × 3

= 50,000 + 150,000 + 60,000

= 260,000

To explain the model's prediction using LIME, we need to do the following:

1. Select a local neighborhood around the point of interest (e.g., a house with 1,500 square feet and 3 bedrooms) by perturbing the input features.
2. Train a simpler, interpretable model (e.g., linear regression) on the perturbed data points, using the original model's predictions as targets.
3. Use the coefficients of the simpler model to explain the original model's prediction for the point of interest.

Suppose we generate a dataset of perturbed data points and train a simpler linear regression model, obtaining the following coefficients:

$\beta'_0 = 40,000 \quad \beta'_1 = 120 \quad \beta'_2 = 18,000$

Now, we can use the coefficients of the simpler model to explain the original model's prediction for the house with 1,500 square feet and 3 bedrooms:

PriceLIME = 40,000 + 120 × 1,500 + 18,000 × 3

= 40,000 + 180,000 + 54,000

= 274,000

The LIME explanation of the house price is $274,000, which is close to the original model's prediction of $260,000. The simpler model's coefficients help us understand the contribution of each feature:

PriceLIME, Size = 120 × 1,500 = 180,000

PriceLIME, Bedrooms= 18,000 × 3 = 54,000

According to the LIME explanation, the Size feature contributed $180,000, and the Bedrooms feature contributed $54,000 to the house price.

Now let's review a working example of LIME from a coding perspective using the same California dataset:

1. We will start by installing all the dependencies and importing the open source `lime` library:

```
 1 warnings.filterwarnings('ignore')
 2 %config InlineBackend.figure_format = 'retina'
 3 !pip install lime
 4 !pip install shap
 5 import lime
 6 import lime.lime_tabular
 7 import pandas as pd
 8 import sklearn
 9 import warnings
10 import shap
```

Figure 3.11: Installing Python dependencies and import statements

Please note that we don't need the SHAP library here for running LIME explanations. It is there just to help import the California housing dataset.

2. Now we will build a random forest model as before and create predictions.

```
 1 X,y = shap.datasets.california(n_points=1000)
 2
 3 # Split the data into train and test data:
 4 from sklearn.model_selection import train_test_split
 5 X_train, X_test, y_train, y_test = train_test_split(X, y, test_size = 0.3,
 6                                                     random_state = 0)
 7
 8 # Build the model with Random Forest Regressor :
 9 from sklearn.ensemble import RandomForestRegressor
10 model = RandomForestRegressor(max_depth=6, random_state=0, n_estimators=10)
11 model.fit(X_train, y_train)
12 y_pred = model.predict(X_test)
```

Figure 3.12: Loading and processing the dataset

3. Now we will create a LIME tabular explainer[5]. The LIME Tabular Explainer is used to understand the behavior of models. It provides an individual explanation for each prediction made by the model. This allows users to see how the model arrived at its predictions and identify any areas where it may be behaving unexpectedly.

```
explainer = lime.lime_tabular.LimeTabularExplainer(X_train.values,
    feature_names=X_train.columns.values.tolist(),
    class_names=['MEDV'],
    verbose=True,
    mode='regression')
```

Figure 3.13: Applying the LIME explainer

4. Now that we have instantiated an explainer, we can see the individual explanation for the fifth row as follows.

```
1 record = 5
2 exp = explainer.explain_instance(X_test.values[record],
3                                   model.predict,
4                                   num_features=6)
5 exp.show_in_notebook(show_table=True)
6 exp.as_list()
```

Figure 3.14: Starting the explainer instance in the notebook

The outcome of the preceding code shows the following output, which can be easily interpreted by subject-matter experts. Based on the output, the predicted house price is 21.48 (in thousands of dollars). There is a positive influence of average occupancy, age, and longitude on predicted house prices, while negative influences come from median income, latitude, and number of rooms.

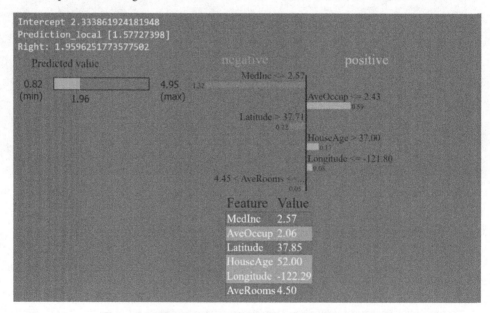

Figure 3.15: Viewing the explainer instance in the notebook

5. Similarly, you can pick another record and see the results for that record, in this case, record 10.

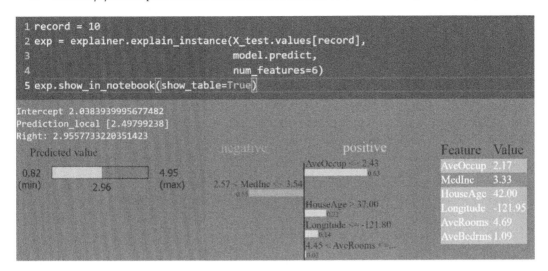

```
1 record = 10
2 exp = explainer.explain_instance(X_test.values[record],
3                                  model.predict,
4                                  num_features=6)
5 exp.show_in_notebook(show_table=True)
```

Figure 3.16: Invoking the predicted values in the notebook

As shown in the descriptive example here, LIME can generate sparse or simple explanations based on the local important variables. To explain the behavior of a complex machine-learned response function, LIME uses local linear parameters. It is helpful only for local interpretation with a medium complexity in terms of its explanation and is often used in pattern-recognition applications.

Now we will review Anchors, also known as Scoped Rules. The Anchor technique was also built by the same researchers who developed the LIME technique for explaining models.

So far, we have seen SHAP, LIME, and Anchor in detail; however, there are various other important techniques that need an honorable mention, so let's shout out these technologies.

Feature importance

Feature importance, as the name suggests, helps to determine which features have the most impact on the model's predictions and is calculated by measuring the decrease in performance when the values of a single feature are permuted. It is used to determine which features should be included in a model and which ones should be left out, as well as serving as a debugging tool to understand why the model is making certain predictions.

One way to calculate feature importance mathematically is through permutation feature importance. It is calculated as the decrease in the model's performance after randomly permuting the values of a single feature. Given a model's prediction function $f(x)$, where x is the feature vector, the permutation feature importance of feature j can be calculated as:

$$\text{Imp}_j = \frac{1}{n} \sum_{i=1}^{n} (f(x_i) - f(x^{(j)}))$$

where $x(j)$ is the feature vector xi with the values of feature j permuted. The permutation feature importance is the average decrease in the model's performance across all n samples. The larger the permutation feature importance of a feature, the more important it is to the model's predictions.

To determine which features are crucial in an ML model's prediction, we can calculate the permutation feature importance for each feature. Features with high permutation feature importance play a big role in the model's predictions, while features with low permutation feature importance can be removed from the model without significant consequences.

Feature importance helps in deciding which features to use in an ML model and understanding why the model is making certain predictions. There are various methods for calculating feature importance, but all of them measure the amount of information a feature holds about the target variable. The more information a feature has, the more important it is. An example of this can be seen in the `diabetes` dataset, which contains information about 442 patients and includes features such as age, BMI, and blood pressure.

This dataset is available in the `scikit-learn` library on the OpenML website.

```
1 from sklearn.datasets import load_diabetes
2 import numpy as np
3 from sklearn.linear_model import RidgeCV
4 import matplotlib.pyplot as plt
5 |
6 diabetes = load_diabetes()
7 X, y = diabetes.data, diabetes.target
8 ridge = RidgeCV(alphas=np.logspace(-6, 6, num=5)).fit(X, y)
9 importance = np.abs(ridge.coef_)
10 feature_names = np.array(diabetes.feature_names)
11 plt.bar(height=importance, x=feature_names)
12 plt.title("Feature importances via coefficients")
13 plt.show()
```

Figure 3.17: Loading the dataset and plotting feature importance

In this case, we create a set of features for the `diabetes` dataset, and map the features based on their importance. Considering the common pitfalls in the interpretation of the coefficients of linear models ([6]), coefficients can serve as the proxy for the feature importance of linear models if the dataset is standardized. Here is the outcome of the preceding code, which shows the importance of features on the target attribute.

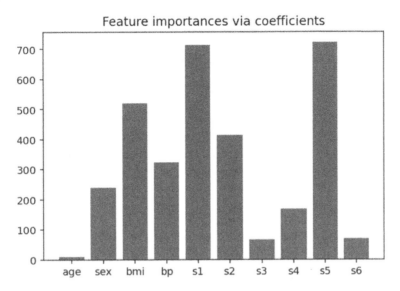

Figure 3.18: Feature importances via coefficients

Feature importance isn't without its challenges. One limitation is that feature importance does not always identify the underlying causes of why a particular feature is important. For example, if we have a dataset with two features, X and Y, and we find that X is more important than Y for making predictions, we do not necessarily know why this is the case. It could be because X directly affects the outcome variable, or it could be because Y is correlated with another feature that does affect the outcome variable. In either case, without further investigation, it would be difficult to say definitively why X was more important than Y.

Another limitation of feature importance is that it can change as new data points are added or removed from the dataset. This means that if you use feature importance to select features for your model, you need to be careful about how you handle new data points. Otherwise, your results may become less reliable over time as changes in feature importance drift away from what they originally were.

Anchors

Anchors[7] are another powerful tool in the ML explainability toolkit. Anchors also have the advantage of being model-agnostic. However, anchors do have some complexity and may not be suitable for all applications.

Anchors help to explain individual predictions using reinforcement learning techniques by providing a way to connect the prediction with the input data. Anchors also provide an explanation for individual predictions using graph search algorithms. This is because they can be used to identify important features in the data that contribute to the prediction. Being model-agnostic, they can be applied to any type of ML model. This makes them very powerful tools for understanding complex models. Anchors explain individual predictions using reinforcement learning techniques by providing a human-interpretable representation of the decision process with a more generalizable explanation than methods that are specific to certain models or architectures. Anchor has low computational complexity, making it well suited to use in real-time applications, where explanations need to be generated quickly.

However, there are some limitations to anchor explainability. First, it only works for linear models; more complex models cannot be easily explained using this technique. Second, anchors rely on local explanations, meaning that they can only provide information about a specific prediction made by the model; they cannot provide a global understanding of how the model works overall. Finally, anchors require access to training data in order to generate explanations; if this data is not available or is not representative of all possible inputs, then the explanations may be inaccurate or misleading.

PDPs

A PDP displays the relationship between the target and a feature by showing the change in predicted probability as a feature changes while keeping other features constant. Unlike feature importance, which only measures the contribution of each feature, PDPs can reveal interactions between features and their effect on the target. This technique can be used for both regression and classification problems and is compatible with any ML algorithm. PDPs provide insights into the workings of an ML model and help in communicating these findings to others.

A PDP serves as a tool used to understand the relationship between a target and a feature in an ML model. It shows how changes in a single feature affect the predicted target, while holding all other features constant. Unlike feature importance, which only provides information about the main effect of a feature, PDPs can also reveal interactions between features. PDPs can be represented as the average change in the predicted target as a function of changes made to a feature, holding all other features constant. This can be expressed as:

$$PDP_j(x) = \frac{1}{n}\sum_{i=1}^{n} f(x^{(i)}1, ..., x^{(i)}j - 1, x\tilde{} j, x^{(i)}j + 1, ..., x^{(i)}p)$$

where f is the ML model, xj is the jth feature, $x\tilde{}j$ is a constant value representing the change in feature, and p is the total number of features in the model.

PDPs can be used with various ML algorithms, including regression and classification, making them versatile and model-agnostic interpretation tools. They help to visualize and communicate the behavior of an ML model and are useful for problem-solving and debugging purposes.

Counterfactual explanations

In ML, a counterfactual explanation is an explanation of the output of a model that considers what would have happened if the input to the model had been different. This type of explanation can be used to understand why a particular prediction was made and can also be used to understand how changing the input data would change the output of the model.

Counterfactual explanations are often used in explainable AI applications such as healthcare, where it is important to understand not only why a particular decision was made but also how changing inputs (such as patient characteristics or medical records) would affect that decision. In this way, counterfactual explanations can help researchers and practitioners identify potential areas for improvement in their models.

Counterfactual explanations provide an intuitive way to understand the output of an ML model by showing how the input features would need to change to alter the prediction. Here, we will present a detailed example of how counterfactual explanations work.

Consider a simple linear regression model that predicts the price of a house based on its size (in square feet) and the number of bedrooms it has. The model's prediction equation can be represented as:

Price = β0 + β1 × Size + β2 × Bedrooms   (3.3)

Suppose we have the following model coefficients:

β0 = 50,000; β1= 100; β2 = 20,000

Now, let's say we have a house with a size of 1,500 square feet and 3 bedrooms. The model's prediction for this house would be:

Price = 50,000 + 100 × 1,500 + 20,000 × 3 = 50,000 + 150,000 + 60,000 = 260,000

The model predicts that the house would cost $260,000. Now, let's say we want to find a counterfactual explanation that shows how the house price would change if the number of bedrooms were different while keeping the size constant.

For example, we want to know the price of the house if it had 4 bedrooms instead of 3:

Counterfactual Price = 50,000 + 100 × 1,500 + 20,000 × 4= 50,000 + 150,000 + 80,000 = 280,000

The counterfactual explanation tells us that if the house had 4 bedrooms instead of 3, its price would be $280,000. This provides an intuitive way to understand the effect of the number of bedrooms on the house price, as predicted by the model.

There are many ways to generate counterfactual explanations for ML models; one popular approach is to use **local interpretable models** (**LIMs**). LIMs are trained on small subsets of data and then applied to larger datasets; they provide both global (overall) and local (specific) insights into how changes in input features affect model predictions. Another approach is through use cases or prototypes; these approaches focus on specific instances where it may be helpful to generate counterfactual explanations. There are many other methods for generating counterfactual explanations, including rule-based systems, decision trees, and saliency maps.

Summary

As organizations increasingly turn to AI to drive critical business decisions, it is becoming increasingly important to understand how and why these systems are making the predictions they are making. This is known as AI explainability. Not only does AI explainability help to build trust in these systems but it also plays a crucial role in debugging and improving AI models. When we can understand how an AI algorithm works, we can have confidence in its results. However, if we cannot explain the workings of an AI system, we cannot be sure that it is making accurate predictions.

In enterprises and any other business setting in which explainability methods must be applied, there is a constant need to question whether the explainability challenges that come with more complex ML models can be justified, particularly when simpler ML models can do almost as good a job predictively.

In this chapter, we reviewed various methods for explaining AI models, including visualizing data inputs and outputs using techniques such as feature importance and PDPs, as well as methods such as LIME, SHAP, and anchors. These techniques help to understand how individual components contribute to the overall behavior of the AI system.

We also examined several key techniques for AI explainability, including local and global explanations, feature importance, decision trees, SHAP, PDP, and LIME. Feature importance provides a ranking of which input features are most important in determining the output of an AI model, while decision trees visually represent how a model makes its predictions by breaking down each decision into smaller steps. LIME creates simplified versions of complex models that are easier for humans to understand while still maintaining accuracy, and SHAP approximates the value that each feature contributes to a prediction using a game theory approach.

To promote fairness and reliability in AI systems, it is essential to understand and properly use these and other explainability techniques. By promoting transparency, accountability, and fairness, organizations can avoid the risks associated with AI misuse. To build trust in mission-critical AI applications, it is crucial that AI predictions are analyzable in a transparent manner and held accountable for their decisions. By explaining AI, trust can be increased, and potential fairness risks can be identified.

And so, as we journey through the vast and mysterious universe of AI, we come upon the next chapter, where we shall embark on a quest to understand the intricacies of operationalizing mode monitoring, MLOPs, and ModelOps – a journey as wondrous as reaching the heart of the Vogon poetry archive.

References and further reading

1. In this book, we use the terms interpretable and explainable AI interchangeably, but it is important to note that there are differences in opinion among the researchers about their definitions. Typically, explainable AI is focused on providing insights into how the AI system arrived at a particular decision, while interpretability is the discipline of making the AI system itself more understandable by making the individual components transparent. Transparency refers to systems where the inner workings are completely open and accessible, while explainable AI

may only require that some level of understanding be possible. Generally speaking, explainable AI is more concerned with human-centered concerns such as usability and trustworthiness, while interpretable AI focuses more on providing information that can be used to improve the model or debug errors. However, both approaches are necessary for creating safe and effective AI systems.

2. `https://arxiv.org/pdf/2101.09429.pdf`

3. `https://shap.readthedocs.io/en/latest/`

4. `https://shap.readthedocs.io/en/latest/generated/shap.datasets.california.html`

5. `https://lime-ml.readthedocs.io/en/latest/lime.html#module-lime.lime_tabular`

6. `https://scikit-learn.org/stable/autoexamples/inspection/plotlinearmodelcoefficientinterpretation.html`

7. *Anchors: High-Precision Model-Agnostic Explanations*: `https://homes.cs.washington.edu/marcotcr/aaai18.pdf`

8. *Why Are We Using Black Box Models in AI When We Don't Need To? A Lesson from an Explainable AI Competition*: `https://hdsr.mitpress.mit.edu/pub/f9kuryi8/release/8`

9. *Model Monitoring in Practice: Lessons Learned and Open Challenges*: `https://dl.acm.org/doi/pdf/10.1145/3534678.3542617`

10. *Interpretable Machine Learning – A Guide for Making Black Box Models Explainable*: `https://christophm.github.io/interpretable-ml-book/`

11. *Explaining Explanations: An Overview of Interpretability of Machine Learning*: `https://arxiv.org/pdf/1806.00069.pdf`

Robust ML – Monitoring and Management

"A computer would deserve to be called intelligent if it could deceive a human into believing that it was human."

– Alan Turing

"The future depends on some graduate student who is deeply suspicious of everything I have said."

– Geoffrey Hinton

"No one has a clue how to build a conscious machine, at all."

– Stuart Russell

"Anything that could give rise to smarter-than-human intelligence – in the form of Artificial Intelligence, brain-computer interfaces, or neuroscience-based human intelligence enhancement – wins hands down beyond contest as doing the most to change the world. Nothing else is even in the same league."

– Eliezer Yudkowsky

"Robust machine learning aims to develop models that maintain high performance even in the presence of adversarial noise, distributional shift, or corrupted inputs, and thereby ensure safety and reliability in critical applications."

– Adnan Masood

Robust **machine learning** (**ML**) focuses on the development and deployment of resilient algorithms capable of withstanding adversarial attacks, data poisoning, model drift, and data drift, while maintaining stable and reliable predictions in mission-critical applications. While the at-scale production of ML models is still diffusing across enterprises, as AI is more widely developed and used, these production processes are being increasingly adopted.

Tied to the need to develop and deploy resilient algorithms is the requirement to ensure that these algorithms comply with any regulations within the jurisdiction and business vertical they are being deployed in. These two requirements go together very effectively when deployed within a framework for ModelOps and MLOps, and this will be discussed further in *Chapter 6*.

Key components of robust ML include ensuring data integrity, preserving privacy with techniques such as differential privacy, monitoring model stability, and detecting drifts in data distribution and model performance. By tackling these challenges, robust ML fosters trust and reliability in AI systems, ultimately driving safer and more equitable outcomes across various domains.

ML model monitoring is a process of regularly evaluating the performance and accuracy of an ML model over time. Operationalizing model monitoring – that is, establishing a structured approach for tracking and measuring a model's accuracy and effectiveness, and identifying any changes in the data or model that could affect its performance – is essential to ensure ongoing performance and precision. This chapter focuses on identifying the key parameters to track the model's performance and setting thresholds to raise alerts. It covers the essential components of model performance monitoring, including maintaining the business purpose of the model and detecting drifts.

The purpose of this chapter is also to underscore the importance of robust ML life cycle management, MLOps, and ModelOps. These technologies support automated monitoring of models running in production, providing comprehensive measures for data drift, model concept drift, statistical performance, ethical fairness monitoring, privacy preservation, and business scenario simulation. They also offer capabilities such as what-if analysis, parallel model execution comparison, and custom metric creation. You will learn how to use various techniques as part of robust model monitoring and develop an understanding of detecting, alerting, and addressing drifts and other challenges.

In this chapter, you will learn about the following.

- Getting started with the ML life cycle
- Model monitoring with operational and business metrics
- Detecting a model's data drift, prior probability drift, and concept drift
- Metrics for drift monitoring – magnitude, top features, and thresholds
- Addressing drift – alerts on incorrect predictions and decisions to reduce costs
- Handling degradation – when to recalibrate, retrain, or replace models

Artificial intelligence (**AI**) is rapidly becoming integrated into our everyday lives, influencing everything from online searches to the ads we see on social media. As AI grows smarter, there is a risk that it could become biased against certain groups of people, based on the data it is trained on and the algorithms it uses. This is why robust ML and enterprise model governance are essential to operationalize ML models in production. Model governance encompasses the processes and controls that an organization implements to ensure its ML models are ethical, reliable, and fit for purpose. In other words, it's a way to make sure AI systems are fair and trustworthy. As organizations increasingly rely on ML models for critical decision-making, ensuring the security and resilience of these models against potential attacks is crucial. By understanding the different types of attacks and their potential impact, organizations can implement appropriate countermeasures to ensure robust ML systems and minimize potential vulnerabilities.

In this chapter, we will do a quick overview of ML-related attacks and countermeasures.

An overview of ML attacks and countermeasures

The development and deployment of robust ML systems demand a comprehensive approach that covers various aspects of the technology. To ensure the security, reliability, and ethical use of ML models, organizations must focus on four key categories – model and data security, privacy and compliance, attack prevention and monitoring, and ethics and responsible AI. By addressing these categories holistically, organizations can mitigate risks, maintain user trust, and ensure the successful integration of AI technologies into their operations.

In the realm of robust ML, model and data security is of paramount importance. Implementing strong authentication methods ensures only authorized users access ML systems, while using interpretable, fair, or private models bolsters transparency and fairness. Thorough model documentation preserves knowledge and enables seamless transfer, whereas model management combines process and technology controls to oversee deployed systems. Techniques such as throttling and watermarking protect against data extraction attacks. It is crucial to be cautious of potential issues in pre-trained/third-party models and to prioritize API endpoint security. Data versioning safeguards data, while regularized and constrained models and L2 regularization and constraints act as countermeasures against attacks.

Privacy and compliance are central to responsible ML. Adherence to regulations and policies ensures legal compliance, while obtaining consent respects user privacy. Employing anonymization techniques protects personal information, and additional measures are necessary for sensitive biometric data. Following retention limits or requirements and accommodating deletion and rectification requests maintain data integrity. Providing an explanation and allowing intervenability in ML decisions fosters transparency and trust, while addressing bias ensures fairness.

Attack prevention and monitoring focus on safeguarding ML systems from various threats. Discussed in more detail later in this chapter, in summary these methods achieve the following. Mitigating general availability attacks and guarding against trojans and malware helps protect system integrity. Employing measures against man-in-the-middle attacks ensures data and result integrity. Addressing unexplainable ML enhances transparency, while securing distributed computing protects entire computing clusters. Defense against adversarial example attacks, backdoor attacks, data poisoning attacks, and impersonation and evasion attacks strengthens ML systems. Monitoring for attacks on ML explanations, model extraction, inversion attacks, and membership inference attacks helps detect potential threats. Effective communication and thorough API documentation deter attackers, while rigorous code review processes identify potential backdoors.

Last but not least, ethics and responsible AI emphasize the importance of monitoring and controlling the use of AI technologies. Addressing abuses of ML raises awareness of potential misuse and promotes the responsible application of AI across industries.

So long, and thanks for all the fish! Now, let's hitch a cosmic ride to swiftly probe the peculiarities of each category and its accompanying members.

Model and data security

Note the following peculiarities for model and data security:

- **Authentication**: Authentication is the process of verifying a user's identity to ensure that only authorized individuals can access high-stakes ML systems. Examples of authentication methods include login credentials, multi-factor authentication, and biometrics. By implementing strong authentication mechanisms, organizations can prevent unauthorized access and reduce the risk of malicious activities.

- **Interpretable, fair, or private models**: Interpretable models are designed to be more transparent and easier to understand, making them simpler to debug and secure. Fair models aim to minimize bias and ensure equitable treatment for all users, reducing potential legal and reputational risks. Private models protect sensitive data, often using privacy-preserving techniques such as differential privacy. By prioritizing accuracy, interpretability, fairness, and privacy in modeling techniques, organizations can increase security and reduce potential vulnerabilities.

- **Model documentation**: Model documentation is the practice of thoroughly recording information about an ML system, including its architecture, training data, hyperparameters, performance metrics, vulnerabilities, and security concerns. Comprehensive documentation helps preserve and transfer knowledge, enabling developers and security teams to better understand and address potential risks.

- **Model management**: Model management involves maintaining an overview of all deployed ML systems and responding quickly to issues that may arise. This process typically combines process controls (such as documentation) with technology controls (such as model monitoring and inventories). Effective model management ensures that organizations can detect and remediate security concerns promptly.

- **Throttling**: Throttling is a technique used to restrict the rate at which users can make predictions or access an ML system. By limiting the number of rapid predictions or increasing prediction latency, organizations can slow down potential attackers and protect against model or data extraction attacks.

- **Watermarking**: Watermarking involves adding subtle markers or patterns to data or predictions that can be used to identify the source or owner of the information. This technique deters theft and makes stolen assets more identifiable, helping to protect intellectual property and sensitive data.

- **API endpoint security**: API endpoint security refers to the measures taken to protect high-risk ML APIs from unauthorized access and malicious activities. This can include implementing anomaly detection, throttling, and strong authentication to prevent unauthorized users from effectively extracting model information or manipulating the system.

- **Pre-trained/third-party model awareness**: Pre-trained and third-party models can introduce security risks, as they may contain vulnerabilities or be susceptible to poisoning attacks. Organizations should be cautious when using these models and thoroughly evaluate them for potential security issues before deployment.

- **Data versioning**: Data versioning is the practice of tracking changes to datasets over time, allowing organizations to monitor and control the data used to train and update their ML models. Implementing data versioning can help counteract data poisoning attempts, as it enables organizations to identify and revert to previous, uncompromised versions of the data.

- **Regularized, constrained models, and L2 regularization**: Regularized models use penalties, such as L2 regularization, on model parameters to prevent overfitting, while constrained models limit the model's architecture or parameters to a predefined space. Although potentially easier to extract, these models offer increased resistance to adversarial example attacks and data poisoning. It is crucial to remember that no single countermeasure is entirely effective against all attacks, so organizations should employ a combination of techniques and best practices for comprehensive security in their ML systems.

Privacy and compliance

- **Regulations and policies**: Regulations and policies refer to data privacy laws and organizational guidelines that dictate how personal data should be handled. Ensuring adherence to these regulations and policies is crucial to maintain trust and avoid legal repercussions. Understanding and adhering to data privacy regulations, such as GDPR and CCPA, as well as organizational privacy policies, helps protect users' data and maintain compliance.

- **Consent**: Consent is the process of obtaining permission from users before collecting, processing, or using their data in ML models. In many jurisdictions, acquiring consent is a legal requirement, and doing so helps ensure ethical data practices. For example, a company might ask for user consent through a clear, concise privacy policy that outlines how their data will be used.

- **Anonymization**: Anonymization is the process of removing, masking, or otherwise obscuring **personally identifiable information** (**PII**) from a dataset to protect users' privacy and reduce the risk of bias in ML models. Techniques such as k-anonymity, differential privacy, and pseudonymization can be used to anonymize data while preserving its utility.

- **Biometric data**: Biometric data refers to unique, measurable physiological or behavioral characteristics, such as fingerprints, facial recognition, and voice patterns, used for identification or authentication purposes. Given the sensitive nature of biometric data, additional security and data privacy controls must be implemented to ensure its protection. For example, encrypting biometric data at rest and in transit can help prevent unauthorized access.

- **Retention limits or requirements**: Data retention limits or requirements are guidelines or legal mandates that dictate how long personal data can be stored or processed. Following these limits ensures compliance with data privacy laws and organizational privacy policies. For example, a company might implement a policy to automatically delete user data after a specific period or upon a user's request.

- **Deletion and rectification requests**: Deletion and rectification requests are user-initiated actions that require an organization to update, correct, or delete personal data. Complying with these requests is often a legal requirement and helps maintain user trust. For example, a company should establish clear procedures for users to submit requests and ensure that their data is updated or deleted as needed.

- **Explanation**: Explanation in ML refers to the ability to understand and interpret the decision-making process of a model. Preparing for potential legal requirements to explain ML decisions to consumers can help organizations maintain compliance and ensure transparency. For example, a company might use techniques such as LIME or SHAP to generate human-understandable explanations for model predictions.

- **Intervenability**: Intervenability is the ability of users or regulators to intervene, appeal, or override ML decisions. Anticipating potential legal requirements for intervenability can help organizations maintain compliance and ensure fairness. For example, a company might establish a clear process for users to contest ML-based decisions, allowing human intervention when necessary.

- **Bias**: Bias in ML refers to systematic errors in model predictions that result from the underlying data or algorithms. Addressing bias in data processing outcomes helps organizations comply with data privacy laws and non-discrimination regulations. For example, a company might use techniques such as re-sampling, re-weighting, or adversarial training to mitigate bias in their ML models.

Attack prevention and monitoring

- **General availability attacks**: General availability attacks are attempts to overwhelm an ML system, causing a denial of service. For example, an attacker might flood a system with numerous requests, rendering it unavailable for legitimate users. To defend against these attacks, secure ML systems with firewalls, filters, reverse DNS lookup, and conduct bias testing during training and deployment.

- **Trojans and malware**: Trojans and malware are malicious software that can infiltrate and compromise an ML system. An attacker might introduce malware into a model's training data to manipulate its behavior. To counteract these threats, scan all software artifacts associated with an ML system for malware and trojans.

- **Man-in-the-middle attacks**: **Man-in-the-middle** (**MITM**) attacks occur when an attacker intercepts and alters the communication between two parties, potentially manipulating the data or model results. For example, an attacker might intercept the data sent to an ML model and manipulate the results returned to the user. To defend against MITM attacks, use encryption, certificates, mutual authentication, or other security measures to ensure the integrity of ML system results.

- **Unexplainable ML**: Unexplainable ML refers to complex models that are difficult to interpret, increasing the risk of unintended consequences and making it harder to detect potential attacks. For example, a deep neural network might produce accurate results but be difficult to understand or validate. To address this issue, use interpretable models and model explanations to reduce complexity and improve transparency.

- **Distributed computing**: Distributed computing attacks involve compromising worker nodes in distributed systems, potentially leading to data or model corruption. For example, an attacker might infiltrate a worker node and manipulate its training data or model parameters. To defend against these attacks, monitor and secure worker nodes in distributed systems and ensure data and model integrity across the entire computing cluster.

- **Adversarial example attacks**: Adversarial example attacks are attempts to manipulate an ML model's input data to produce incorrect or harmful predictions. For example, an attacker might add imperceptible noise to an image to cause a classification model to misidentify it. Implement robust ML models that are less sensitive to small changes in input data to counteract these attacks.

- **Backdoor attacks**: Backdoor attacks involve inserting hidden functionality into an ML model or its training data to trigger a specific behavior when certain conditions are met. For example, an attacker might insert a specific pattern into training data that causes a model to produce incorrect predictions when encountered. To defend against these attacks, harden code review processes and monitor for unusual input-output combinations.

- **Data poisoning attacks**: Data poisoning attacks occur when an attacker manipulates training data to compromise an ML model's performance or behavior. For example, an attacker might introduce incorrect labels or corrupted samples into the training data. To counteract these attacks, implement data versioning, monitor data changes, and avoid excessive columns in ML models.

- **Impersonation and evasion attacks**: Impersonation and evasion attacks involve an attacker attempting to impersonate a legitimate user or evade detection by an ML model. For example, an attacker might mimic the behavior of a legitimate user to gain access to a system protected by an ML model.

  To counteract these attacks, monitor for suspicious input patterns and enhance model robustness.

- **Attacks on ML explanations**: Attacks on ML explanations involve manipulating the explanations provided by an ML model to hide or mislead users about its behavior. For example, an attacker might alter the explanation of a model's decision to conceal a bias or malicious intent. To defend against these attacks, validate the accuracy of explanations and monitor for suspicious explanation patterns.

- **Model extraction and inversion attacks**: Model extraction attacks aim to reverse-engineer or steal an ML model, while inversion attacks attempt to recover the original training data from the model's output. For example, an attacker might send numerous queries to an API and analyze the responses to recreate the underlying model or data. To defend against these attacks, limit access to the model's API, implement strong authentication, and monitor for unusual API usage patterns.

- **Membership inference attacks**: Membership inference attacks involve determining whether a specific data point was used in the training set of an ML model. For example, an attacker might use the model's predictions to infer sensitive information about individuals in the training data. To counteract these attacks, enhance model robustness, monitor for unusual API usage patterns, and implement privacy-preserving techniques such as differential privacy. Although membership inference attacks can be difficult to execute, they should not be overlooked. Focus security resources on more feasible attacks, while still monitoring for potential signs of these attacks and implementing privacy-enhancing techniques to minimize their impact.

- **Communication**: Communication in the context of ML security involves clearly documenting findings and effectively communicating them to the security team in charge of hosting the models. This helps ensure that potential vulnerabilities and concerns are addressed promptly.

- **API documentation**: Thorough and transparent API documentation can help deter model extraction attacks and make manipulation attempts obvious. By providing clear instructions and guidelines, users can better understand how to interact with the API securely and responsibly.

- **Code review processes**: Hardening code review processes helps account for potential backdoors in ML scoring artifacts. By carefully reviewing code and ensuring that best practices are followed, organizations can minimize the risk of vulnerabilities being introduced into ML systems.

Ethics and responsible AI

- **Abuses of ML**: As ML and AI technologies continue to advance, there is an increasing risk that they may be misused or abused for malicious purposes. To mitigate these risks, it is essential to monitor and control the use of AI technologies, ensuring that they are only employed in ethical and responsible ways. This includes raising awareness about the potential for abuse among stakeholders, such as developers, users, and regulators. Additionally, organizations should establish clear guidelines and best practices for the ethical use of ML systems and promote transparency and accountability in their development and deployment. By fostering a culture of responsibility and ethics in the AI community, we can help to prevent the abuse of ML technologies and ensure their positive impact on society.

As we transition from discussing potential attacks in the ML context, let's now delve into the crucial role of the ML life cycle and MLOps in mitigating these threats and maintaining secure, robust AI systems.

The ML life cycle

Reproducibility is crucial in ML to ensure consistent and replicable results. Integrating the MLOps life cycle promotes reproducibility, auditability, ethics, reliability, and trustworthiness in ML models. Auditability ensures the model behaves as expected and provides transparency of its workings and data usage. Ethical guidelines addressing privacy rights, data accuracy, and transparency are essential when deploying AI systems. A well-defined ML life cycle facilitates adherence to these guidelines. Model monitoring guarantees reliability by operationalizing the trustworthiness of ML models, particularly in high-risk applications and regulated industries. Implementing routine testing, validation by outside experts, and ongoing performance monitoring is essential. Clear explanations for decision-making and user control over their own data ensure a transparent, repeatable, and auditable AI system.

Adopting an ML life cycle

ML operationalization is the process of making ML models available for production use, enabling them to be utilized at scale. This involves moving beyond a **works-on-my-machine** or, in this case, **works-on-my-Jupyter-notebook** approach, requiring a robust, reliable, secure, and reproducible implementation of an ML model suitable for enterprise deployment. Operationalization typically encompasses user interface creation, model training and deployment management, and performance monitoring.

The productionization of ML models and AI systems presents a significant challenge for modern enterprises, demanding substantial cultural shifts as well as the adoption of new technologies and methodologies. Organizations that successfully navigate this transformation can effectively produce and deliver AI at scale, reaping the associated business benefits. Moreover, these capabilities facilitate data-driven model governance and AI assurance processes.

To effectively productionize AI in an enterprise setting, an AI system must transition from a prototype to a full-fledged product, necessitating considerable engineering efforts to enhance robustness, performance, and integrate domain-specific features. This process often involves collaboration with domain experts to embed domain knowledge into a system.

The ML life cycle typically consists of many elements, including the following:

- **Preprocessing** refers to the task of cleaning up raw data so that it can be used by ML algorithms.

- **Feature engineering** is the process of selecting relevant features (variables) from the dataset for use in building the models.

- **Model selection** involves choosing between different types of models (for example, support vector machines or decision trees) based on their performance on a given dataset. Model selection is the process of choosing an ML model that best suits the data and the task at hand. There are many different types of models to choose from, so it is important to select one that will work well with the data and produce accurate results.

- **Training** is the process of fitting a model to data so that it can learn from it. This involves adjusting the model's parameters so that it accurately predicts outcomes based on new input data.

- **Tuning** or **optimization** is the process of fine-tuning a model's parameters in order to improve its performance.

- **Evaluation** or **testing** is used to assess how well a trained model performs on unseen data. This allows for an objective assessment of a model's accuracy and helps identify any areas where improvements could be made.

At this stage, we should highlight that the ML life cycle and data science life cycle are connected yet distinct concepts, designed to ensure the responsible and efficient development and deployment of AI models. The data science life cycle primarily focuses on the process of extracting insights from data, and then using learning, which may subsequently lead to the development of an ML model. The ML life cycle refers to the distinct set of processes that address the development, training, evaluation, and deployment of ML models.

The **Cross-Industry Standard Process for Data Mining (CRISP-DM)** and **Team Data Science Process (TDSP)** are examples of frameworks used to manage these life cycles. CRISP-DM is a process model for data mining projects, while TDSP is a framework that streamlines the collaborative efforts of data science teams. Both are instrumental in providing structure and guidance to develop, deploy, and maintain ML models and data-driven solutions. The ML counterpart, the MLLifecycle, comprises several steps:

1. Define the business problem to be solved with ML.

2. Understand and ensure the quality and representativeness of the data used for model training.

3. Split the data into training, validation, and test sets to assess model performance on unseen data.

4. Choose appropriate ML algorithms or employ automated ML tools.

5. Train the model on the training set and evaluate it on the validation set.

6. Tune hyperparameters if needed and repeat *steps 4–6* until satisfied with the model's performance.

7. Test the final model on the test set.

8. Deploy the model into production.

9. Monitor the model, gather feedback, and assess its ongoing performance.

Splitting data into training, validation, and test sets immediately prior to modeling is standard when building an ML model. Doing so enables a data scientist or ML engineer to validate and test the power and validity of the built model, determining its performance in terms of prediction accuracy.

An ML model consists of parameters and hyperparameters. The model parameters are fixed values that are determined when the model is trained. The model hyperparameters can be adjusted (either manually or automatically) to tune the model with the aim of improving its performance.

Having established the importance of a well-defined ML life cycle to ensure ethical, safe, and fair development of AI models, we will now turn our attention to ModelOps and MLOps. These disciplines emphasize model monitoring, drift detection, and other aspects of the ML life cycle that have significant implications for explainable and interpretable AI. As we progress, we will explore model monitoring techniques to track ML model performance and examine the phenomenon of model drift, which results from shifts in data distribution or the underlying algorithm. Before delving into the intricacies of model drift and strategies to maintain consistent models, we will first review some key concepts associated with the ML life cycle.

MLOps and ModelOps

MLOps, also known as DevOps for ML, is a practice to operationalize and manage ML workflows, with the goal of increasing the speed, quality, and reliability of ML applications. Conversely, ModelOps is a set of best practices to manage ML models throughout their life cycle, covering aspects from model development and training to deployment and monitoring.

Although MLOps and ModelOps share similarities in their focus on the operational aspects of ML development, MLOps encompasses elements of data engineering and model management as well. Key components of MLOps include **continuous integration/delivery (CI/CD)**, infrastructure as code, and monitoring and logging.

Successful ModelOps involves automation in building, testing, and deploying models, as well as setting up monitoring systems to track model performance in production and identify issues early on. While MLOps specifically targets the management of ML models, ModelOps covers a broader range of best practices to manage any type of software application throughout its life cycle. However, both terms are often used interchangeably.

Implementing ModelOps involves four main components – data management, environment management, code management, and pipeline management. Each component plays a vital role in ensuring smooth operations and preventing errors during each stage of the model life cycle. Popular automation tools such as Jenkins, **CircleCI**, **AWS CodePipeline**, and **Azure DevOps** help automate various tasks related to each stage of the model life cycle, such as building, testing, and deployment.

In MLOps, the focus is on the operationalization and management of AI models specifically within production systems. Conversely, ModelOps is considered a superset of MLOps. The advantage of ModelOps over MLOps lies in its broader scope, as it aims to operationalize not only ML models but also all AI models.

Implementing MLOps and ModelOps within an enterprise can be challenging due to the required cultural changes. Successful implementation requires buy-in from all stakeholders, including business leads, IT teams, subject matter experts, and operations team members. Initiatives tend to succeed when connected to the upskilling of data scientists and engineers working within an enterprise, where their implementation facilitates key business innovations. It is recommended to start small, prove value, and then migrate all existing and new ML models and other advanced analytics onto the delivery platform, rather than opting for a "big bang" approach, which often fails in practice.

The ML life cycle, MLOps, and ModelOps are distinct yet interrelated concepts, each playing a critical role in the development, deployment, and management of AI models. While the ML life cycle outlines the process of building, training, evaluating, and deploying ML models, MLOps specifically focuses on the operational aspects of managing these models in production systems. ModelOps, conversely, serves as a more comprehensive framework that encompasses the operationalization of all AI models, extending beyond just ML models.

Despite their similarities and overlaps, these concepts have important distinctions. MLOps is primarily concerned with the management of ML models, while ModelOps covers a broader range of practices to manage any type of software application throughout its life cycle. The ML life cycle, however, provides the structure and steps to build and deploy ML models effectively.

Having understood the distinctions and connections between these concepts, we will now shift our attention to a key aspect of robust ML – model monitoring. In particular, we will delve into **model drift**, **concept drift**, and **data drift**, which are crucial to maintain consistent and accurate models in production environments.

Model drift

Model drift occurs when the performance of an ML model degrades over time, often due to changes in the underlying data distribution or the relationships between input features and the target variable. Detecting and addressing model drift is essential to maintain the accuracy and reliability of a model in production environments.

There are two main types of model drift:

- **Concept drift**: This happens when the relationship between the input features and the target variable changes over time. It may be caused by evolving trends, changing customer preferences, or other external factors that affect the underlying data patterns. Concept drift requires updating a model to capture these changes and maintain its performance.

- **Data drift**: Data drift occurs when the distribution of the input features changes over time, even if the relationship between the input features and the target variable remains constant. This could be due to changes in data collection processes, shifts in user behavior, or other factors that affect the input data. Detecting data drift allows for timely adjustments to the data preprocessing and feature engineering steps, ensuring a model remains accurate and relevant.

To measure model drift, you can employ several techniques:

- **Performance metrics monitoring**: Regularly monitor key performance metrics (e.g., accuracy, F1-score, precision, and recall) on new, unseen data to detect any significant drop in a model's performance, which may indicate drift

- **Statistical tests**: Conduct statistical tests (e.g., the Kolmogorov-Smirnov test and chi-squared test) to compare the distributions of the input features in the training data and the new data, identifying significant differences that may indicate data drift

- **Drift detection algorithms**: Implement drift detection algorithms (e.g., ADWIN, DDM, and EDDM) that monitor a model's error rate or other performance indicators over time, and raise alarms when drift is detected

By proactively measuring model drift and addressing it through model retraining, data preprocessing adjustments, or other interventions, you can ensure the continued accuracy and reliability of your ML models in production environments.

The primary distinction between model decay and model drift lies in the source of performance reduction. Model decay stems from technical degradation, impacting ease of use, whereas model drift signifies a semantic change or conceptual shift. To put it succinctly, all decaying models undergo some form of drifting, but not all drifting models experience decay. It is worth noting that these terms are sometimes used interchangeably, which can undoubtedly lead to confusion.

Detection, correction, and prevention are crucial aspects to consider when addressing model drift.

Data drift

Data drift occurs when the distribution of the input features in an ML model changes over time, even if the relationship between the input features and the target variable remains constant. This can lead to a decrease in model performance, as the model might have been trained on data that is no longer representative of the current data. Detecting and addressing data drift is crucial to maintain the accuracy and reliability of a model in production environments.

Data drift can be categorized into the following types:

- **Covariate drift**: This type of drift occurs when the distribution of the input features changes over time, while the relationship between the input features and the target variable remains constant. Covariate drift can result from changes in data collection processes, shifts in user behavior, or other factors that affect input data.

- **Prior probability drift**: In this case, the distribution of the target variable changes over time, which can indirectly affect the relationship between input features and the target variable. This type of drift might require adjusting a model's decision threshold or updating the model entirely.

To measure data drift, you can employ several techniques:

- **Distribution comparison**: Compare the distribution of input features in the training data and the new data using visualizations, such as histograms or density plots. Significant differences may indicate data drift.

- **Statistical tests**: Conduct statistical tests (e.g., the Kolmogorov-Smirnov test and chi-squared test) to compare the distributions of the input features in the training data and the new data, identifying significant differences that may indicate data drift.

  The **chi-squared test** is a statistical test used to determine whether there is a significant difference between the expected frequencies and the observed frequencies in categorical data. It can be used to detect data drift by comparing the distribution of categorical features in the reference and test data.

Let Oi j denote the observed frequency in category i for group j, and let Ei j denote the expected frequency under the null hypothesis (no difference between groups). The chi-squared test statistic, χ2, is given by the following:

$$\chi 2 \qquad k \quad m \quad (Oi\, j - Ei\, j\,)2$$

$$= \sum \sum$$

Assuming i=1, j=1,

Ei j   (4.1)

where k is the number of categories and m is the number of groups. The null hypothesis is that the observed frequencies are consistent with the expected frequencies, meaning there is no difference between the groups. If the calculated χ2 value is greater than the critical value at a given significance level, the null hypothesis is rejected, indicating data drift. For example, we can use the chi-squared test to compare the distribution of customer purchase categories in two different months. If the test indicates a significant difference, it may suggest data drift, and the model should be retrained with the new purchase data. We will describe the Kolmogorov-Smirnov test in the following section.

- **Monitoring feature importance**: Track the importance of input features over time. If the importance of certain features changes significantly, it may be an indication of data drift.

  By proactively measuring data drift and addressing it through data preprocessing adjustments, feature engineering, or model retraining, you can ensure the continued accuracy and reliability of your ML models in production environments.

Concept drift

Concept drift refers to the change in the underlying relationships between input features and target variables in an ML model over time. This change can lead to a decrease in model performance as the model's assumptions become less accurate. There are different types of concept drift:

- **Abrupt drift**: Sudden changes in the underlying concept, often caused by unforeseen events or rapid shifts in the environment

- **Gradual drift**: Slow and steady changes in the underlying concept that occur over a longer period

- **Incremental drift**: Continuous and progressive changes in the underlying concept that occur over time

- **Recurring drift**: The underlying concept changes cyclically or periodically, returning to previous states

Measuring concept drift typically involves monitoring the performance metrics of a model over time and detecting any significant changes in these metrics. Some common methods for measuring concept drift include the following:

- **Performance monitoring**: Regularly evaluate the model's performance on new, unseen data and compare it to a predefined threshold or the model's historical performance.

- **Statistical tests**: Apply statistical tests, such as the Kolmogorov-Smirnov test or the Page-Hinkley test, to detect changes in the data distribution or the model's error rates.

- The **Kolmogorov-Smirnov (KS)** test is a non-parametric[1] test to compare the distributions of two samples. It is used to detect data drift by measuring the maximum difference between the **cumulative distribution functions (CDFs)** of the reference and test data. Mathematically, let $F_n(x)$ and $G_m(x)$ denote the empirical CDFs of the reference data with n samples and test data with m samples, respectively. The KS test statistic, Dnm, is given by the following:

$$Dnm = \sup_x |F_n(x) - G_m(x)| \qquad (4.2)$$

The null hypothesis is that both samples are drawn from the same distribution. If Dnm is greater than the critical value at a given significance level, the null hypothesis is rejected, indicating data drift. For example, we can use the KS test to compare the distributions of daily temperatures in two different months. If the test indicates a significant difference, it may suggest data drift, and the model should be retrained with new temperature data.

- The **Page-Hinkley (PH)** test is a change-point detection method to detect concept drift in a time-series data stream by monitoring the cumulative sum of deviations from the mean.

  The test statistic, PH_t, is given by the following:

$$PH_t = \sum_{i=1}^{T}(X_i - \bar{X}t) - \min_{i=1}^{i} \sum_{j=1}^{i}(X_j - \bar{X}t) \qquad (4.3)$$

where X_i is the observation at time i, $\bar{X}t$ is the mean of the observations up to time t, and PH_t is the PH test statistic at time t. A change is detected if PH_t exceeds a user-defined threshold, λ. For example, we can apply the PH test to detect changes in the error rate of a classifier. If a change is detected, it may indicate concept drift, and the model should be updated or retrained accordingly.

- **Drift detection algorithms**: Employ specific drift detection algorithms such as ADWIN, DDM, or EDDM to identify concept drift in streaming data.

- **Adaptive Window (ADWIN)** is a change detection algorithm based on a sliding window with a variable size. It maintains two windows, W1 and W2, and continually compares the average of the elements in each window. When the absolute difference in averages exceeds a predefined threshold, a change is detected.

Mathematically, let μ_1 and μ_2 denote the averages of the elements in W_1 and W_2, respectively. A change is detected if:

$$|\mu_1 - \mu_2| > \varepsilon_{cut} \qquad (4.4)$$

where ε_{cut} is the total number of elements in both windows, and δ is a user-defined confidence parameter.

- **Drift Detection Method (DDM)** monitors the error rate of a classifier and raises an alarm when the error rate increases significantly. Let p_i be the error rate at instance i, and $s_i = p_i(1 - p_i)/i$. DDM calculates the minimum error rate p_{min} and its standard deviation s_{min} up to instance i. A warning is raised if:

$$p_i + s_i \geq p_{min} + \alpha \cdot s_{min} \qquad (4.5)$$

and a drift is detected if:

$$pi + s_i \geq p_{min} + \beta \cdot s_{min} \qquad (4.6)$$

where α and β are user-defined thresholds, with $\beta > \alpha$.

- **Early Drift Detection Method (EDDM)** is an extension of DDM that is more sensitive to gradual changes. It measures the average distance pi between classification errors, with the standard deviation s_i. For each instance i, EDDM calculates the maximum distance between errors p_{max} and its standard deviation s_{max}. A warning is raised if:

$$p_i + s_i \leq p_{max} \cdot (1 - \alpha \cdot s_{max}) \qquad (4.7)$$

and a drift is detected if:

$$p_i + s_i \leq p_{max} \cdot (1 - \beta \cdot s_{max}) \qquad (4.8)$$

where α and β are user-defined thresholds, with $\beta > \alpha$.

When concept drift is detected, it's essential to update the model or retrain it on the latest data to maintain its accuracy and effectiveness.

Monitoring and mitigating drift in ML models

All three types of drift (model, data, and concept) are important to measure, as they impact the performance and accuracy of ML models. Monitoring and mitigating each type of drift is essential to maintain model performance over time:

- As discussed, model drift occurs when a model's performance degrades as it becomes outdated due to changes in the underlying data distribution or concept.

  Mitigation: Regularly retrain the model with fresh, representative data to maintain its performance. For example, retrain a sales prediction model with new sales data to capture recent trends and changes in customer behavior.

- Data drift occurs when the input data distribution changes over time, making the model's training data less representative of the current data.

  Mitigation: Continuously monitor the distribution of input features and compare them to the training data. If significant deviations are detected, retrain the model using updated data. For example, if an image recognition model is trained on outdoor images taken in summer, it may not perform well on winter images due to different lighting conditions. Retrain the model with a diverse dataset covering all seasons to improve its performance.

- Concept drift occurs when the relationship between input features and the target variable changes over time, rendering the model's learned patterns less relevant.

  Mitigation: Use online learning or adaptive models that can update their parameters as new data becomes available. For example, if a credit scoring model is affected by changing economic conditions, adapt the model to account for these changes, such as incorporating new features or adjusting model parameters in real time.

To sum it all up, it is crucial to monitor and mitigate all types of drift to ensure the continued effectiveness of ML models. Regularly updating the models, monitoring input feature distributions, and employing adaptive learning techniques are practical ways to address drift and maintain model performance.

"The most important aspect of a statistical analysis is not what you do with the data, it's what data you use."

– Andrew Gelman

Before concluding this section and moving on to drift detection examples, we will discuss model bias and model drift, two related concepts in the context of ML, but they refer to different aspects of model performance and behavior.

Model bias refers to a model's assumptions about the underlying data and the relationships between input features and the target variable. A biased model makes systematic errors when attempting to generalize from the training data to new, unseen data points. High bias typically indicates that the model is too simple and does not capture the complexity of the underlying data patterns, leading to underfitting. Conversely, low bias suggests that the model can accurately capture the relationships in the training data. Model drift, conversely, refers to the degradation of a model's performance over time due to changes in the underlying data distribution, input features, or the relationship between input features and the target variable (concept drift). Model drift is not an inherent property of the model itself but, rather, a consequence of the evolving environment in which the model operates.

Understanding the relationship between model bias and model drift is essential to build resilient ML models. A high-bias model may be more sensitive to drift due to its simplistic assumptions, while a low-bias model that accurately captures underlying patterns may be more adaptable. To mitigate model drift, it is crucial to address model bias by selecting an appropriately complex model and retraining it regularly with fresh, representative data.

In the following code examples, we will demonstrate practical approaches to detect and manage data and model drift to maintain optimal model performance over time.

Simple data drift detection using Python data drift detector

`DataDriftDetector` is a Python package that contains tools to detect and compare statistical differences between two structurally similar pandas DataFrames. The function is intended to detect data drift – when an input variable's statistical properties change over time. The main `DataDriftDetector` class compares and analyzes the differences between two pandas datasets and provides a few useful methods.

You can install the package using the following command:

```
pip install data-drift-detector
```

Once installed, you should now import all the required libraries, including `sklearn` for the diabetes dataset and `DataDriftDetector`.

```
1 import pandas as pd
2 import json
3 from sklearn.datasets import load_diabetes
4 from data_drift_detector import DataDriftDetector
```

Figure 4.1: Importing the libraries and datasets

For this analysis, we'll use the diabetes dataset from the widely used scikit-learn library, which offers a diverse collection of data points specifically designed to train models to predict the presence of diabetes in patients. The dataset encompasses crucial features, including the patient's age, weight, and blood sugar levels, which together enable the development of more accurate and reliable predictive models while harnessing the power of the `scikit-learn` library.

```
1 data = load_diabetes()
2 df = pd.DataFrame(data.data, columns=data.feature_names)
3 df['target'] = pd.Series(data.target)
4 df.head()
```

	age	sex	bmi	bp	s1	s2	s3	s4	s5
0	0.038076	0.050680	0.061696	0.021872	-0.044223	-0.034821	-0.043401	-0.002592	0.019908
1	-0.001882	-0.044642	-0.051474	-0.026328	-0.008449	-0.019163	0.074412	-0.039493	-0.068330
2	0.085299	0.050680	0.044451	-0.005671	-0.045599	-0.034194	-0.032356	-0.002592	0.002864
3	-0.089063	-0.044642	-0.011595	-0.036656	0.012191	0.024991	-0.036038	0.034309	0.022692
4	0.005383	-0.044642	-0.036385	0.021872	0.003935	0.015596	0.008142	-0.002592	-0.031991

Figure 4.2: Loading the diabetes dataset

Now that we have loaded the dataset (see the sample data in the preceding figure), we will need to split the dataset into two segments. We have learned that data drift is the gradual change in the distribution of a dataset over time. In order to use the diabetes dataset for data drift, we split it into two concurrent segments. Measuring data drift between multiple datasets can be done by calculating summary statistics for each dataset and then comparing them using a statistical test, such as a chi-squared test or ANOVA, and by using distance measures, such as Euclidean distance (we will discuss these further in the following list).

The following code is used to split the data into two different segments, `prior` and `post`.

```
1 split_ = int(len(df)/2)
2 df_prior, df_post  = df.iloc[:split_], df.iloc[split_:]
```

Figure 4.3: Splitting the dataset into segments

Now, we can proceed and initialize the data drift detector.

```
2 detector = DataDriftDetector(df_prior=df_prior,
3                              df_post=df_post,
4                              categorical_columns=cat_columns,
5                              numeric_columns=[c for c in df.columns
6                                               if c not in cat_columns])
```

Figure 4.4: Loading DataDriftDetector

The `DataDriftDetector` instance takes two pandas DataFrames and a set of columns (categorical or numerical) to compare these datasets.

Distance measures are used in statistics and probability theory to assess the differences between statistical objects, such as data points, data samples, and probability distributions. As such, they have an obvious application when it comes to measuring and monitoring data and model drift.

Various distance measures can be used to assess the similarity or dissimilarity between two data points or data samples:

- **Euclidean distance** is a measure of the straight-line distance between two points in a Euclidean space.

- **Manhattan distance**, also known as the city block distance, is the sum of absolute differences of a point or sample coordinates.

- **Hamming distance** is the number of positions at which the corresponding elements of points or samples are different. This is used to compare the binary representation of data.

- **Minkowski distance** is a generalization of both Euclidean and Manhattan distances.

- **Jensen-Shannon distance** is a measure of how close two probability distributions are to each other.

- **Wasserstein distance**, also known as the earth mover's distance, measures the amount of work required to transform one probability distribution into another.

Each of these has its own advantages and disadvantages, so it is important to choose the right one for your dataset and problem.

In this case, statistical tests are performed to determine whether the columns are similar, with Jensen-Shannon distances and Wasserstein distances calculated for each column. These distance measures are preferred in data drift detection because they are more robust, capable of capturing subtle changes, and provide a comprehensive view of the changes in the data. Data drift is more likely to exist when distance values are high, and this is indicated by lower p-values:

```
1 print(json.dumps(detector.calculate_drift(), indent=4))
```

```json
{
    "categorical": {
        "bmi": {
            "chi_square_test_statistic": Infinity,
            "chi_square_test_p_value": 0.0,
            "kl_divergence_post_given_prior": Infinity,
            "kl_divergence_prior_given_post": Infinity,
            "jensen_shannon_distance": 0.4645821001845946,
            "wasserstein_distance": 0.000666241012686339
        }
    },
    "numerical": {
        "age": {
            "ks_2sample_test_statistic": 0.16,
            "ks_2sample_test_p_value": 0.1548386665118475,
            "jensen_shannon_distance": 0.06786036225010543,
            "wasserstein_distance": 0.0008626574628176742
        },
        "sex": {
            "ks_2sample_test_statistic": 0.07,
            "ks_2sample_test_p_value": 0.9684099261397212,
            "jensen_shannon_distance": 0.028831354643951746,
            "wasserstein_distance": 0.00030124328424485257
```

Figure 4.5: The JSON output from statistical tests

Let's briefly discuss the statistics shown in the preceding figure. These are a combination of distance measures and statistical tests (where each has a null hypothesis that there is no evidence of data drift, against the alternative hypothesis that there is evidence that data drift is present).

The Jensen-Shannon distance and Wasserstein distance are reported for each feature of the dataset.

The KS^2 sample test statistic (or the Kolmogorov-Smirnov test for a better fit) measures the difference between the two datasets under the null hypothesis. If this statistic is large, it means that there is evidence against the null hypothesis.

The chi-squared sample test statistic is another means of comparing the differences between two datasets and determining whether there is evidence of significant differences. Low p-values are indicative of such significant differences.

While we can discern evidence of differences from some of the statistics associated with each of these statistical tests and distance measures, plotting and visualizing these outputs can make any evidence of differences more straightforward to discern.

```
1 detector.plot_numeric_to_numeric(
2     plot_kws={'alpha': 0.4},
3     diag_kws={'common_norm': False},
4     plot_numeric_columns=['age', 'sex', 'bmi', 'bp']
5 )
```

Figure 4.6: Building a numeric plot of the features

A picture is worth a thousand words. Upon plotting these statistics, we can see the difference between the original and the new dataset drift visually, and how it changes between the PRIOR and POST datasets.

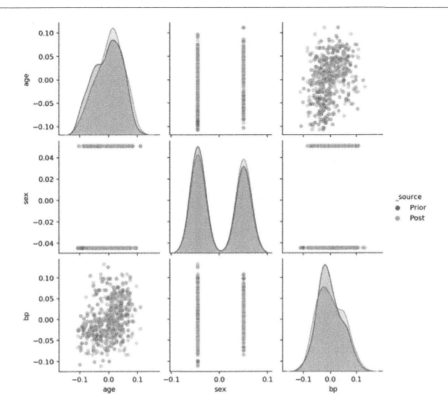

Figure 4.7: A visual representation of dataset drift between the original and new
datasets, showing the difference between PRIOR and POST datasets

Along with the visual representation of the feature differences, we can also discover the ML efficacy, which is essentially a way of finding out how a dataset behaves on multiple models. Efficacy is the ability of something to produce a desired or intended result. In other words, it's the effectiveness of a given action or intervention. When it comes to ML, efficacy refers to how well a model can learn from and make predictions based on data. In this case, it compares the prior and the post datasets, and then outputs standard metrics such as the **Root mean squared error** (**RMSE**), the **mean absolute error** (**MAE**), and the **coefficient of determination** (R^2) regression score function.

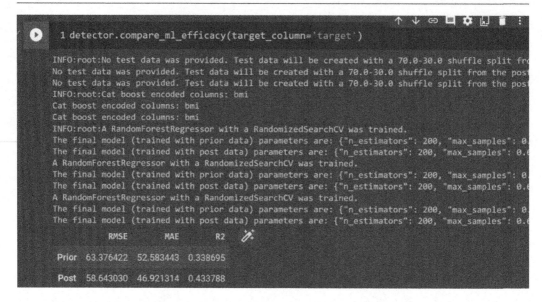

Figure 4.8: Calculating RMSE, MAE, and the coefficient of determination, R^2

The **ML Efficacy** (**MLE**) score measures how accurate the models are in predicting outcomes. The higher the MLE score, the better models are at making predictions. There are different ways to calculate MLE scores, but they all essentially compare predicted values with actual values. In this case, we compare the efficacy with RMSE, MAE, and R^2, and it is evident that there is a noteworthy difference in R^2 between the prior dataset and the post dataset (0.64), suggesting retraining may improve an existing model built using the prior dataset to improve performance.

Up until now, we have examined the data drift detector and discovered that the open source `data-drift-detector` is a compact, user-friendly tool for nominal DataFrame comparisons. While this tool serves its purpose, more advanced options exist, which we will delve into later. In the upcoming section, we will turn our attention to another open source package, known as Evidently.

Housing price data drift detection using Evidently

Like `data-drift-detector`, **Evidently** is an open source resource for data scientists and ML engineers that provides support to evaluate, test, and monitor the performance of ML models. Designed for use with both tabular and text data, Evidently adopts a modular approach, offering three interfaces on top of its shared metrics functionality. The library is simple to implement, with installation instructions provided, and the entire code base can be downloaded, as shown in the following screenshot.

```
1 !pip install evidently
2 !pip install data-drift-detector
3 new_samples = 500
4 verbose = False
5 %config InlineBackend.figure_format='retina'
6 import warnings
7 warnings.filterwarnings('ignore')
8 warnings.simplefilter('ignore')
```

Figure 4.9: Installing and detecting data drift using Evidently

Once installed, we will perform drift detection on the California housing dataset. The California housing dataset is a well-known ML dataset that contains median home prices, based on the eight different characteristics of the housing blocks in California in 1990. Here are the features of the dataset.

- `MedInc`: Median income

- `HouseAge`: Median house age

- `AveRooms`: Average number of rooms per household

- `AveBedrms`: Average number of bedrooms per household

- `Population`: Group population

- `AveOccup`: Average number of household members

- `Latitude`: Block group latitude

- `Longitude`: Block group longitude

```
1 import pandas as pd
2 from sklearn.datasets import fetch_california_housing
3
4 from evidently.dashboard import Dashboard
5 from evidently.pipeline.column_mapping import ColumnMapping
6 from evidently.dashboard.tabs import DataDriftTab, NumTargetDriftTab
7 from evidently.model_profile import Profile
8 from evidently.model_profile.sections import DataDriftProfileSection, \
9                                              NumTargetDriftProfileSection
```

Figure 4.10: Imports for the Evidently components

The California housing dataset is a part of the `sklearn` dataset collection, and it will be important as part of the pandas DataFrame. As we saw earlier, `pandas` DataFrames are two-dimensional arrays with labeled rows and columns. They can be used to store and manipulate tabular data and are often used in data analysis and ML.

```
1 ca = fetch_california_housing(as_frame=True)
2 ca_frame = ca.frame
```

Figure 4.11: Building the California DataFrame

Once the data is retrieved as part of the DataFrame, we will identify the categorical and numerical features, as shown in the following figure. Categorical features are those that can be divided into groups or categories. Examples of categorical features include **gender**, **race**, and **eye color**. In the case of the California housing dataset, there are none.

```
1 target = 'MedHouseVal'
2 numerical_features = ['MedInc', 'HouseAge', 'AveRooms', 'AveBedrms',
3                       'Population', 'AveOccup','Latitude', 'Longitude']
4 categorical_features = []
5 features = numerical_features
```

Figure 4.12: Defining the numerical features

However, we do have a set of numerical features, those that can be quantified or measured. Examples of numerical features include height, weight, and age. The difference between categorical and numerical features is that categorical features can only be divided into groups while numerical features can be quantified.

At this stage, we can create the drift dashboard to show the data drift.

```
[22]  1 ca_data_and_target_drift_dashboard = Dashboard(tabs=[DataDriftTab(verbose_level=verbose),
      2                                          NumTargetDriftTab(verbose_level=verbose)])
      3 ca_data_and_target_drift_dashboard.calculate(ref_data_sample, prod_data_sample,
      4                                          column_mapping=column_mapping)
      5 ca_data_and_target_drift_dashboard.show(mode="inline")
```

Figure 4.13: Setting up the drift dashboard

A drift dashboard is a tool that allows you to monitor changes in your numerical features over time. These model-monitoring dashboards can be used for a variety of purposes, including monitoring performance, tracking goals, or identifying trends. They can also be augmented to create alerts.

Drift is detected for 77.78% of features (7 out of 9). Dataset Drift is detected.

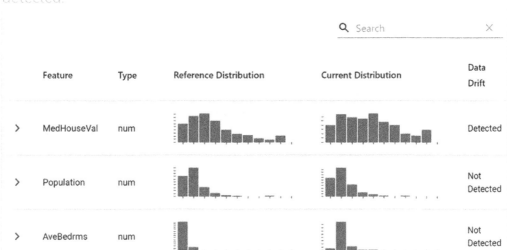

Figure 4.14: The Evidently dashboard

In this dashboard, you can see the plot for reference and current distribution, and also identifiers for data drift detection (the median house value). You can also search for specific columns. Evidently also shows visualizations for the p-value of the Kolmogorov-Smirnov test, which measures the probability that a given sample comes from a population with a specific distribution. You can check out more of Evidently's visualizations, reports, and dashboards here: `https://docs.evidentlyai.com/examples`.

There are various other model monitoring tools, however; hyperscalers or cloud providers have mastered the art of either developing or making the best-of-breed tools part of their cloud marketplace as partners. This makes it hard to not use them, especially when they come standard with most of the cloud ML offerings. In the next section, we will review the Azure ML model drift tool.

Analyzing data drift using Azure ML

Azure ML started out as a cloud-based service to build predictive models using data analytics tools such as R and Python. It has evolved to become one of the most comprehensive sets of ML tools for the end-to-end ML life cycle. From ML model design and development to deployment and monitoring, Azure ML supports notebooks, state-of-the-art compute and storage clusters, automated ML, and fairness algorithms.

To work with Azure ML for data drift detection, we will use one of the following tutorials provided as part of the ML notebooks:

1. In order to get started, you need to clone the ML notebook repository and pull all the files from GitHub to your local machine. At this point, your folder should look like the following screenshot.

```
Developer Command Prompt for VS 2022
C:\dev\MachineLearningNotebooks>dir /ad
 Volume in drive C is OS
 Volume Serial Number is C6DD-24BB

 Directory of C:\dev\MachineLearningNotebooks

10/24/2022  02:45 PM    <DIR>          .
10/24/2022  02:44 PM    <DIR>          ..
10/24/2022  02:45 PM    <DIR>          .git
10/24/2022  02:45 PM    <DIR>          contrib
10/24/2022  02:45 PM    <DIR>          Dockerfiles
10/24/2022  02:45 PM    <DIR>          how-to-use-azureml
10/24/2022  02:45 PM    <DIR>          Licenses
10/24/2022  02:45 PM    <DIR>          setup-environment
10/24/2022  02:45 PM    <DIR>          tutorials
               0 File(s)              0 bytes
               9 Dir(s)  3,189,874,262,016 bytes free

C:\dev\MachineLearningNotebooks>cd how-to-use-azureml\work-with-data\datadrift-tutorial
```

Figure 4.15: Cloning the repository

2. Now, open an Azure ML notebook. You will need to provision an Azure environment, workspace, and compute target.

3. This setup is beyond the scope of this book, but you can find an excellent quick-start tutorial by Microsoft (`https://learn.microsoft.com/en-us/azure/virtual-machines/windows/quick-create-portal?context=%2Fazure%2Fazure-portal%2Fcontext%2Fcontext`) that walks you through the steps. For reference, we used a `Standard DS12_v2` compute resource for this exercise, and it worked fine.

● Select from recommended options   ○ Select from all options

Name ↑	Category	Workload types	Available quota ⓘ	Cost ⓘ
○ Standard_DS11_v2 2 cores, 14GB RAM, 28GB storage	Memory optimized	Development on Notebooks (or other IDE) and light weight testing	20 cores	$0.15/hr
○ Standard_DS3_v2 4 cores, 14GB RAM, 28GB storage	General purpose	Classical ML model training on small datasets	20 cores	$0.23/hr
⊘ Standard_DS12_v2 4 cores, 28GB RAM, 56GB storage	Memory optimized	Data manipulation and training on medium-sized datasets (1–10GB)	20 cores	$0.30/hr
○ Standard_D13_v2 8 cores, 56GB RAM, 400GB storage	Memory optimized	Data manipulation and training on large datasets (>10 GB)	20 cores	$0.60/hr

Figure 4.16: Selecting the Azure virtual machine

4. Once the environment is created and provisioned, you can upload the entire folder in Azure ML, as shown in the following figure.

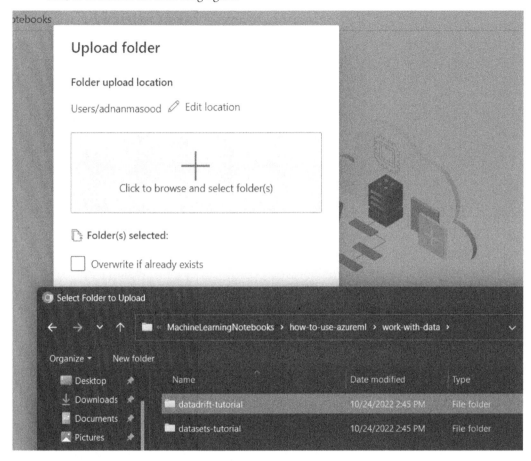

Figure 4.17: Uploading the cloned folders from the repository

5. Once you upload the entire datadrift-tutorial folder, which includes data and notebooks, you can open the notebook by double-clicking on the file.

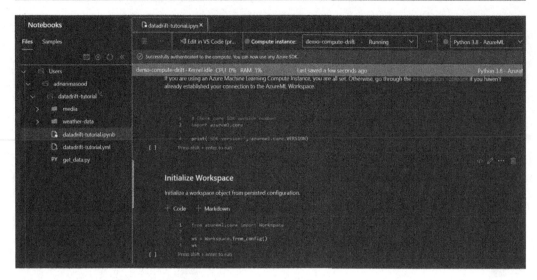

Figure 4.18: Running the uploaded Python notebook

AnAzure notebook is like any Jupyter notebook, with seamless and tight integration with Azure compute, experimentation, storage, and CI/CD pipelines. Now, you can run the entire notebook from the hamburger menu. We will only review the data drift portion of the notebook.

The first step to monitor the data drift is to create a data drift monitor. In this example, we'll operate on the weather dataset.

```
Create data drift monitor

See our documentation for a complete description for all of the parameters.

1   from azureml.datadrift import DataDriftDetector, AlertConfiguration
2
3   alert_config = AlertConfiguration(['user@contoso.com']) # replace with your email to recieve alerts from the scheduled
4
5   monitor = DataDriftDetector.create_from_datasets(ws, 'weather-monitor', baseline, target,
6                                                    compute_target='cpu-cluster',    # compute target for schedul
7                                                    frequency='Week',                # how often to analyze targe
8                                                    feature_list=None,               # list of features to detect
9                                                    drift_threshold=None,            # threshold from 0 to 1 for
10                                                   latency=0,                       # SLA in hours for target da
11                                                   alert_config=alert_config)       # email addresses to send al
[9]   ✓ 25 sec
```

Figure 4.19: Creating the data drift monitor

We will use the weather dataset from NOAA Integrated Surface Dataset. A typical weather dataset is a collection of data points that describe various aspects of past weather events. This information can be used to build models that predict future weather patterns. The most common types of data included in these datasets are temperature, precipitation, wind speed, and air pressure. However, more specialized datasets may also include information on humidity, barometric pressure changes over time, solar activity, and so on. The information from this dataset is in the `weather-data` folder and limited to station names that had the string `FLORID'` in them to reduce the data size. The data curation is a document in the `get_data.py` script.

The `create_from_datasets` method creates a weather monitor alert that monitors for data drift changes.

```
1   # get monitor by name
2   monitor = DataDriftDetector.get_by_name(ws, 'weather monitor')
3
4   # create feature list - need to exclude columns that naturally drift or increment over time, such as year, day, index
5   columns  = list(baseline.take(1).to_pandas_dataframe())
6   exclude  = ['year', 'day', 'version', '__index_level_0__']
7   features = [col for col in columns if col not in exclude]
8
9   # update the feature list
10  monitor  = monitor.update(feature_list=features)
✓ 5 sec
```

Figure 4.20: Executing the data drift monitor

You will also want to eliminate the columns that naturally change over time, such as date and time variables. Now that the data is loaded, you can monitor the data drift results, comparing them against 2019 weather data. This is set up to use January as the monitoring baseline.

```
1 # backfill for one month
2 backfill_start_date = datetime(2019, 9, 1)
3 backfill_end_date = datetime(2019, 10, 1)
4 backfill = monitor.backfill(backfill_start_date, backfill_end_date)
5 backfill
```

Figure 4.21: Backfill the monitor for testing

The following drift overview shows how much the drift contribution happens by feature (temperature being the main driver here), and how the data drift magnitude changes over time.

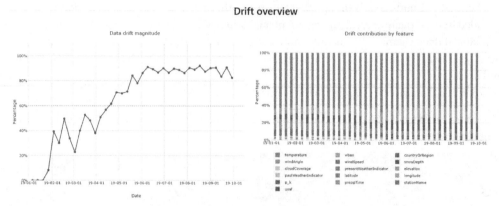

Figure 4.22: Drift overview in the dashboard

With this dashboard and various other APIs, you can create alerts for data drift and take mitigation steps as necessary. You can create real-time alerts for data drift and monitor model performance. The Azure ML Python SDK contains a data drift package that contains excellent functionality to compare against baseline and target datasets. This was a quick introduction to the Azure ML data drift monitoring capabilities. To explore further, you can look into Microsoft Learn's free module on monitoring data drift with Azure ML.

Other hyperscalers such as AWS and Google also provide the same features. You can build event-triggered detection of data drift in ML workflows using Google Vertex AI, or detect data drift using Amazon SageMaker quite easily.

Which tool you should use to perform data and model drift detection and to manage your MLOps workflow is an age-old question, which we cannot really answer for you. However, we can provide you with some guidelines. There are many different MLOps tools and ML frameworks available, so it can be difficult to know which one to use for your project. The best way to decide is to first understand your needs and then compare the various options against those needs. Some factors you may want to consider include the following:

- **Adjacencies**: Is this MLOps tool supported or already provided by your hyperscaler's ML toolchain? If yes, then you are probably better off using your cloud provider's version, since it will be closer to your data and in most cases won't have any extra cost.

- **Ease of use**: How easy is the MLOps tool or framework to learn and use? If you and your team are new to MLOps or ML, you'll want something that's relatively straightforward.

- **Support**: Does the MLOps tool or framework have good documentation and support? This is especially important if you're just starting out. Make sure there are resources available should you run into any problems. Also, check whether the community is active – this can be a valuable source of help and advice.

- **Functionality**: What features does the tool or framework offer? Make sure it has everything you need for your MLOps needs, including any specific features that are important to you.

- **Cost**: Is the tool or framework free or paid? If it's paid, how much does it cost? Keep in mind that some tools and frameworks offer free versions with limited functionality.

Summary

Data and model drift refer to a phenomenon that occurs when the statistical properties of a dataset or underlying model change over time. In this chapter, we reviewed how this can have an adverse impact on the predictions of models and, hence, on business outcomes. To make sure models function as desired, companies implement an ML life cycle that ensures design, development, deployment, and monitoring best practices are in place. Drifts can happen for a variety of reasons, including changes in the underlying population and changes in the way data is collected. When data drift happens, it can create bias in ML models that are trained on this data, which can be quite problematic for regulations and compliance.

In this chapter, we reviewed several ways to detect and mitigate bias due to data or model drift, and to monitor your training and validation error rates closely using different tools, including open source and commercial hyperscaler products. There are various other techniques available, including visualizing training and validation datasets side by side and using validation to get multiple estimates of errors. The proper understanding and use of these tools and other techniques help with transparency, accountability, and fairness to avoid risks associated with AI misuse.

In the next chapter, we will delve into the topic of model governance audit and compliance standards and recommendations. The chapter will explore the essential components of AI governance for trustworthy AI, including the implementation of model governance standards recommendations, the measurement of AI governance through the use of guiding principles for the model framework, the importance of algorithmic audits, and the creation of an enterprise roadmap for AI governance. We aim to provide you with a comprehensive understanding of the best practices and steps needed to ensure the responsible and ethical use of AI in an enterprise setting.

References and further reading

1. A non-parametric test is a statistical test that does not make any assumptions about the underlying distribution of the data. Non-parametric tests are useful when data does not follow a specific distribution, such as a normal distribution, or when the distribution is unknown. These tests rely on the ranks or order of the data rather than the actual values, making them more robust to outliers and less sensitive to the shape of the data distribution. Examples of non-parametric tests include the Wilcoxon rank-sum test, Kruskal-Wallis test, and the KS test.

2. The coefficient of determination, often denoted as R^2, is a statistical measure that represents the proportion of the variance in the dependent variable that can be explained by the independent variable(s) in a regression model. In other words, R^2 indicates how well the regression model fits the observed data. It ranges from 0 to 1, with a higher value suggesting a better fit. If R^2 equals 1, the model explains 100% of the variance in the dependent variable, indicating a perfect fit. Conversely, an R^2 of 0 means the model does not explain any of the variance, suggesting that the model is not useful for prediction.

3. *Model Monitoring in Practice: Lessons Learned and Open Challenges*: `https://dl.acm.org/doi/pdf/10.1145/3534678.3542617`

4. *Explainable Artificial Intelligence Approaches: A Survey*: `https://arxiv.org/pdf/2101.09429.pdf`

5. *Operationalizing Model Monitoring – MLOps Model Ops: A Guide to Measuring and Monitoring Model Drift*: `https://mlops.org/model-monitoring/`

6. *Model Drift Detection Using ML*: `https://ieeexplore.org/abstract/document/8916375`

7. *Monitoring ML Models in Production*: `https://medium.com/towards-data-science/monitoring-ml-models-in-production-768b6a74ee51`

8. *A Guide to Model Drift Detection in ML*: `https://towardsdatascience.com/a-guide-to-model-drift-detection-in-machine-learning-b3a3dd3f4d9f`

9. *An Introduction to MLOps: Best Practices for Running ML Workflows*: `https://towardsdatascience.com/an-introduction-to-mlops-best-practices-for-running-machine-learning-workflows-6f1b6c9b6f8c`

10. *Managing Model Risk in ML*: `https://www.kdnuggets.com/2021/04/managing-model-risk-machine-learning.htm`

5

Model Governance, Audit, and Compliance

"In this era of profound digital transformation, it's important to remember that business, as well as government, has a role to play in creating shared prosperity – not just prosperity. After all, the same technologies that can be used to concentrate wealth and power can also be used to distribute it more widely and empower more people."

– Erik Brynjolfsson, director of the MIT initiative on the digital economy

"Some cultures embrace privacy as the highest priority part of their culture. That's why the U.S., Germany, and China may be at different levels in the spectrum. But I also believe fundamentally that every user does not want his or her data to be leaked or used to hurt himself or herself. I think GDPR is a very good first step, even though I might disagree with the way it was implemented and the effect it has on companies. I think governments should put a stake in the ground and say this is what we're doing to protect privacy."

– Kai-Fu Lee, chairman and chief executive officer, Sinovation Ventures

"If the government regulates against use of drones or stem cells or artificial intelligence, all that means is that the work and the research leave the borders of that country and go someplace else."

– Peter Diamandis

"Artificial intelligence is growing up fast, as are robots whose facial expressions can elicit empathy and make your mirror neurons quiver."

– Diane Ackerman

Automated decision-making is becoming commonplace in all walks of life. In everyday life, it not only impacts how and what we buy, see, or eat but also more critical parts of our lives. These systems decide who gets a loan, who can or cannot open a bank account or do a wire transfer, who gets healthcare services, and who gets admission to college – these life-impacting decisions are now being managed by automated decision management systems, powered by AI and **machine learning** (**ML**) systems.

In the previous chapters, you read about all the ways AI can cause – and has caused – harm to humans. Therefore, it is crucial to have guardrails, best practices, governance, regulations, policy, and compliance requirements around automated decision-making. However, lawmakers around the world are struggling to define, validate, and test such policy measures due to their inherent complexity and black-box nature. Due to the diverse nature of automated systems, there has been a wide array of standards, policies, and recommendations proposed by governments, professional organizations, universities, and various commercial organizations. The standards try to address the risks that may emerge from a biased model by either enforcing validation testing for harmful bias, reviewing dangerous design choices with humans in the loop, or ensuring that models meet some well-defined enforceable policies for privacy, fairness, disparate impact, human oversight, transparency, and accountability.

AI and its uses within an enterprise have been developing at a pace over the past decade. At the time of writing, the coverage and mainstream interest of generative AI such as ChatGPT and Bard are exploding. The pace of AI proliferation is currently happening at such a pace that government regulation – stating what AI should and should not do and how it should be controlled – is at risk of never being able to keep up.

It currently seems likely that a significant part of the responsibility for the development and application of AI services that are fair, ethical, and harmless will be placed on the businesses and public sector agencies doing so, with guidelines stated and monitored by the relevant industry regulator.

Where does this leave those in an enterprise who see that AI can benefit their business area significantly and who want to ensure that they do this fairly and ethically? We believe the answer lies in comprehensive frameworks for **responsible AI** (**RAI**) that are embedded into business processes and supporting technologies, which we will discuss further in *Chapter 6*.

Before that, in this chapter, we will provide an overview of the current standards landscape. Be warned that, for the previously stated reasons, these standards are currently something of a movable feast! At the time of writing, they include the following:

- Policies and regulations
- Professional bodies' industry standards
- Technology toolkits
- Auditing checklist measures

Policies and regulations

In this section, we will review the national policies and regulations pertaining to AI in various countries and regions. It is important to note the nuances, in similarities as well as differences, in these policies, since AI has a wide-ranging global impact.

United States

The **United States** (.U.S.) currently lacks a comprehensive regulation for AI at a national (federal) level. There have been a few different initiatives in the pipeline, including the Algorithmic Accountability Act, which aims to address the issues surrounding AI bias and discrimination. One notable effort is the **National Institute of Standards and Technology** (**NIST**) initiative called *Towards a Standard for Identifying and Managing Bias in Artificial Intelligence*. This initiative seeks to develop a framework to assess and mitigate biases in AI systems, focusing on transparency, explainability, and fairness. In the absence of an all-encompassing national standard to govern AI models, states have made their own initiatives.

NIST Framework (AI RMF 1.0)

NIST is a U.S. agency dedicated to promoting innovation and industrial competitiveness by advancing measurement science, standards, and technology. One of their initiatives, *Towards a Standard for Identifying and Managing Bias in Artificial Intelligence*[1], aims to address the challenge of AI bias, taking into account not only computational factors, such as dataset representativeness and algorithm fairness, but also human and systemic institutional and societal factors that contribute to bias. By adopting a socio-technical perspective, this initiative seeks to provide guidance on how to connect existing practices for RAI development to societal values, ultimately fostering public trust in AI systems. NIST intends to develop flexible and easily communicated methods to increase assurance and governance and practice improvements in identifying, understanding, measuring, managing, and reducing bias across different industries and stakeholder groups.

NIST has published the NIST AI **Risk Management Framework** (**RMF**), a risk-based, resource-efficient, pro-innovation, and voluntary framework that has been developed through a consensus-driven and open process, inviting contributions from all stakeholders. It employs clear, plain language that is understandable by a wide audience while maintaining technical depth for practitioners. The AI RMF provides a common language to manage AI risks, offering taxonomy, terminology, definitions, metrics, and characterizations. It is designed to be easily usable, fitting well with other aspects of risk management and being adaptable to an organization's broader risk management strategy. The framework is applicable across various perspectives, sectors, and technology domains, focusing on outcomes rather than prescribing one-size-fits-all requirements. The AI RMF builds on existing standards, guidelines, best practices, methodologies, and tools while remaining law- and regulation-agnostic. As a living document, it can be updated to reflect changes in technology, understanding, and AI risk management approaches.

The AI RMF Core – governing, mapping, measuring, and managing AI risks

The key components of the AI RMF Core are four high-level functions that enable dialogue, understanding, and activities to manage AI risks and responsibly develop trustworthy AI systems.

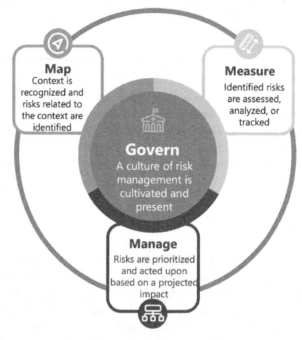

Figure 5.1: AI RMF Core (courtesy of NIST)

These functions are as follows:

- **Govern**: A cross-cutting function that informs and is infused throughout the other three functions, focusing on governance aspects

- **Map**: This function helps in mapping risks and identifying potential challenges associated with AI systems

- **Measure**: This function focuses on measuring the performance, trustworthiness, and other relevant aspects of AI systems to assess their risks

- **Manage**: This function deals with the management of identified risks and the implementation of appropriate mitigation strategies

Each function is further broken down into categories and subcategories, which are subdivided into specific actions and outcomes. These functions should be carried out continuously, timely, and throughout the AI system life cycle, while incorporating diverse and multidisciplinary perspectives.

The NIST standard addresses various aspects of AI bias and provides guidance to mitigate its negative effects. The standard is divided into several sections:

- **Testing, evaluation, validation, and verification (TEVV) challenges and guidance**: This section covers the challenges related to AI system testing and evaluation, offering guidance on how to ensure the reliability and performance of AI models while minimizing bias

- **Human factors in AI bias**: This part focuses on the human aspects involved in AI decision-making and discusses the challenges and guidance to mitigate bias arising from human involvement in AI systems

- **Governance and AI bias**: This section deals with the management and oversight of AI systems, providing governance guidance to ensure RAI development and deployment

Human-AI interaction guidelines

The NIST AI RMF emphasizes the importance of understanding human-AI interaction and its limitations in order to enhance AI risk management. It highlights the need to define and differentiate human roles and responsibilities when using, interacting with, or managing AI systems. The framework acknowledges that representing complex human phenomena in mathematical models can lead to a loss of context, which makes understanding individual and societal impacts crucial for AI risk management efforts. Issues to consider include the clear definition of human roles in decision-making and oversight, the influence of cognitive and systemic biases, the variability in human-AI interaction results, and the complexity of presenting AI system information to humans. The **Govern** and **Map** functions of the framework help organizations clarify roles, responsibilities, and decision-making processes to counter biases, improve internal competency, and promote interdisciplinarity and diverse teams. Ongoing research and evaluation will further augment AI risk management approaches for human-AI configurations.

Distinctive challenges in AI risk management

The NIST AI RMF highlights that AI-based technology risks can differ from traditional software risks and may not be comprehensively addressed by current risk frameworks. Compared to traditional software, AI-specific risks include issues with data representation, ground truth, harmful bias, data dependency, changes during training, detachment from the original context, system scale and complexity, the use of pre-trained models, the unpredictability of failure modes, privacy risks, maintenance requirements, opacity, reproducibility concerns, underdeveloped testing standards, computational costs, and difficulty in predicting or detecting side effects. While privacy and cybersecurity risk management approaches, such as the NIST Cybersecurity Framework and the NIST Privacy Framework, can inform AI risk management, they may not comprehensively address harmful bias, generative AI risks, ML attacks, complex attack surfaces, or risks associated with third-party AI technologies and transfer learning. The AI RMF aims to address these unique AI risks while also acknowledging the need to monitor and adapt to rapid technological innovation.

The standard concludes by summarizing the importance of addressing AI bias across all these areas and provides a glossary for key terms used throughout the document. Figures throughout the standard help visualize and clarify various concepts, such as categories of AI bias, the AI development life cycle, and human-centered design processes for AI systems.

This is a guidance document that is part of NIST's AI RMF. While the guidance is voluntary and does not establish any legal standard or requirement, it is intended to advance the trustworthiness of AI technologies by providing reference information and technical guidance on terminology, processes, and procedures. The NIST AI RMF addresses risks in the design, development, use, and evaluation of AI products, services, and systems, including the risk of bias.

Through a multi-stakeholder approach, NIST aims to create and maintain actionable practice guides that are broadly adoptable, thereby enhancing the trustworthiness of AI systems and responsible practices when designing, developing, and deploying them.

Algorithm Accountability Act

Originally proposed in the congressional session 2019–2020, the H.R.2231[2] – Algorithmic Accountability Act of 2019 was reintroduced by Senators Wyden, Booker, and Clarke again in 2022. The bill requires "AI assessments" for companies that deal with personal information or use AI and ML techniques to automate their decision-making.

The Algorithmic Accountability Act of 2022 is a legislative effort to address the potential risks and biases that arise from the increasing use of automated systems in critical decision-making processes in various sectors. The act aims to provide more transparency, accountability, and consumer empowerment concerning the automation of critical decisions. The key provisions of the bill include the following:

- **Baseline requirements**: The act mandates companies to assess the impacts of automating critical decision-making processes, including those that have already been automated.

- **FTC regulations**: This requires the **Federal Trade Commission (FTC)** to create regulations that provide structured guidelines for the assessment and reporting of automated systems' impacts.

- **Responsibility allocation**: The act ensures that both companies making critical decisions and those building the enabling technology are responsible for assessing the impact of automation.

- **Reporting to the FTC**: The bill mandates companies to report select impact-assessment documentation to the FTC.

- **Transparency and consumer information**: The act requires the FTC to publish an annual anonymized aggregate report on trends and to establish a repository of information, where consumers and advocates can review which critical decisions have been automated by companies. This repository will also include details such as data sources, high-level metrics, and how to contest decisions, where applicable.

- **Additional resources and enforcement**: The bill provides resources for the FTC to hire 50 additional staff and establishes a Bureau of Technology to enforce the act, supporting the commission in its technological aspects.

The Algorithmic Accountability Act of 2022 has received endorsements from several organizations, including Access Now, Accountable Tech, **Center for Democracy and Technology** (**CDT**), Color of Change, Consumer Reports, EPIC, Fight for the Future, IEEE, **Open Technology Institute** (**OTI**), and US PIRG.

California Consumer Privacy Act

California, which is usually on the cutting edge of technology regulation, introduced the **California Consumer Privacy Act** (**CCPA**)[3] in 2018. California's concentration of tech companies and start-ups in Silicon Valley has led to a culture of innovation, early adoption of new technologies, and a willingness to experiment with and regulate emerging technologies, resulting in the state becoming a leader in enacting legislation that seeks to protect consumer privacy and promote the responsible use of technology. Its regulatory actions often serve as a model for other states and countries.

A cursory overview of the CCPA may show that it is influenced by the **European Union** (**EU**)'s **General Data Protection Regulation** (**GDPR**); however, there are differences. In order to collect personal information, the GDPR requires a legal basis and consent. The CCPA, on the other hand, mandates that users be informed of the personal information that a business collects about them, and how that information is used and shared. The CCPA stipulates that users have the right to opt out of the collection of their personal information and to request its deletion. Additionally, they are entitled to non-discrimination in accordance with the CCPA. GDPR is applicable to any person located within the EU, whereas the CCPA is applicable to residents of California.

Consumer Financial Protection Circular 2022–03

The **Consumer Financial Protection Bureau** (**CFPB**), in order to prevent digital redlining and theft discrimination, has announced that it will clamp down upon practices in banking that use AI, which can be used to discriminate against individuals. There is good reason for doing so, as Federal Reserve economists found that algorithmic systems for mortgage underwriting led to higher denial rates for minority borrowers in a 2021 paper.[4]

In its recent circular, the agency discussed adverse action notification requirements in connection with credit decisions based on complex algorithms[5], and it proposed a regulation that requires lenders to provide a statement detailing why an adverse action has been taken against an applicant. If creditors make these decisions based on complex and difficult-to-understand models, it can be difficult – if not impossible – to pinpoint the precise reasons for denying credit or taking other negative actions. As a result of ECOA and Regulation B, creditors are not permitted to use complex algorithms when it means that they cannot specify and provide accurate reasons for adverse actions.

Virginia Consumer Data Protection Act 2021

In March 2021, the **Virginia Consumer Data Protection Act (VCDPA)**[6] became law, protecting consumer privacy and data security law in the state of Virginia. Similar to the **California Privacy Rights and Enforcement Act (CPRA)**, the law governs the data usage between consumers and businesses and, therefore, impacts AI model development using this data.

San Francisco City's Ethics Algorithms Toolkit

The city of San Francisco and its affiliates proposed a risk management framework[7] for government leaders and staff. The toolkit contains an algorithmic assessment process and how to address the underlying risks. One of the quotes on their website is very relevant and notable in the scope of AI work. The purpose of the toolkit is to help government bodies understand the implications of using algorithms, articulate potential risks, and identify ways to mitigate them. It is designed to promote transparency and accountability in the implementation of algorithms by governments.

The toolkit was created through a collaboration between GovEx, the city and county of San Francisco, Harvard DataSmart, and Data Community DC.

The toolkit is used by following the provided documents:

- **Overview and Introduction**: Read this section to understand the background information, real-life scenarios, and relevant definitions.

- **Part 1: Assess Algorithm Risk**: Go through the six major steps/questions to help characterize an algorithm. Use the worksheet to track responses and overall risk values.

- **Part 2: Manage Algorithm Risk**: Identify specific techniques to address the considerations identified in *Part 1*.

- **Appendices**: Consult these resources for additional context and depth, particularly to understand data and address bias.

To effectively use the toolkit, it is assumed that the user has some knowledge of data science concepts or experience with algorithms and largely understands their data.

It is essential to involve various stakeholders, data analysts, information technology professionals, or vendor representatives during the process, as completing the toolkit may require considerable discussion and collaboration. This thought-provoking quote from San Francisco City's Ethics Algorithms Toolkit serves as a reminder that the adoption of algorithmic decision-making is inevitable, and the critical focus should be on determining the right time to embrace these technologies while ensuring ethical considerations and responsible practices:

"The question isn't whether you should, but when will you start?"

Now, let us venture across the Atlantic to explore the AI governance landscape in Europe, specifically focusing on their laws and regulations.

European Union

The **EU** is a political and economic union of 27 member states located primarily in Europe. It is the world's largest trading bloc, and its regulations and policies impact numerous industries globally. One area where the EU has recently been active is in the regulation of AI. The EU has recognized the need for AI to be developed and used in a responsible and ethical manner and has proposed regulations to ensure that AI systems are transparent, accountable, and safe. These proposed regulations aim to balance innovation and development with the protection of individuals' rights and freedoms. Therefore, the EU is working toward establishing a framework for the ethical and responsible development and use of AI. In this section, we will discuss some of the EU's AI-related regulations.

The EU's AI Act

The EU's AI Act[8] is a proposed piece of EU legislation that represents the first law concerning AI to emerge from a major regulatory body. In this regulation, which was announced by Brussels in April 2022, AI applications are assigned to three risk categories. First of all, applications and systems with unacceptable risks, such as the government-run social scoring systems used in China, are prohibited. A second consideration is for high-risk applications, such as a résumé scanner to rank candidates, will be subject to certain legal and regulatory requirements to monitor and control bias. Last but not least, applications that are not explicitly banned or listed as high-risk are largely unregulated.

European Commission's guidelines for trustworthy AI

The Ethics Guidelines for Trustworthy AI is an expert document prepared in 2018, identifying components of trustworthy AI (lawful, ethical, and robust) and providing a framework to achieve trustworthy AI. The guideline document outlines the foundation of trustworthy AI, explains the underlying requirements, and also provides guidance on how to access trustworthy AI. The guidelines outline the seven key requirements.

- Human agency and oversight
- Technical robustness and safety
- Privacy and data governance
- Transparency
- Diversity, non-discrimination, and fairness
- Societal and environmental well-being
- Accountability

These guidelines for trustworthy AI can be deemed the foundational document upon which the EU's AI Act is based.

GDPR

GDPR[9], dubbed the "toughest privacy and security law in the world," is one of the most prominent and wide-reaching regulations for consumer privacy. GDPR ensures the privacy and security of data related to those living in EU countries, including but not limited to the processing, storage, and transit of such data.

GDPR is aimed at protecting an individual's personal data, which includes the right to know how their data is being used and to request its erasure. However, the black-box nature of deep learning models can make it difficult to comply with GDPR's transparency requirements. To address this issue, researchers and practitioners have developed techniques to interpret the decisions made by these models. By providing transparency and accountability, these deep learning explainability techniques can help organizations build trust with their customers and ensure the ethical use of personal data in automated decision-making processes.

You can also thank GDPR for all those "accept cookie" messages you get nowadays. In 2008, Professor Emeritus of computer science and engineering at the University of Washington, Dr. Pedro Domingos, tweeted this controversial statement:

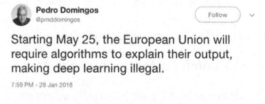

Figure 5.2: GDPR will outlaw deep learning

In this tweet, he alluded to the "right of explainability" clause of GDPR, which is a subject of much legal debate[10]. Even though it is safe to say that deep learning isn't necessarily illegal in the EU, it is heavily frowned upon if a human-impacting decision cannot be sufficiently explained, especially if its outcomes are adverse or harmful.

United Kingdom

In the **United Kingdom** (**UK**), the regulatory landscape for AI is evolving as technology advances and its impact on society becomes more apparent. While the UK was once subject to EU regulations, the country's departure from the EU in 2020, commonly known as Brexit, means that EU regulations are no longer directly applicable. As a result, the UK is in the process of developing its own policies and regulations surrounding AI and other emerging technologies. This involves striking a balance between fostering innovation and ensuring ethical, safe, and RAI use. Although the UK may still draw inspiration from EU guidelines and best practices, it is now responsible for establishing its own distinct regulatory framework for AI.

UK Data Protection Act

The Data Protection Act of 2018[11] is the UK version of GDPR; it is very similar to the GDPR provisions, with some minor differences. The law ensures that those dealing with data use it fairly, lawfully, and in a transparent manner. Protected classes and attributes such as race, ethnic background, political and religious beliefs, health and genetic information, sexual orientation, and biometrics are safeguarded and not used for any discriminatory purposes. Like GDPR, it also gives consumers the right to be aware of how their data is used and opt out if needed. The UK exited the EU on January 31, 2020, and the implications of GDPR for the UK depend on ongoing negotiations between the UK and the EU, hence the new law.

The UK government's Data Ethics Framework

The UK government's Data Ethics Framework[12] is a set of guidelines around the appropriate and responsible use of data. The overarching principles outlined in this framework are those of transparency, accountability, and fairness, with accompanying self-assessment tables. This framework heavily overlaps with the European Commission's Ethics Guidelines for Trustworthy AI and provides the seven key elements for ethical AI specified previously.

Singapore

A small nation-state, Singapore is at the forefront of AI use and regulations. The country has drafted several regulations and guidance for the pragmatic, ethical use of AI.

Personal Data Protection Act

The **Personal Data Protection Act** (**PDPA**) of 2012 (revised in 2020)[13] not only regulates the use of consumer personal data but also addresses telemarketing preferences, such as a "do not call" registry. The PDPA establishes a data protection framework to balance the need for organizations to collect, use, and disclose personal data for legitimate purposes with the need to protect an individual's personal data from misuse. The PDPA applies to all organizations that collect, use, or disclose personal data in Singapore, regardless of whether they are based in Singapore or not. It provides individuals with the right to access and correct their personal data and outlines the consequences for non-compliance with the law, including financial penalties and reputational damage. The PDPA is designed to help build trust in the digital economy and ensure the responsible use of personal data in Singapore.

The Protection from Online Falsehoods and Manipulation Act

The Protection from Online Falsehoods and Manipulation Act 2019[14], commonly known as the fake news law, ensures that information communicated in or outside Singapore is based on facts and not prejudicial. The law also regulates bot (AI agent)-based communication and safeguards online communication and manipulation.

AI Verify – an AI governance testing framework and toolkit

In 2019, the Singapore Personal Data Protection Commission released the Model AI Governance Framework to provide guidance for addressing ethical and governance-related issues encountered by organizations. These guidelines were updated in 2020, with a second edition focused on guiding principles such as explainability, transparency, fairness, and human-centricity. In May 2022, Singapore launched AI Verify[15], an industry-government-led effort being called the "world's first AI testing framework and toolkit to promote transparency."[16] The AI governance testing framework and toolkit is at its **minimum viable product (MVP)** stage and proposes a set of ethical AI principles and pillars to show how developers and stakeholders can build trust.

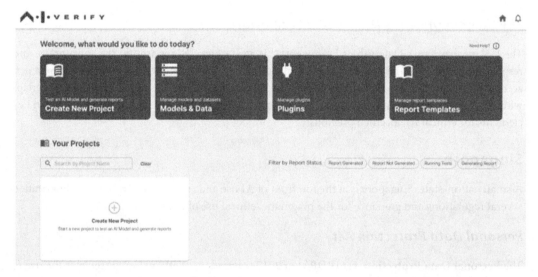

Figure 5.3: The Singapore government's AI Verify toolkit

United Arab Emirates

The United Arab Emirates, particularly Dubai, is rapidly advancing in the field of digital transformation, AI, and ML. The /digital Dubai initiative has published an Ethical AI Toolkit[17] that provides guidelines around fairness, accountability, transparency, and explainability. The toolkit comprises practical guidance, including principles, guidelines, and a self-assessment tool. The target audience for this toolkit includes government entities, private sector organizations, and individuals.

Toronto Declaration – protecting the right to equality in ML

Published in 2018, the Toronto Declaration[18] was one of the first statements aimed at protecting human rights in the face of the inevitable age of AI. The declaration emphasizes utilizing the framework of international human rights law to establish the right to equality and non-discrimination in the age of machines. The Toronto Declaration seeks to have states fulfill their human rights obligations, promote equality, and ensure that private sectors are accountable for their use of AI.

Professional bodies and industry standards

Professional bodies for computer and information sciences have provided their own code of conduct and standards for AI. Here is a brief overview of these standards.

Microsoft's Responsible AI framework

The Microsoft Responsible AI Standard, v2[19], is a comprehensive framework designed to guide the development, deployment, and maintenance of AI systems in an ethical, reliable, and inclusive manner. It encompasses a broad range of goals and requirements addressing critical aspects, such as system reliability and safety, ongoing monitoring, feedback and evaluation, privacy, security, and inclusiveness. The standard emphasizes the importance of conducting thorough impact assessments, adhering to transparency, and incorporating guidelines for human-AI interactions to mitigate potential risks and failures. Furthermore, the framework entails regular evaluations, documentation updates, and collaboration with the Office of Responsible AI to ensure continuous improvement and alignment with the company's RAI principles. This standard demonstrates Microsoft's commitment to upholding ethical AI practices, promoting transparency, and fostering a secure and accessible AI ecosystem.

Goals, requirements, and practices

The following are the ongoing monitoring, privacy, security, and inclusiveness goals for RAI at Microsoft:

- **Fairness** – strive to reduce biases in AI systems and ensure equal treatment for all user groups:

  - Conduct bias and fairness assessments

  - Implement robust testing and validation processes

  - Continuously update AI systems to reduce biases

- **Reliability and safety** – develop AI systems that perform consistently and safely under varying conditions:

  - Perform thorough risk assessments and address potential hazards
  - Conduct **Failure mode and effects analysis (FMEA)**
  - Follow the **Guidelines for Human-AI Interaction** when designing a system

- **Privacy and security** – protect users' data and privacy while maintaining secure AI systems:

  - Comply with the Microsoft Privacy Standard and Microsoft Security Policy
  - Implement strong data encryption and access control measures
  - Regularly monitor and update security protocols

- **Inclusiveness** – design AI systems that are accessible and cater to diverse user needs:

  - Follow the Microsoft Accessibility Standards
  - Continuously evaluate and improve a system's accessibility
  - Encourage diverse representation in AI system development

- **Transparency** – provide clear and accurate information about AI system capabilities and limitations:

  - Publish detailed documentation and transparency notes
  - Regularly update documentation as system functionality evolves
  - Communicate system changes to stakeholders, customers, and partners

- **Accountability** – hold developers and users of AI systems responsible for their actions and decisions:

  - Establish a clear chain of responsibility for AI system development and deployment
  - Collaborate with the Office of Responsible AI for guidance and review
  - Encourage feedback and implement corrective measures when necessary

Goals to safeguard AI systems

Fairness goal: The goal of fairness is to create AI systems that treat all user groups equitably, minimizing biases in both data and algorithms. This involves designing, developing, and deploying AI systems that are inclusive and impartial, thus providing equal opportunities and benefits to users irrespective of their backgrounds. Continuous evaluation of these systems and addressing potential biases are critical to achieving fairness.

Reliability and safety goal: The objective of reliability and safety is to ensure AI systems perform consistently and securely under various conditions. This involves rigorous risk assessments, thorough testing, and adherence to best practices, such as FMEA and the *Guidelines for Human-AI Interaction*. Ongoing monitoring, feedback, and evaluation help maintain a system's dependability and safety.

Privacy and security goal: The privacy and security goal focuses on protecting users' data and privacy while securing AI systems against potential threats. This requires adherence to the Microsoft Privacy Standard and Microsoft Security Policy, implementing strong encryption and access control measures, and continuous monitoring of an AI system's security posture to identify and address vulnerabilities.

Inclusiveness goal: The inclusiveness goal aims to develop AI systems that are accessible and cater to the diverse needs of all users. This involves following the Microsoft Accessibility Standards and promoting diverse representation in AI system development. Regular evaluation and improvement of a system's accessibility help ensure a more inclusive user experience.

Transparency goal: The transparency goal entails providing clear, accurate, and comprehensive information about AI system capabilities, limitations, and intended uses. This involves publishing detailed documentation, transparency notes, and regular updates as system functionality evolves. Communication with stakeholders, customers, and partners is essential to maintain transparency.

Accountability goal: The objective of accountability is to hold developers, users, and organizations responsible for AI system decisions and actions. This involves establishing a clear chain of responsibility, collaborating with the Office of Responsible AI for guidance and review, and encouraging feedback from users to identify and implement corrective measures when necessary.

Enterprise adaption of Microsoft's Responsible AI framework

An enterprise can adapt the Microsoft Responsible AI Standard, v2, by integrating its six core principles – fairness, reliability and safety, privacy and security, inclusiveness, transparency, and accountability – into its AI development, deployment, and maintenance processes. This involves establishing clear goals, requirements, and recommendations aligned with each principle, while incorporating continuous monitoring, feedback, and evaluation systems. By tailoring the standard to their specific needs and industry contexts, enterprises can build an RAI culture, ensuring ethical, reliable, and safe AI systems across the organization.

The Microsoft Responsible AI Standard provides practical guidelines and concrete steps that go beyond high-level concepts to facilitate the implementation of RAI practices. Some of these actionable recommendations include the following:

- Conducting *impact assessments* to identify potential risks and benefits associated with AI systems and their applications
- Defining and documenting clear requirements, responsibilities, and processes to evaluate, monitor, and maintain AI systems

- Ensuring compliance with *privacy, security,* and *accessibility standards* in the AI system development process

- Implementing *FMEA* to identify and manage potential system failures

- Following the *Guidelines for Human-AI Interaction* to design systems that can manage failures and provide a positive user experience

- Establishing channels for *customer* and *public feedback* to improve AI systems continuously

These guidelines and steps help organizations develop AI systems that are **ethical, transparent**, and **accountable**, while minimizing the risks associated with AI deployment.

Also, you do not have to use Microsoft Azure to implement the Responsible AI Standard. Although the standard is designed with Microsoft AI systems in mind, its core principles and guidelines can be applied to any AI development process, irrespective of the platform or technology used. Organizations can adapt the standard to suit their specific needs, adopting RAI practices and fostering ethical, reliable, and safe AI systems across various platforms and technologies.

The Microsoft Responsible AI Standard, v2, is a comprehensive framework designed to guide the development, deployment, and maintenance of ethical, reliable, and safe AI systems. It is organized around six core principles – fairness, reliability and safety, privacy and security, inclusiveness, transparency, and accountability. Each principle is supported by a set of goals, with corresponding requirements and recommendations to operationalize the principles. The standard applies to all AI systems, with some goals specifically tailored to contexts where certain policies, such as the Microsoft Privacy Standard or Microsoft Security Policy, apply. The standard emphasizes a continuous improvement process, involving ongoing monitoring, feedback, and evaluation to ensure that AI systems meet ethical and performance expectations throughout their life cycle.

IEEE Global Initiative for Ethical Considerations in AI and Autonomous Systems

IEEE is one of the oldest and most established professional organizations. The initiative's mission is as follows:

> *"To ensure every stakeholder involved in the design and development of autonomous and intelligent systems is educated, trained, and empowered to prioritize ethical considerations so that these technologies are advanced for the benefit of humanity."*

The initiative seeks to build accountability, accelerate transparency, and reduce bias in AI models. The IEEE standards are focused on ethical design principles and intend to create specifications and certifications around ethical AI.

IEEE has several working groups addressing AI and ethical concerns, such as the **IEEE 7000-2021** Standard Model Process for Addressing Ethical Concerns during System Design, the **IEEE 7001-2021** Standard for Transparency of Autonomous Systems, the **P7015** Standard for Data and AI Literacy, Skills, and Readiness, the **P7014** Standard for Ethical Considerations in Emulated Empathy in Autonomous and Intelligent Systems, the **P7012** Standard for Machine Readable Personal Privacy Terms, the **P7011** Standard for the Process of Identifying and Rating the Trustworthiness of News Sources, the **P7010.1** Recommended Practice for **Environmental Social Governance** (**ESG**) and **Social Development Goal** (**SDG**) for Action Implementation and Advancing Corporate Social Responsibility, the **P7009** Standard for Fail-Safe Design of Autonomous and Semi-Autonomous Systems, Sources, the **P7010.1** Recommended Practice for **Environmental Social Governance** (**ESG**) and **Social Development Goal** (**SDG**), the **P7008** Standard for Ethically Driven Nudging for Robotic, Intelligent, and Autonomous Systems, the **IEEE 7007-2021** Ontological Standard for Ethically Driven Robotics and Automation Systems, the **IEEE 7005-2021** Standard for Transparent Employer Data Governance, the **P7004.1** Recommended Practices for Virtual Classroom Security, Privacy and Data Governance, the **P7004** Standard for Child and Student Data Governance, the **P7003** Algorithmic Bias Considerations, the **IEEE 7002-2022** Standard for Data Privacy Process, and the **IEEE 7001-2021** Standard for Transparency of Autonomous Systems. Select the right standard based on your industry application and data governance requirements.

ISO/IEC's standards for AI

ISO is the international organization for standards and has published several standards across big data, IT, and AI. Some of the key AI-related standards include the following:

- **ISO/IEC TR 24027:2021**: Bias in AI systems and AI-aided decision-making

- **ISO/IEC TR 24028:2020**: Overview of trustworthiness in AI

- **ISO/IEC TR 24029-1:2021**: Assessment of the robustness of neural networks

- **ISO/IEC TR 24030:2021**: AI use cases

- **ISO/IEC TR 24372:2021**: Overview of computational approaches for AI systems

- **ISO/IEC 38507:2022**: Governance implications of the use of AI by organizations

The ISO standards regarding the overview of trustworthiness in AI and bias in AI systems and AI-aided decision-making are highly relevant to automated decision-making for enterprises. We will discuss these standards in more detail in *Chapter 6*.

ISO offers AI and ML standards, such as ISO/IEC TS 4213:2022 AI – Assessment of ML classification performance, ISO/IEC 23053:2022 – Framework for Artificial Intelligence (AI) Systems Using Machine Learning (ML), ISO/IEC TR 24027:2021 – Bias in AI systems and AI aided decision-making, ISO/IEC TR 24028:2020 – Overview of trustworthiness in AI, ISO/IEC TR 24029-1:2021 – Assessment of the robustness of neural networks, ISO/IEC TR 24368:2022 – Overview of ethical and societal concerns, ISO/IEC TR 24372:2021 – Overview of computational approaches for AI systems, and ISO/IEC 38507:2022 – Governance of IT – Governance implications of the use of AI by organizations. Ensure your team is acquainted with these guidelines and principles for compliance with the ethics, privacy, safety, trust, and cybersecurity aspects of AI.

The ISO report ISO/IEC TR 24028 is about standardization efforts related to the use of AI. The report provides guidelines for the ethical and socially responsible implementation of AI systems. Its key elements include the identification of potential ethical issues, the establishment of RAI practices, and the promotion of transparency and accountability in AI development and deployment. The ISO/IEC TR 24028:2020 report provides an overview of trustworthiness in AI systems. It aims to analyze the factors that can impact the trustworthiness of systems providing or using AI. The report covers various topics related to trustworthiness in AI systems, including the following:

- Approaches to assess and achieve availability, resiliency, reliability, accuracy, safety, security, and privacy in AI systems

- Engineering pitfalls, typical threats, risks associated with AI systems, and possible mitigation techniques and methods

- Approaches to establish trust in AI systems through transparency, explainability, controllability, and more

The report briefly surveys existing approaches that can support or improve trustworthiness in technical systems and discusses their potential application to AI systems. It also addresses possible approaches to mitigating AI system vulnerabilities related to trustworthiness and suggests ways to improve the trustworthiness of AI systems.

OECD AI Principles

The **Organization for Economic Co-operation and Development (OECD)** is an international organization that aims to promote policies that improve the economic and social well-being of people around the world. Established in 1961, it currently consists of 38 member countries that collaborate on a range of issues, including economic growth, education, health, and innovation.

Adopted in May 2019, the OECD AI Principles represent a comprehensive set of guidelines for the responsible and human-centric development and deployment of AI systems. These principles aim to ensure that AI technologies are beneficial and trustworthy and respect human values and rights.

The OECD AI Principles consist of the following five key recommendations:

- **Inclusive growth, sustainable development, and well-being**: AI should be designed to promote inclusive growth, sustainable development, and well-being, while considering the potential impact on economic, social, and environmental aspects.

- **Human-centered values and fairness**: AI systems should respect human rights, democratic values, and the rule of law. They should be designed to prevent discrimination, ensure fairness, and promote diversity and inclusiveness.

- **Transparency and explainability**: AI systems should be transparent, and their functioning should be explainable to individuals, especially those directly affected by AI decisions. This will help build trust and allow users to challenge or appeal AI-driven outcomes.

- **Robustness, security, and safety**: AI systems should be robust, secure, and safe throughout their operational lifetime. They should be designed to prevent and minimize unintended consequences, ensuring resilience against attacks and addressing potential vulnerabilities.

- **Accountability**: Organizations and individuals responsible for the development, deployment, and use of AI systems should be accountable for their proper functioning. This includes complying with existing laws, adopting appropriate governance mechanisms, and being responsible for AI's impact on society.

Asilomar AI Principles

The Asilomar AI Principles were established during the 2017 Asilomar Conference[20] and consist of guidelines that steer the development of AI. These principles are categorized into research issues, ethics and values, and longer-term issues. The research issues emphasize creating beneficial intelligence, funding for AI research, fostering a healthy exchange between researchers and policymakers, promoting a cooperative and transparent research culture, and ensuring safety standards. The ethics and values category focuses on safety, transparency, responsibility, value alignment, human values, personal privacy, liberty, shared benefits, shared prosperity, human control, non-subversion, and avoiding an AI arms race. Lastly, the longer-term issues category includes being cautious about AI capabilities, recognizing the importance of advanced AI, planning and mitigating AI risks, ensuring strict safety and control measures for recursive self-improvement, and developing superintelligence for the common good. Together, these principles form a comprehensive framework to guide the development and deployment of AI in a responsible and beneficial manner.

The University of Oxford's recommendations for AI governance

The University of Oxford's Future of Humanity Institute has provided a set of recommendations[21] and overviews of current standards. Even though this report doesn't provide any groundbreaking new approaches, it is an excellent survey and overview of existing techniques and research in the space.

PwC's Responsible AI Principles/Toolkit

PwC's Responsible AI Toolkit[22] provides a set of principles and a point of view around the governance, compliance, risk management, bias and fairness, interpretability and explainability, privacy, security, robustness, safety, AI ethics, and policy and regulation of AI. It discusses a strategy for performance and security measures and provides an architectural review with associated risks, such as the risk of errors, bias and discrimination, and a lack of interpretability and robustness.

Alan Turing Institute guide to AI ethics

With a focus on AI ethics, safety, and responsible design, the Alan Turing Institute has released a comprehensive guide[23] to assist with the responsible design and implementation of AI systems in the public sector, known as the FAST guidelines.

The FAST guide presents a set of principles that focus on fairness, accountability, sustainability, safety, and transparency, covering topics such as non-discriminatory fairness, pre- and post-model deployment accountability, stakeholder impact, safety measures, and transparent AI. It provides a process-based governance framework and is one of the few resources to define transparent and interpretable AI, making it a valuable guide for anyone working with AI technology.

Now that we've explored the laws, regulations, and guidelines impacting AI implementation worldwide, let's delve into some of the available tools.

Technology toolkits

Along with guidance documents and PowerPoint, enterprises need toolkits that can actually parse the datasets, models, and code to identify the underlying biases and provide practical ways to address these concerns. The following subsections explain some such tools and libraries that offer these capabilities.

Microsoft Fairlearn

Microsoft Fairlearn[24] is an open source Python library to assess and improve the fairness of ML models, and it has a wide range of algorithms to compare and mitigate bias in predictive models, as well as visualization tools to explore and analyze model performance. Fairlearn is designed to help data scientists and developers build more equitable and inclusive ML models by providing them with the tools to measure and address unfairness in their models. The library is part of Microsoft's RAI efforts and is freely available for use by anyone.

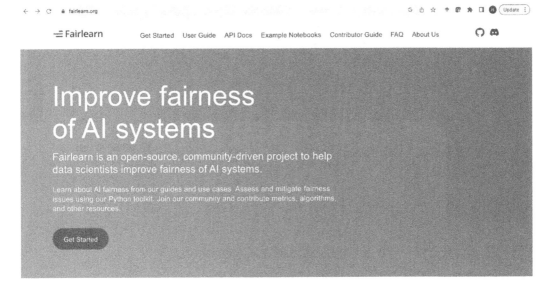

Figure 5.4: The Fairlearn toolkit

In *Chapters 8* and *9*, we will discuss using this toolkit in further detail.

IBM's AI Explainability 360 open source toolkit

IBM's AI Explainability toolkit[25] is one of the most mature offerings in the marketplace.

IBM's AI Explainability toolkit is a comprehensive offering that provides built-in algorithms, examples, quantitative metrics, and tutorials to help developers and data scientists better understand and interpret their ML models. The toolkit is one of the most mature offerings on the market and offers a range of features to enhance model explainability, including global and local explainability, fairness indicators, and counterfactual explanations. It also offers guidance, research papers, videos, tutorials, and event guides to help users navigate the complex landscape of AI explainability.

In addition to its built-in features, the AI Explainability toolkit is designed to be flexible and customizable, allowing users to develop their own custom explainability metrics and integrate the toolkit with other ML tools and frameworks. The toolkit is part of IBM's broader RAI initiatives and is designed to promote the responsible use of AI, which is achieved by providing users with the tools and resources to enhance the interpretability and transparency of their ML models.

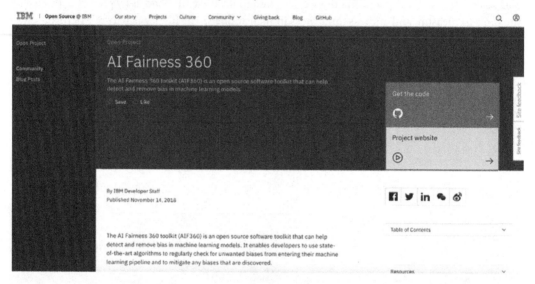

Figure 5.5: IBM's AI Fairness 360

IBM's AI Explainability toolkit is one of many tools and frameworks available to promote AI explainability and transparency. Other tools include AIF360, an open source toolkit to assess and mitigate bias in ML models, and Microsoft Fairlearn, an open source library to assess and improve the fairness of ML models. These tools and frameworks are essential to promote the responsible development and deployment of AI systems and ensure that these systems are transparent, interpretable, and fair.

In the upcoming chapter, we will discuss using the AIF360 toolkit in further detail.

Credo AI Lens toolkit

The Credo AI Lens toolkit[26] is an open source RAI assessment framework (with a commercial counterpart), designed for data scientists to quickly assess models and generate results for governance review within the Credo AI app.

With a focus on RAI, Lens allows comprehensive AI assessments to be streamlined, structured, and interpretable by diverse audiences. It provides **RAI** assessment reports that reduce the time spent on manual documentation and allows for easy stakeholder review. The framework allows for assessment with respect to various RAI considerations, including fairness, performance, and security. Lens uses a governance object to connect with the Credo AI governance platform for programmatic assessment and immediate translation into digestible reports. It can be run in a notebook, a CI/CD pipeline, or anywhere else ML analytics are performed, and it is easily customizable to support an organization's specific assessments. When paired with the Credo AI app, Lens shows its full value by supporting multi-stakeholder alignment, AI assessment, and AI risk assessment.

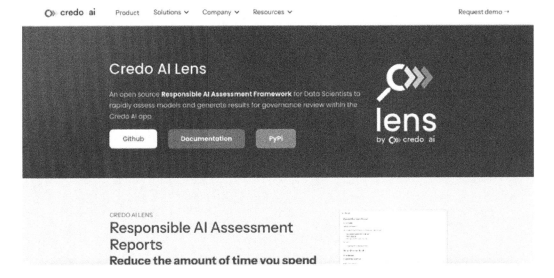

Figure 5.6: The Credo AI Lens RAI toolkit

PiML – the integrated Python toolbox for interpretable ML

The PiML (-ML) Python toolbox[27] is an open source platform to develop and validate interpretable ML models. It supports a growing list of inherently interpretable ML models, including GLM, GAM, decision tree, FIGS, XGB2, EBM, GAMI-Net, and ReLU-DNN, as well as arbitrary supervised ML models for regression and binary classification settings. PiML offers a range of outcome testing, including accuracy metrics, explainability via global and local explainers, fairness through disparity tests and segmented analysis, the identification of weak regions and overfitting, the assessment of prediction uncertainty, and the evaluation of performance degradation under covariate noise perturbation and different out-of-distribution scenarios.

Figure 5.7: The GitHub repo for PiML

Created by Agus Sudjianto, the head of model risk at Wells Fargo and responsible for enterprise model risk management, this platform offers both low-code interfaces and high-code APIs to support users with varying levels of coding experience. With its range of features and interpretability, PiML offers a powerful tool to develop and validate ML models in various domains.

FAT Forensics – algorithmic fairness, accountability, and transparency toolbox

FAT is an acronym for **fairness, accountability**, **and transparency**. **FAT Forensics** (**fatf**) is a Python toolbox[28], built using SciPy and NumPy and licensed under the new BSD license[29], which can be used to evaluate the fairness, accountability, and transparency of AI systems.

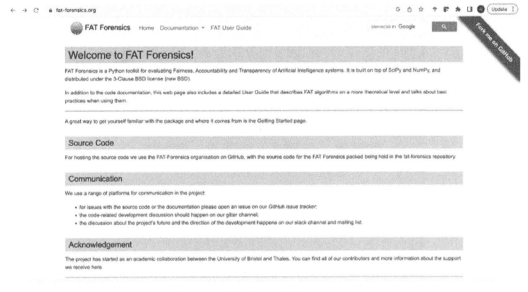

Figure 5.8: The fatf toolkit home page

The fatf tools implement state-of-the-art algorithms, addressing three key aspects of the ML pipeline – data, models, and inference. The package can be used in interactive research mode for **exploratory data analysis** (**EDA**) by researchers, and also in deployment mode for practitioners to monitor a model's attribute post-deployment.

Aequitas – the Bias and Fairness Audit Toolkit

Aequitas[30] is one of the first (and most-cited) open source toolkits in the AI audit and bias landscape. Developed by the Center for Data Science and Public Policy at the University of Chicago[31], Aequitas created an open source bias audit report for ML models and allows users to identify biases. With explainable visuals and detailed tree-based outputs, it helps understand a model's risk to make equitable decisions.

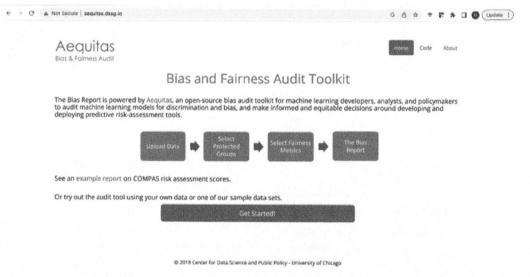

Figure 5.9: The University of Chicago's Aequitas Bias and Fairness Audit Toolkit

AI trust, risk, and security management

AI trust, risk, and security management (AI TRiSM)[32] is a concept introduced by Gartner that focuses on AI model governance, trustworthiness, fairness, reliability, efficacy, security, and data protection. This framework encompasses solutions, techniques, and processes for model interpretability and explainability, privacy, model operations, and adversarial attack resistance.

AI TRiSM helps with AI governance by ensuring that AI models are built and operated safely, ethically, and in compliance with regulations. It aims to prevent failures that could lead to reputational, legal, or financial losses. Key aspects of AI TRiSM include the following:

- **Guided documentation**: Ensuring proper documentation of AI models, their testing, and associated risks, which simplifies the risk management process and makes it more efficient

- **Automated risk and bias checks**: Regular monitoring of AI models for biases and risks, so that errors and discriminatory behavior can be detected and corrected early on

- **Transparency**: Providing audit and comment trails, so that stakeholders can have a clear understanding of a model's development, testing, and decision-making processes

AI TRiSM is essential for organizations to achieve better AI adoption, improved business outcomes, and increased user acceptance. It helps organizations build AI models that are not only effective but also safe and compliant, ensuring long-term success in leveraging AI technologies.

Having explored various XAI toolkits, let's proceed to the *Auditing checklists and measures* section, where we provide a comprehensive set of tools and techniques to quantify model bias and build accountable ML systems.

Auditing checklists and measures

Along with compliance standards and code reviews, quantifying the results for model bias is a critical step in building accountable ML systems. In this section, we will provide a list of some of these checklists and measures.

Datasheets for datasets

Datasheets for datasets is an initiative aimed at improving transparency, accountability, and an understanding of the datasets used in the development and training of ML models. Introduced by Timnit Gebru, an AI ethicist and former co-leader of Google's ethical AI team, as well as Kate Crawford and others, this initiative proposes using a standard way to report datasets, which its creators refer to as *datasheets*[33]. Their rationale was inspired by the electronics industry, where datasheets provide important information about the components being used:

> *"In the electronics industry, every component, no matter how simple or complex,
> is accompanied with a datasheet that describes its operating characteristics, test
> results, recommended uses, and other information."*

For ML, datasheets for datasets outlines essential information about a dataset, including its purpose, composition, collection process, data preprocessing, intended uses, limitations, and ethical considerations. By providing this information, datasheets help developers, researchers, and users understand the context in which a dataset was created, its potential biases, and the appropriateness of its use for specific tasks.

By promoting transparency and encouraging developers to think critically about the data they use, datasheets for datasets contributes to the responsible and ethical development of AI and ML systems. It can help identify potential issues related to fairness, accuracy, and bias, and encourage the creation of more robust, reliable, and equitable AI models.

An example of such a datasheet in use could be for traffic data used for smart city initiatives, such as the one developed and used by Bristol City Council in the UK. This datasheet provides essential information about the dataset, which contains urban traffic patterns to help develop intelligent transportation systems. This datasheet outlines the dataset's purpose, composition, collection process, preprocessing steps, intended uses, limitations, and ethical considerations. The dataset includes data from various sources, such as traffic cameras, vehicle counts, and GPS data from smartphones. It has been preprocessed to ensure data quality and protect user privacy. While the dataset is intended for use in developing traffic prediction models and traffic management systems, it comes with certain limitations, such as potential biases and data quality issues.

The datasheet will highlight the importance of ethical considerations, such as data anonymization and adherence to local data protection regulations, ensuring transparency and fostering responsible AI development in the urban transportation domain.

Model cards for model reporting

Model cards for model reporting[34] are a standardized framework designed to improve transparency and accountability in the development and deployment of ML models. Introduced by Margaret Mitchell, Timnit Gebru, and their team, model cards aim to provide comprehensive and easily understandable information about a model's performance, limitations, and potential biases across a range of conditions and demographic groups. These conditions may include cultural, demographic, or phenotypic groups, such as race, geography, or sex, which are relevant to the intended use domain of the model.

By offering a clear and concise description of a model's behavior, model cards enable developers, users, and other stakeholders to better understand its strengths and weaknesses, as well as its ethical implications. This increased transparency can help to ensure that ML models are used responsibly and ethically, and that potential biases and limitations are acknowledged and addressed.

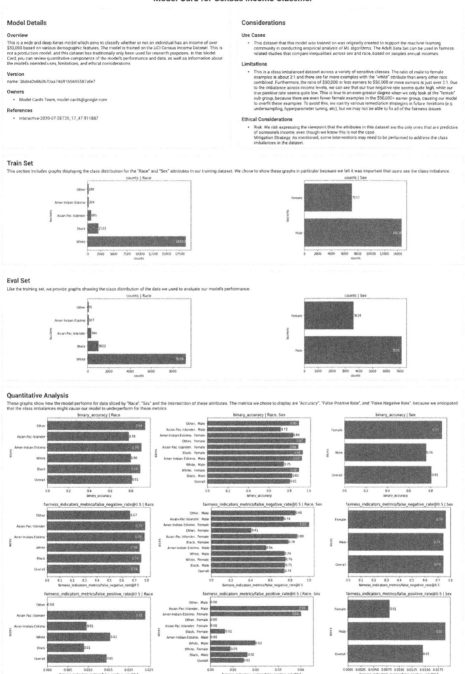

Figure 5.10: This is an example model card for the Census Income Classifier (courtesy of Google: https://ai.googleblog.com/2020/07/introducing-model-card-toolkit-for.html) This image is for demonstration purposes only and the detail in the text is not essential.

A great example of this is a **Generative Pre-trained Transformer 3 (GPT-3)** model card[35]. Model cards for GPT-3 offer a transparent and standardized method to evaluate and communicate the performance, intended use, limitations, and biases of OpenAI's **GPT-3** model. As a state-of-the-art language model, GPT-3 is designed for various natural language processing tasks, such as text completion, question-answering, summarization, and translation. The model card for GPT-3 highlights its limitations, including potential biases and the possibility of generating plausible-sounding but incorrect or nonsensical answers. It also provides performance metrics such as perplexity and an F1 score, and acknowledges the lack of specific performance information for different demographic groups, urging users to be cautious when dealing with sensitive or controversial topics. In this way, model cards for GPT-3 serve as an essential tool to understand the model's strengths, weaknesses, and appropriate use cases.

Here are some other notable mentions of ethical AI and ML toolkits:

- **Inclusive AI – ODEP's checklist for employers**: EARN and PEAT provide a checklist[36] for inclusive AI-based recruitment.

- **Santa Clara University ethical toolkit for engineering/design practice**: The Markkula Center offers an Ethical OS Toolkit[37] to implement ethical judgment in workflows.

- **IETF Ethical OS Toolkit**: IETF provides a toolkit[38] to identify risk zones and for ethical decision-making strategies.

- **Deon – ethics checklist for data scientists**: The Deon command-line tool[39] aids in adding ethical checklists to data science projects, allowing the creation and appending of checklists in various formats.

- **AI-RFX procurement framework**: The Institute for Ethical AI Machine Learning[40] has published eight responsible ML principles. The AI-RFX procurement framework builds on these principles, creating a checklist to improve AI safety, quality, and performance.

Summary

In this chapter, we reviewed the current standards landscape. You saw how different countries, professional bodies, and organizations implement best practices, governance, regulations, and policies around automated decision management systems. We provided an overview of national policies and regulations, attempts from professional bodies to establish industry standards, the contemporary landscape of technology toolkits, and auditing checklist metrics.

In many ways, the sheer number of different standards, regulatory frameworks, and guides for best practice is daunting. This is perhaps particularly true for those enterprise leaders who are non-technical regarding data science and ML, but who are seeking to lead their businesses to achieve the benefits that AI-driven service improvement can facilitate. This is one of the main reasons we wrote this book! We seek to demystify these assurance processes. At the core of all the frameworks and starter kits outlined previously is a set of processes that, when followed, enable an enterprise to ensure that they develop and deploy AI responsibly.

In the upcoming chapter, we will do a deep dive into an enterprise starter kit for fairness, accountability, and transparency, where we will discuss the importance of governance, compliance, and regulations in the current business landscape, with a specific focus on AI. As organizations seek robust and successful outcomes while adhering to regulations in the geographies they operate in, governance and compliance are critical components for success. We will explore the practical aspects of AI governance, compliance regulations, and the key elements of an enterprise AI governance framework.

Adhering to ethical AI principles is also essential as part of corporate social responsibility. By developing and implementing a well-designed governance process, organizations can ensure they adhere to their core values, ethical standards, and legal obligations, ultimately protecting the public interest and maintaining the trust of stakeholders.

The next chapter awaits, like a Vogon fleet hovering over your planet with the threat of bureaucratic paperwork. Stay tuned!

References and further reading

1. NIST Special Publication 1270 *Towards a Standard for Identifying and Managing Bias in AI*: `https://nvlpubs.nist.gov/nistpubs/SpecialPublications/NIST.SP.1270.pdf`.

2. H.R.2231 – Algorithmic Accountability Act of 2019: `https://www.congress.gov/bill/116th-congress/house-bill/2231`.

3. CCPA: `https://oag.ca.gov/privacy/ccpa`.

4. *How Much Does Racial Bias Affect Mortgage Lending? Evidence from Human and Algorithmic Credit Decisions*: `https://papers.ssrn.com/sol3/papers.cfm?abstractid=3887663`.

5. Consumer Financial Protection Circular 2022-03: `https://www.consumerfinance.gov/compliance/circulars/circular-2022-03-adverse-action-notification-requirements-in-connection-with-credit-decisions-based-on-complex-algorithms/`.

6. SB 1392 Consumer Data Protection Act; establishes a framework for controlling and processing personal data: `https://lis.virginia.gov/cgi-bin/legp604.exe?211+sum+SB1392`.

7. Ethical AI Toolkit: `https://ethicstoolkit.ai/`.

8. Proposal for a *REGULATION OF THE EUROPEAN PARLIAMENT AND OF THE COUNCIL LAYING DOWN HARMONISED RULES ON ARTIFICIAL INTELLIGENCE (ARTIFICIAL INTELLIGENCE ACT) AND AMENDING CERTAIN UNION LEGISLATIVE ACTS*: `https://eur-lex.europa.eu/legal-content/EN/TXT/?uri=CELEX%3A52021PC0206`.

9. GDPR: `https://gdpr.eu/what-is-gdpr`.

10. *Is there a right to explanation for ML in the GDPR?*: https://iapp.org/news/a/is-there-a-right-to-explanation-for-machine-learning-in-the-gdpr/.

11. The Data Protection Act: https://www.gov.uk/data-protection.

12. UK Government's Data Ethics Framework: https://www.gov.uk/government/publications/data-ethics-framework.

13. *PERSONAL DATA PROTECTION ACT 2012*: https://sso.agc.gov.sg/Act/PDPA2012.

14. *PROTECTION FROM ONLINE FALSEHOODS AND MANIPULATION ACT 2019*: https://sso.agc.gov.sg/Acts-Supp/18-2019.

15. AI Verify: https://file.go.gov.sg/aiverify.pdf.

16. *Singapore launches world's first AI testing framework and toolkit to promote transparency*: https://www.imda.gov.sg/news-and-events/Media-Room/Media-Releases/2022/Singapore-launches-worlds-first-AI-testing-framework-and-toolkit-to-promote-transparency-Invites-companies-to-pilot-and-contribute-to-international-standards-development.

17. *ARTIFICIAL INTELLIGENCE PRINCIPLES ETHICS*: https://www.digitaldubai.ae/initiatives/ai-principles-ethics.

18. The Toronto Declaration protecting the right to equality and non-discrimination in ML systems: https://www.torontodeclaration.org/declaration-text/english/.

19. AI accountability: Microsoft's principles and requirements for responsible AI development and deployment: https://query.prod.cms.rt.microsoft.com/cms/api/am/binary/RE5cmFl.

20. Beneficial AI 2017: https://futureoflife.org/event/bai-2017/.

21. Standards for AI Governance: International Standards to Enable Global Coordination in AI Research Development: https://www.fhi.ox.ac.uk/wp-content/uploads/Standards-FHI-Technical-Report.pdf.

22. PwC Responsible AI Toolkit: https://www.pwc.com/gx/en/issues/data-and-analytics/artificial0intelligence/what-is-responsible-ai.html.

23. Understanding AI ethics and safety: https://www.turing.ac.uk/research/publications/understanding-artificial-intelligence-ethics-and-safety.

24. Microsoft Fairlearn: https://github.com/fairlearn/fairlearn.

25. IBM's AI Explainability Toolkit: http://aix360.mybluemix.net/ https://www.ibm.com/opensource/open/projects/ai-fairness-360/.

26. https://github.com/credo-ai/credoailens.

27. PiML: `https://github.com/SelfExplainML/PiML-Toolbox`.

28. fatf: `https://github.com/fat-forensics/fat-forensics`.

29. The new BSD license, also known as the simplified BSD license, is a permissive open source license that allows users to modify, distribute, and use software under the conditions outlined in the license, with the requirement that the original copyright notice and disclaimer of warranty remain intact. The new BSD license is similar to the original BSD license but is shorter and simpler. To learn more, visit the new BSD license page at `https://opensource.org/licenses/BSD-2-Clause`.

30. Aequitas – the Bias and Fairness Audit Toolkit: `https://github.com/dssg/aequitas`.

31. Center for Data Science and Public Policy: `http://www.datasciencepublicpolicy.org/our-work/tools-guides/aequitas/`.

32. AI TRiSM: `https://www.gartner.com/en/articles/what-it-takes-to-make-ai-safe-and-effective`.

33. Datasheets for datasets: `https://arxiv.org/abs/1803.09010`.

34. *Model Cards for Model Reporting*: `https://arxiv.org/abs/1810.03993`.

35. GPT-3 model card: `https://github.com/openai/gpt-3/blob/master/model-card.md`.

36. `https://www.peatworks.org/wp-content/uploads/2020/10/EARN_PEAT_eRecruiting_Checklist.pdf`.

37. `https://www.scu.edu/ethics-in-technology-practice/ethical-toolkit/`.

38. `https://ethicstoolkit.ai/`.

39. `https://deon.drivendata.org/`.

40. `https://ethical.institute/index.html`.

41. NIST (2021). NIST AI Framework: A Guide for Developing and Using AI Systems. Retrieved from `https://nvlpubs.nist.gov/nistpubs/SpecialPublications/NIST.SP.2100-5.pdf`.

42. Algorithm Accountability Act. (2021): `https://www.congress.gov/bill/116th-congress/senate-bill/1057`.

43. Info-communications Media Development Authority (IMDA) (2021). AI Ethics Governance Framework. Retrieved from `https://www.imda.gov.sg/regulations-licensing-and-consultations/regulations/industry-guidance/ai-ethics-and-governance-framework`.

44. European Union (2021). Regulation (EU) 2019/881 of the European Parliament and of the Council of 17 April 2019 on the European Agency for the Cooperation of Energy Regulators and repealing Regulation (EC) No 713/2009. Retrieved from `https://eur-lex.europa.eu/legal-content/EN/TXT/HTML/?uri=CELEX:32019R0881&from=EN`.

45. Ministry of Electronics Information Technology (MEITY) (2021). Ethical Guidelines for AI. Retrieved from `https://meity.gov.in/writereaddata/files/Ethical_Guidelines_for_Artificial_Intelligence.pdf`.

46. Office of the Privacy Commissioner of Canada (2021). AI and Privacy: Challenges and Best Practices. Retrieved from `https://www.priv.gc.ca/en/privacy-topics/artificial-intelligence-and-privacy/`.

47. AI Now Institute (2021). Model Governance and Compliance Standards. Retrieved from `https://ainowinstitute.org/model-governance-compliance.html`.

Regulations and compliance standards are constantly evolving. Please check the official websites for the latest updates and changes.

6

Enterprise Starter Kit for Fairness, Accountability, and Transparency

"The real problem is not the existential threat of AI. Instead, it is in the development of ethical AI systems."

– Rana El Kaliouby

"We're seeing a kind of a Wild West situation with AI and regulation right now. The scale at which businesses are adopting AI technologies isn't matched by clear guidelines to regulate algorithms and help researchers avoid the pitfalls of bias in datasets. We need to advocate for a better system of checks and balances to test AI for bias and fairness, and to help businesses determine whether certain use cases are even appropriate for this technology at the moment."

– Timnit Gebru, research scientist, Google AI

Streamlined operations in compliance with regulations are essential for any company looking to run a successful business. Companies need to ensure that their operations are efficient and compliant with all relevant regulations. This requires careful planning and management, as well as ongoing monitoring of the company's design, development, and operations of its core business. By ensuring that their operations are up to par, companies can avoid costly fines and penalties, which could ultimately damage the bottom line.

There is no doubt that AI regulations are on the way; the question then becomes what can companies do about that? In this chapter, we will provide practical advice and tools to explain what companies can do to prepare themselves for upcoming regulatory needs.

In this chapter, we will learn about the following:

- How to get started with AI governance in a company for trustworthy AI
- Enterprise roadmap for AI governance – guiding principles for the model framework
- AI impact assessments and algorithmic audits
- Building an AI center of excellence
- Real-world use cases and recommendations

Getting started with enterprise AI governance

In some business settings such as finance and healthcare, the machine learning algorithms that underpin AI are already regulated. For example, in the UK, the **Financial Conduct Authority** (**FCA**) is responsible for ensuring that credit agencies who use risk modeling (typically logistic regression) to estimate the likelihood of a customer defaulting on a loan do so in ways that are consistently fair to the customer. The credit agency must assure the FCA that the machine learning models they use for this are not biased for certain customer groups, are robust estimators of default risk, and similar assurances.

So, we can say that in some instances, AI Assurance Frameworks already exist and are used regularly in business today. However, as the use of AI grows exponentially across industry and the machine learning models used to produce this AI increase in their power and complexity, there is arguably a growing requirement for AI Assurance in those business sectors where it is currently either light-touch or non-existent. At the time of writing, the US, UK, and EU are all recognizing that current regulatory approaches for AI require development and implementation. The requirement for enterprises to develop and use AI Assurance Frameworks will follow. Indeed, it is our appreciation of this that led us to write this book!

For these reasons, AI Assurance Frameworks in enterprises today either do not exist or are focused on specific business areas such as credit risk modeling. One of our intentions with this book is to provide a general approach to AI Assurance and to provide a framework to do so.

Enterprises seek paths for robust and successful business outcomes while staying compliant with regulations in the geographies in which they operate. Governance is the process of decision-making and the process by which decisions get implemented, while compliance refers to an organization's adherence to laws, regulations, guidelines, or specifications. A regulation (reg) is a specific requirement that an organization must adhere to in order to be in compliance. AI regulations refer to the body of laws, regulations, and guidelines governing artificial intelligence. An AI governance standard is a set of requirements that organizations must meet in order to ensure the safety and ethical use of artificial intelligence.

There is currently no comprehensive set of AI governance standards, but it is crucial that leadership prepare their organizations for upcoming regulations by taking practical steps to upskill, self-regulate, and put in place the necessary procedures, tools, and standards. This includes educating their staff about AI safety concerns related to the potential risks posed by artificial intelligence technologies. These risks may include unintended harm caused by errors or the malicious use of AI systems. Leadership must also educate themselves and their workforce about AI ethics and principles in their domain; which refer to the moral principles that guide the development and application of artificial intelligence technologies. Adhering to ethical AI principles is part of **corporate social responsibility (CSR)**.

Throughout this chapter, you will explore topics related to governance, compliance, and regulations in today's business environment with a specific focus on **Artificial Intelligence (AI)**. In particular, we will discuss practical aspects of AI Governance, compliance regulations, and the key elements of an enterprise AI Governance framework. It goes without saying that governance and compliance are critical to the success of any organization. A well-designed and implemented governance process helps ensure that an organization adheres to its core values, ethical standards, and legal obligations. Such a framework enables compliance with laws and regulations, which is essential to protect the public interest and maintain the trust of stakeholders.

> **Note**
>
> The board of directors is responsible for overseeing the management of the company and ensuring that it operates in the best interests of its shareholders. They set the strategy, approve major decisions and transactions, and appoint and remove executive officers. The board also has a fiduciary duty to act in good faith and in the best interests of the shareholders. AI governance and policy have quickly become part of the purview of the board, which has to establish guidelines around how AI can be made to operate within the company's boundaries.

An effective AI governance process has some key characteristics. First of all, it provides transparency into an organization's automated decision-making systems, and makes their respective stakeholders accountable.

This process ensures that all stakeholders are aware of the challenges of ethical AI and consider the effects of bias, model drift, and decay when shaping the direction of the organization's workflow, keeping it in line with the organization's values. This governance process enables a strong compliance program, and this protects against potential algorithmic risks by identifying problems early on and developing corrective action plans to address them.

Artificial intelligence workflows and model governance can become tangled up in technical details, and it is important to ensure that this process does not become murky and hard to understand. The importance of creating an easy-to-follow process in AI governance and compliance cannot be overstated. By establishing clear guidelines for automated decision-making and holding all members of the organization accountable to these standards, organizations can safeguard against unethical or illegal behavior while promoting a positive culture within the workplace.

There are some key factors to consider when creating an enterprise AI governance framework. First, you need to identify what your organization's goals are for using AI. Once you know your goals, you can start to develop policies and procedures around data collection, storage, and processing; algorithm development and training; model deployment and management; and monitoring and auditing. You also need to create a process for continuous improvement so that your governance framework evolves as your AI program grows. Lastly, it is important to ensure that everyone in your organization understands the governance framework and their role in adhering to it. By taking these steps, you can create a strong foundation for success with enterprise AI.

> **Note**
>
> **CSR** is a company's commitment to manage the impact of its activities on the environment and the communities in which it operates. All businesses have a responsibility to operate in an ethical and sustainable way. This refers to a company's efforts to positively impact society through its business practices, but besides traditional endeavors such as reducing pollution, supporting local charities, or improving working conditions for employees, it now involves building and establishing ethical AI policies.

As discussed in earlier chapters, the machine learning development lifecycle and MLOps play an important role in AI governance by providing a framework for managing and deploying AI applications. MLOps helps to ensure that AI applications are deployed securely and efficiently, while also providing a way to monitor and optimize model bias, drift, decay, and performance. By automating the management of AI deployments, MLOps can help organizations to reduce the risk of human error and improve the overall efficiency of their operations.

Risk management is a key pillar of any governance program and involves identifying AI model-related risks, mitigating risks, and monitoring risks. To effectively manage the risks associated with AI, organizations need to have a clear understanding of the potential risks involved. AI model risk management requires that the governance framework provides the following:

- An understanding of how the model works and what it is trying to achieve
- Clear communication between those who create and use the model
- Documentation of the assumptions made during development and testing
- Regular monitoring of performance against expectations

When these requirements are met, organizations can more effectively manage the risks associated with using machine learning models. Since model bias is a socio-technical problem, model risk assessment likewise becomes a domain-specific human-centered problem.

> **Note**
>
> We cannot emphasize enough the importance of a domain expert's involvement in reviewing the business use cases and helping identify algorithmic bias. AI bias is a socio-technical problem because it is caused by the interaction of social and technical factors. Technical factors include the algorithms used to create and train AI models, which can be biased against certain groups of people. Social factors include the data that is used to train AI models, which can also be biased against certain groups of people. Human experts need to address AI model bias because they are ultimately responsible for creating and training AI models, and they are the only ones with the ability and will to change the algorithms and data that are used to create and train AI models.

Once these risks have been identified, steps can be taken to mitigate them. It's equally important to continuously monitor AI systems for any new or emerging risks. Continuous monitoring is a critical aspect of AI risk management to minimize the impact of potentially harmful events and ensure that their AI systems are safe and reliable.

Assurance is the confirmation that something is safe or secure. In the context of AI, model assurance refers to the confidence that an AI system has in its predictions and decisions. This can be achieved through various means, such as verifying and validating the data used to train the model, testing the model against known datasets, and monitoring the performance of deployed models. By ensuring that AI models are accurate and reliable, we can help build trust in these systems and ensure that they are ethically sound. AI assurance requires measures to be put in place for the safety, security, privacy, and trustworthiness of AI models. Each of these areas is critical to ensuring that AI technologies are developed and used responsibly. Together, they become part of the AI Governance framework for building automated decision-making systems that are safe, secure, and trustworthy.

So far, we have discussed many different aspects of AI governance frameworks, which can get overwhelming. To simplify this, we provide a draft of the Masood-Heather AI governance framework **AI STEPS FORWARD** in the next section.

AI STEPS FORWARD – AI governance framework

Our proposed framework[1] encapsulates the salient aspects of **S**ecurity, **T**ransparency, **E**xplainability, **P**rivacy, **S**afety, **F**airness, **O**versight (an internal AI board with SMEs), **R**eliability, **W**orkforce (upskilling and education), **A**I CoE, **R**egulations (external AI governance and regulations), and **D**iversity (inclusivity).

The STEPS FORWARD framework aims to promote ethical AI, auditability, and trust as overarching themes that permeate each component. By integrating these principles into AI systems, organizations can create more responsible, effective, and beneficial AI solutions.

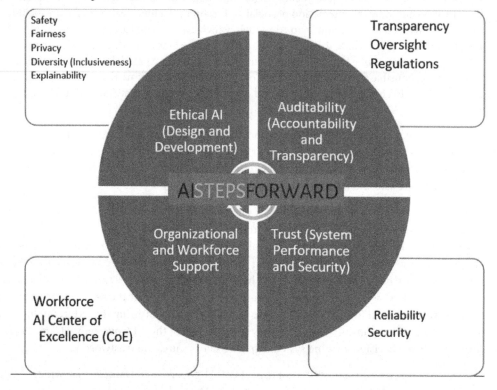

Figure 6.1: AI STEPS FORWARD governance framework

Incorporating **Ethical AI**, **Auditability**, and **Trust** as overarching themes, the AI STEPS forward framework principles are categorized into the following four categories:

1. **Ethical AI (Design and Development):**

   - **Safety**: Prioritize the identification and mitigation of risks associated with AI systems. Implement measures to prevent harm and ensure the safe operation of AI systems across their lifecycles.

   - **Fairness**: Detect, mitigate, and prevent biases in AI systems. Ensure that AI systems are equitable and do not unfairly discriminate against or favor any specific group.

   - **Privacy**: Uphold data protection standards, ensuring that user and stakeholder information is anonymized and secure. Incorporate privacy-by-design principles to minimize privacy risks.

- **Diversity** (inclusivity): Encourage inclusive AI development by involving diverse perspectives, ensuring equal representation, and making AI systems accessible to all users.

- **Explainability**: Develop AI systems that can provide human-understandable rationales for their outputs and decisions. Maintain clear documentation of the AI system's design, functionality, and decision-making processes.

2. **Auditability (Accountability and Transparency):**

- **Transparency**: Maintain openness in AI development, disclosure of AI system capabilities, and stakeholder communication. Ensure that users and affected parties have a clear understanding of the AI system's goals, limitations, and potential impacts.

- **Oversight**: Establish internal AI boards with subject-matter experts to monitor AI system performance, ensure compliance, and manage AI system lifecycles. Provide guidance and expertise throughout the development and deployment process.

- **Regulations**: Adhere to external AI governance and regulations, maintain compliance with relevant laws and standards, and coordinate with regulatory bodies to ensure responsible AI deployment.

3. **Trust (System Performance and Security):**

- **Reliability**: Ensure AI systems are accurate, consistent, and resilient under various conditions. Continuously improve AI system performance and stability.

- **Security**: Implement robust cybersecurity measures to protect AI systems and data from unauthorized access, tampering, or malicious activities. Ensure the integrity of AI system operations.

4. **Organizational and Workforce Support:**

- **Workforce**: Invest in upskilling and education, fostering talent development, and promoting AI awareness and literacy. Build a workforce capable of understanding, developing, and maintaining ethical AI systems.

- **AI CoE**: Create a centralized body for AI strategy development, research, and best practices. Support organizational AI initiatives and drive innovation.

The AI STEPS FORWARD framework aims to promote ethical AI, auditability, and trust as overarching themes that permeate each component in the framework. By integrating these principles into AI systems, organizations can create more responsible, effective, and beneficial AI solutions.

Implementing AI STEPS FORWARD in an enterprise

Implementing the AI STEPS FORWARD framework in an enterprise involves a series of steps to ensure that AI systems are developed and deployed ethically, responsibly, and in compliance with relevant regulations. Here's a detailed guide to implementing the framework:

1. **Assess the current state**: Evaluate your organization's existing AI systems, projects, and initiatives to identify the strengths, weaknesses, and gaps in relation to the STEPS FORWARD framework components.

2. **Establish a clear AI strategy**: Develop an AI strategy that aligns with the organization's objectives and incorporates the principles of the STEPS FORWARD framework. Define goals, timelines, and **key performance indicators** (**KPIs**) to measure progress.

3. **Create an AI CoE**: Set up a centralized body responsible for AI strategy development, research, best practices, and innovation. The AI CoE should include cross-functional teams and subject-matter experts.

4. **Form an internal AI oversight board**: Assemble a board of experts, stakeholders, and decision-makers to oversee AI initiatives, ensure compliance, and provide guidance throughout the development and deployment process.

5. **Develop AI policies and guidelines**: Draft clear policies and guidelines that cover each aspect of the STEPS FORWARD framework. These documents should provide guidance on responsible AI development and deployment and should be regularly reviewed and updated.

6. **Incorporate external regulations**: Stay informed about relevant external AI governance, regulations, and standards. Ensure your organization's AI systems and processes comply with these requirements.

7. **Build a diverse and skilled workforce**: Invest in upskilling and education programs to build AI awareness and literacy among employees. Encourage diversity and inclusivity by involving individuals with various backgrounds, expertise, and perspectives in AI initiatives.

8. **Implement AI system development best practices**: Incorporate the principles of the STEPS FORWARD framework during AI system design, development, and testing. This includes ensuring safety, transparency, explainability, privacy, security, fairness, and reliability throughout the process.

9. **Monitor and audit AI systems**: Continuously monitor AI systems to assess their performance, safety, and compliance with the framework principles. Regular audits should be conducted to identify and mitigate risks and to ensure adherence to ethical standards.

10. **Encourage stakeholder engagement and communication**: Foster open communication channels with internal and external stakeholders to ensure transparency, gather feedback, and address concerns. Keep stakeholders informed about the AI system's capabilities, limitations, and potential impacts.

11. **Iterate and improve**: Regularly review the organization's AI initiatives in light of the STEPS FORWARD framework. Identify areas for improvement and implement changes as needed to align with the framework's principles and objectives.

By following these steps, an enterprise can successfully implement the AI STEPS FORWARD framework, ensuring responsible AI development and deployment while fostering trust, ethical behavior, and compliance with relevant regulations.

The strategic principles of AI STEPS FORWARD

In today's rapidly evolving AI landscape, organizations must prioritize responsible AI development and deployment to build trust, ensure ethical behavior, and comply with regulations. The AI STEPS FORWARD framework offers a comprehensive approach to achieving this goal. Here are five key strategic principles of the framework:

- **Holistic approach to responsible AI**: The AI STEPS FORWARD framework takes a holistic approach, encompassing various aspects of responsible AI development, such as safety, transparency, explainability, privacy, security, fairness, reliability, inclusivity, and compliance with internal and external regulations. This comprehensive perspective ensures that organizations address all relevant factors when deploying AI systems, minimizing potential risks and maximizing benefits.

- **Establishing a robust governance structure**: A crucial aspect of the framework is the creation of a robust governance structure, including an AI CoE and an internal AI oversight board. This structure ensures effective management of AI initiatives, provides guidance throughout the development process, and fosters cross-functional collaboration, promoting innovation and adherence to responsible AI practices.

- **Continuous improvement and learning**: The AI STEPS FORWARD framework emphasizes the importance of continuous improvement and learning. By staying informed about new developments, best practices, and emerging risks, organizations can refine their AI policies, guidelines, and practices to ensure responsible AI adoption. This also includes learning from past experiences and iterating on existing systems and processes to optimize their performance and ethical impact.

- **Stakeholder engagement and transparent communication**: Engaging with stakeholders and maintaining transparent communication are central principles of the AI STEPS FORWARD framework. Organizations should actively involve stakeholders in the AI development process, address their concerns, and maintain open communication channels to build trust and foster collaboration. Transparent communication helps stakeholders understand the AI system's capabilities, limitations, and potential impacts, enabling them to make informed decisions and contribute to responsible AI practices.

- **Building a diverse and skilled workforce**: Investing in upskilling and education programs to build AI awareness and literacy among employees is vital to ensure responsible AI development. The AI STEPS FORWARD framework encourages organizations to foster diversity and inclusivity, involving individuals with various backgrounds, expertises, and perspectives in AI initiatives. A diverse and skilled workforce contributes to more robust AI systems, ensures that potential risks are identified and mitigated, and drives innovation while promoting ethical behavior.

By adopting these five key strategic principles, organizations can successfully implement the AI STEPS FORWARD framework, ensuring responsible AI development and deployment while fostering trust, ethical behavior, and compliance with relevant regulations. Embracing this framework paves the way for organizations to leverage the full potential of AI technologies while minimizing risks and maximizing societal benefits.

AI STEPS FORWARD in enterprise governance

In the rapidly evolving world of AI, organizations must prioritize responsible and ethical AI implementation. The AI STEPS FORWARD framework offers a comprehensive governance approach tailored to key stakeholders, including executive leaders, data scientists, legal and compliance teams, HR and the workforce, IT and security, and ethics committees. By adhering to specific objectives and checklists, these stakeholders contribute to a robust governance structure that encourages transparency, fairness, and trust, ultimately fostering a responsible AI ecosystem for the benefit of all.

Stakeholder	Purpose	Checklist Title
Executive Leaders	Ensure alignment with AI strategy and objectives	AI Strategy and Business Objectives
Data Science Teams	Validate models and data	Model Validation and Data Quality
Legal & Compliance	Ensure regulatory compliance	Regulatory Compliance and Legal Review
HR & Workforce	Evaluate AI workforce development and upskilling	AI Workforce Training and Upskilling
IT & Security	Assess AI system safety, privacy, and security	AI Safety, Privacy, and Security
Ethics Committee	Review AI system fairness, transparency, and ethics	AI Ethics, Fairness, and Transparency

Table 6.1: Governance checklists for AI projects

In the context of AI governance, the stakeholder groups listed in the preceding table each have specific skills, knowledge, and responsibilities. The AI STEPS FORWARD framework introduces tailored governance dashboards for these stakeholder groups, providing actionable insights related to stakeholder-specific responsibilities and expertise, enabling them to track and optimize the responsible implementation of AI across an organization together.

Stakeholder	Measure	Purpose
Executive Leaders	AI Project Status	Track progress and status of AI initiatives
Data Science Teams	Model Performance Metrics	Monitor and evaluate AI model accuracy and effectiveness
Legal & Compliance	Compliance Status	Assess adherence to regulations and ethical guidelines
HR & Workforce	Workforce Training Metrics	Evaluate AI-related training and upskilling progress
IT & Security	Security and Privacy Metrics	Monitor safety, privacy, and security of AI systems
Ethics Committee	Fairness and Bias Metrics	Review AI system fairness, transparency, and ethical behavior

Table 6.2: AI STEPS FORWARD framework – enterprise governance dashboards

The actionable insights reported to each key stakeholder group within their respective dashboards allow executive leaders to track AI initiatives' progress and status; data scientists to monitor and evaluate AI models' accuracy and effectiveness; legal and compliance teams to assess adherence to regulations and ethical guidelines; HR and the workforce to evaluate AI-related training and upskilling progress; IT and security to monitor AI systems' safety, privacy, and security; and the ethics committee to review AI systems' fairness, transparency, and ethical behavior.

By leveraging such reporting processes, organizations can ensure that the relevant stakeholders have access to the information they need to make informed decisions and contribute to responsible AI practices.

The AI STEPS FORWARD maturity model

The AI STEPS FORWARD maturity model provides a structure for evaluating an organization's progress in implementing responsible AI practices. It helps organizations understand their current state and outlines the path toward achieving full maturity in the ethical use of AI.

Here's a detailed explanation of each level in the AI STEPS FORWARD maturity model:

- **Level 1 – Awareness**: At this stage, an organization is beginning to recognize the importance of responsible AI practices. Key actions include the following:

    - Building awareness of AI ethics and the AI STEPS FORWARD framework among leadership and employees

    - Identifying opportunities and challenges related to responsible AI implementation

    - Conducting initial assessments of the organization's AI systems and initiatives against the AI STEPS FORWARD framework

- **Level 2 – Experimentation Exploration**: Organizations at this level are starting to experiment with responsible AI practices and exploring potential applications. Key actions include the following:

    - Developing an AI strategy that incorporates the principles of the AI STEPS FORWARD framework

    - Forming an AI **CoE** to drive research, best practices, and responsible AI initiatives

    - Launching pilot projects to test and refine responsible AI practices, such as fairness, explainability, and security

    - Investing in upskilling and education programs to build AI awareness and literacy among employees

- **Level 3 – Operational**: At this level, organizations are operationalizing responsible AI practices, moving beyond experimentation to integrate ethical AI into their processes. Key actions include the following:

    - Implementing AI policies and guidelines that cover each aspect of the STEPS FORWARD framework

    - Establishing an internal AI oversight board to ensure compliance and provide guidance throughout the development and deployment process

    - Embedding responsible AI practices into ongoing AI projects and initiatives

    - Monitoring and auditing AI systems to assess their performance, safety, and compliance with the framework principles

- **Level 4 – Systemic/Embedded**: Organizations at this level have fully embedded responsible AI practices into their operations, making ethical AI an integral part of their culture. Key actions include the following:

  - Ensuring that all AI systems and initiatives are aligned with the STEPS FORWARD framework

  - Continuously improving responsible AI practices by learning from past experiences and staying informed about new developments and best practices

  - Fostering a culture of transparency, accountability, and ethical behavior across the organization

  - Engaging with stakeholders, including employees, customers, and regulators, to ensure open communication and continuous feedback

- **Level 5 – Transformational**: At this level, organizations are leveraging responsible AI to drive significant transformation and innovation. Key actions include the following:

  - Expanding the use of responsible AI practices to drive business growth, optimize operations, and create new value propositions

  - Collaborating with other organizations, industry bodies, and regulators to shape the future of responsible AI development and deployment

  - Actively sharing knowledge, best practices, and lessons learned with the broader community to promote responsible AI adoption across industries

  - Continuously refining and advancing the organization's responsible AI capabilities to stay at the forefront of ethical AI innovation

As organizations progress through these maturity levels, they will become increasingly adept at implementing responsible AI practices and harnessing the full potential of AI systems.

Risk management in AI STEPS FORWARD

In the AI STEPS FORWARD framework, risk management is a fundamental component that ensures AI systems are developed and deployed responsibly. By proactively identifying, assessing, and mitigating the potential risks associated with AI technologies, the framework enables organizations to maintain ethical, safe, and compliant AI implementations, fostering trust and promoting responsible innovation. The following are some of the key elements of AI risk management in the framework.

- **Safety**: The framework prioritizes the identification and mitigation of risks associated with AI systems. This involves conducting thorough risk assessments during the development and deployment process to recognize potential hazards, implement appropriate mitigation strategies, and continuously monitor AI systems to ensure safe operation.

- **Transparency**: By promoting transparency in AI development and communication, the framework helps stakeholders understand the potential risks and limitations of AI systems, allowing them to make informed decisions and manage risks more effectively.

- **Explainability**: Ensuring that AI systems are explainable enables users to better comprehend the rationale behind AI outputs and decisions. This understanding helps in identifying potential risks and taking corrective action when needed.

- **Privacy**: The framework emphasizes data protection and privacy by design, which helps manage risks related to unauthorized access, data breaches, and misuse of sensitive information.

- **Security**: By incorporating strong cybersecurity measures, the framework reduces risks related to unauthorized access, tampering, or malicious activities that could compromise AI systems and data.

- **Fairness**: By addressing biases and promoting fairness, the framework mitigates risks associated with discriminatory AI systems that could harm certain groups or individuals.

- **Oversight**: Establishing an internal AI oversight board ensures that risks are continuously monitored and managed throughout the AI system's lifecycle. The board provides guidance on risk mitigation strategies and ensures compliance with relevant policies and regulations.

- **Reliability**: The framework encourages the development of reliable AI systems that are accurate, consistent, and resilient, reducing the risk of unintended consequences or system failures.

- **Regulations**: Adhering to external AI governance and regulations helps manage risks related to legal and regulatory non-compliance, which could result in fines, reputational damage, or other negative consequences.

- **Inclusivity**: By fostering diversity and inclusivity, the framework mitigates risks related to overlooking the needs and perspectives of various stakeholders, which could lead to biased or ineffective AI systems.

The AI STEPS FORWARD framework addresses risk management holistically, incorporating safety, transparency, explainability, privacy, security, fairness, oversight, reliability, regulations, and inclusivity. By applying the framework, organizations can effectively identify, assess, mitigate, and monitor risks associated with their AI systems, ensuring responsible AI development and deployment.

Measures and metrics of AI STEPS FORWARD

While the AI STEPS FORWARD framework[2] provides a comprehensive outline of principles for responsible AI development, it doesn't offer specific quantitative metrics or formulas by default, intentionally avoiding prescriptive measures for tools and metrics. This is by design. This flexibility caters to the unique contexts and objectives of various organizations and industries, acknowledging the rapidly evolving AI landscape. By promoting innovation and customization, the framework allows organizations to adopt the latest tools and metrics that align with their needs and responsible

AI practices, ensuring relevance and ethical behavior across different levels of maturity, resources, and capabilities.

Organizations can develop their own metrics and **KPIs** tailored to their context and objectives.

All that said, whenever we start a new project, we are acutely aware of the value of boilerplate frameworks and code so that we can avoid having to start completely from scratch. As such, we have developed a **Common Data Model** (**CDM**) for AI Assurance using the AI STEPS FORWARD framework[3]. While the CDM is likely to require continued redesign and updates until AI regulatory frameworks and AI standards reach a mature state, it is available for reference and use within enterprise AI governance process and AI system development, deployment, and maintenance. The CDM will not provide the specific quantitative measures that are reported within a given enterprise's AI Assurance processes. Rather the CDM is intended to provide the framework by which the data that underpins all the requisite metrics can be captured, facilitating the automation of the audit and dashboard creation processes as much as possible:

- **Overall AI project overview**: A high-level view of ongoing AI projects, their progress, and status. This can help stakeholders understand the overall AI landscape within an organization and track the development and deployment of AI systems.

- **Performance metrics**: KPIs and metrics related to AI models' accuracy, precision, recall, and other relevant measures, providing insights into the effectiveness of AI systems.

- **Fairness and bias**: Metrics and visualizations that track potential biases and fairness across different demographic groups, enabling stakeholders to identify and address issues related to algorithmic fairness.

- **Explainability and transparency**: Documentation, model cards, and data sheets that offer insights into AI system design choices, training processes, limitations, and potential impacts, promoting transparency and explainability.

- **Safety and reliability**: Metrics related to AI systems' robustness, testing procedures, and potential failure modes, providing stakeholders with an understanding of the system's safety and reliability.

- **Regulatory compliance**: An overview of an organization's adherence to applicable laws, regulations, and ethical guidelines, highlighting any areas of concern or non-compliance.

- **AI model lifecycle**: A visual representation of the AI model lifecycle, including data acquisition, preprocessing, training, validation, deployment, monitoring, and maintenance, offering stakeholders a comprehensive view of AI system development processes.

- **Workforce development and upskilling**: Metrics and indicators related to workforce training, education, and upskilling programs, showing the organization's progress in building AI awareness and capabilities among employees.

- **Risk management**: An overview of identified risks, their severity, and mitigation actions, providing stakeholders with insights into the organization's AI risk management efforts.

By offering customizable dashboards with relevant measures for different stakeholders, the AI STEPS FORWARD framework ensures that all parties have access to the information they need to monitor, evaluate, and contribute to responsible AI practices within an organization.

Here, we suggest possible metrics for each element of the framework:

Feature	Measure
Safety	- Percentage of identified risks mitigated. - Number of incidents related to AI system safety. - Mean time between AI system failures.
Transparency	- Percentage of AI systems with publicly available documentation. - Number of communications with stakeholders regarding AI systems. - Stakeholder satisfaction scores related to transparency.
Explainability	- Explainability index or score based on how understandable the AI system's rationale is to users. - Percentage of AI system outputs accompanied by human-understandable explanations. - User satisfaction scores related to AI system explainability.
Privacy	- Number of data breaches or privacy incidents. - Percentage of anonymized data used in AI systems. - Compliance score with privacy regulations and standards.
Security	- Number of security incidents or breaches involving AI systems. - Compliance score with security standards and best practices. - Mean time to detect and respond to security threats.
Fairness	- Bias detection and mitigation scores, based on disparity in AI system performance across different groups. - Stakeholder satisfaction scores related to AI system fairness. - Compliance with fairness-related regulations and standards.
Oversight	- Number of AI system audits conducted/total number of live AI systems - Compliance score with internal policies and guidelines. - Percentage of AI projects reviewed by the internal AI oversight board.

Reliability	- AI system accuracy rate.
	- AI system consistency score, based on the variance of outcomes under similar conditions.
	- System resilience index, measuring the ability to maintain performance under stress or changing conditions.
Workforce	- Percentage of employees who have completed upskilling or education programs.
	- Employee AI literacy scores.
	- Employee engagement scores related to AI initiatives.
AI Center of Excellence	- Number of AI best practices implemented.
	- Proportion of AI projects supported or driven by the CoE.
	- Innovation index, measuring the CoE's contribution to AI advancements within the organization.
Regulations	- Compliance score with external AI governance and regulations.
	- Number of regulatory violations or penalties.
	- Engagement index with regulatory bodies.
Diversity (Inclusiveness)	- Diversity index or score, measuring the representation of various demographics within the AI development team.
	- Percentage of AI systems designed with accessibility features.
	- Stakeholder satisfaction scores related to AI system inclusiveness.

Table 6.3: Framework metrics

AI STEPS FORWARD – taxonomy of components

The AI STEPS FORWARD framework presents a comprehensive and systematic approach to responsible AI governance, with each component expanding into specific sub-components that address diverse aspects of AI development and deployment. By encompassing Safety, Transparency, Explainability, Privacy, Security, Fairness, Oversight, Reliability, Workforce development, AI CoE, Regulations, and Diversity, the framework ensures organizations tackle various challenges in AI ethics, compliance, and trust. This comprehensive structure enables organizations to harness AI's transformative power by implementing a holistic approach that considers every facet of responsible AI, fostering ethical behavior and maximizing benefits while minimizing potential harm to stakeholders and society at large.

Component	Sub-components
S - Safety	Risk assessment Hazard mitigation AI system monitoring
T - Transparency	Openness in AI development Disclosure of AI system capabilities Stakeholder communication
E - Explainability	AI system rationale Human understandable outputs AI system documentation
P - Privacy	Data protection Anonymization Privacy by design
S - Security	Data security AI system protection Cybersecurity measures
F - Fairness	Bias detection Bias mitigation Equitable AI system impact
O - Oversight	Internal AI board with SMEs AI system performance monitoring AI system lifecycle management
R - Reliability	AI system accuracy AI system consistency AI system resilience
W - Workforce	Upskilling and education Talent development AI awareness and literacy
A - AI CoE	AI strategy development AI best practices AI research and development
R - Regulations	External AI governance and regulations Compliance with laws and standards Coordination with regulatory bodies
D - Diversity	Inclusiveness in AI development Representation of diverse perspectives Accessible AI systems and tools

Table 6.4: Structure and hierarchy of the AI STEPS FORWARD framework

Salient capabilities for AI Governance

By addressing the following key capabilities, the AI STEPS FORWARD framework provides a comprehensive approach to AI governance, helping organizations manage AI systems responsibly, mitigate risks, and ensure compliance with relevant regulations and ethical standards:

- **Comprehensive AI lifecycle governance**: The framework ensures the end-to-end governance of AI systems by cataloging and monitoring AI models with metadata capture, identifying successful outcomes, and assessing remediation requirements. It provides a structured approach to managing AI projects throughout their lifecycle, from inception to deployment and maintenance, ensuring consistency, accountability, and traceability in AI development processes.

- **Robust risk management**: The framework promotes the use of automated tools and processes to identify, monitor, and report on factors and workflows at scale, mitigating potential biases and drift in AI systems. By continuously evaluating AI systems and addressing potential risks proactively, organizations can ensure the safe, ethical, and responsible deployment of AI technologies.

- **Streamlined regulatory compliance**: The AI STEPS FORWARD framework facilitates the translation of external AI regulations into organizational policies for automated enforcement. It encourages the use of customizable dashboards to improve stakeholder collaboration and visibility, enabling organizations to monitor and maintain compliance with applicable laws, regulations, and ethical guidelines.

The AI STEPS FORWARD framework is an attempt to offer a comprehensive approach to operationalizing AI governance, managing risk, and satisfying stakeholder expectations. By implementing robust oversight structures, the framework ensures data, models, metadata, and pipelines are traceable and documented at scale. Through continuous monitoring and automated tools, it addresses fairness, bias, and drift by enabling corrective actions and ensuring compliance with regulations. The framework promotes transparency, explainability, and collaboration, streamlining AI lifecycle management and enhancing visibility for stakeholders. Ultimately, STEPS FORWARD optimizes AI strategy and planning, balancing people, processes, and technology to drive efficiency and responsible AI adoption across organizations.

For the remainder of this chapter, we will look into the practical aspects of how to achieve the aforementioned goals of the AI STEPS FORWARD framework.

The indispensable role of the C-suite in fostering responsible AI adoption

As generative AI continues to transform the business world, companies are increasingly exploring and utilizing diverse AI resources to enhance resilience, optimize costs, and navigate ongoing economic uncertainty. To fully capitalize on AI's potential while mitigating its associated risks, CEOs must champion the responsible deployment of AI systems, known as **Responsible AI (RAI)**. RAI ensures the alignment of AI systems with a company's purpose, values, and risk management frameworks, while addressing regulatory, customer trust, and ethical concerns. By adopting RAI, companies can accelerate innovation, differentiate their brands, and build customer trust.

To successfully implement RAI, CxOs must take the following steps:

1. **Develop a clear RAI strategy**: CxOs need to establish a comprehensive strategy that aligns RAI with their organization's values, purpose, and business objectives. This includes articulating how the company will operationalize RAI across governance, processes, tools, and culture.

2. **Appoint a senior leader accountable for executing RAI**: CxOs must select a suitable senior leader to oversee the implementation of the RAI program and hold them accountable for its success. Potential candidates for this role could include the chief risk officer, ESG leader, or chief AI officer, or the CEO could create a new role, such as chief AI ethics officer.

3. **Integrate RAI into cross-functional risk/governance processes**: As companies plan AI projects, leaders should seek input from multidisciplinary teams to assess risks and set appropriate guardrails and oversight measures. RAI should be incorporated into existing governance processes, with clear escalation paths leading to the CEO.

4. **Communicate RAI priorities effectively**: CxOs must emphasize the importance of RAI in speeches, emails, board meetings, and other forms of communication. They should explain the rationale behind RAI to stakeholders and initiate conversations about RAI with customers, partners, industry groups, and regulators.

By actively supporting and implementing an RAI program, C-suite leaders can help their organizations harness AI's transformative potential while fostering responsible innovation. This commitment to RAI not only enhances AI deployments but also strengthens the organization as a whole, contributing to long-term success in an increasingly competitive business landscape.

An AI Center of Excellence

An AI Center of Excellence is a special facility where artificial intelligence and machine learning technologies are developed and perfected. These centers are usually staffed by experts in the field who can develop new algorithms and software to improve the performance of AI systems. Additionally, these centers often have access to powerful computing resources that can be used to train machine learning models. There are many ways to make an AI center of excellence, but one common approach is to establish it as a **research and development (R&D)** institute within a company or organization. This allows for dedicated resources to be devoted to developing new AI technologies and applications. Another way to make an AI center of excellence is through partnerships between companies, universities, and other organizations. These partnerships can help pool resources and expertise, which can accelerate the development of new technologies.

The question then becomes, why do you need an AI center of excellence and, what is the **return on investment (ROI)** behind it? There are many factors to consider when developing an enterprise AI governance strategy, but at its core, a company wants a strategy that will help with two key factors: staying competitive within its market, and staying compliant with AI regulations. To do this, companies need to have a clear understanding of their data and how it is used by AI systems. Additionally, companies need policies and procedures for managing AI-related risks, and established mechanisms for monitoring and auditing AI usage to ensure compliance with internal rules and external regulations.

An AI center of excellence is a facility to champion all the technical aspects of this AI governance framework – this is where experts in AI and machine learning work together to develop and apply AI technologies and provide tools for SMEs to understand the bias and transparency aspects of algorithms. An AI center of excellence helps with machine learning bias prevention by providing a repeatable process for identifying bias in training and testing data sets and models. This allows for more accurate results and better insights into how different algorithms perform. Per its mandate, the center can help identify issues early on and provide guidance on how to avoid them in the future.

The aim of an AI center of excellence is to promote collaboration between different disciplines, share best practices, and advance the state of the art in AI and machine learning. One of the primary goals of an AI center of excellence is to prevent bias in machine learning models. This can be accomplished by ensuring that datasets used for training are diverse and representative of the real-world population. The experts at the AI CoE build tools and help train data engineers and SMEs to ensure that they do not inadvertently introduce bias into their models. The CoE's mandate is to streamline AI operationalization and prevent bias in machine learning algorithms. Machine learning algorithms are often trained on data that contains biases, which can lead to discriminatory results when the algorithm is applied in the real world. By identifying these biases early on during development, in collaboration with SMEs, they can be removed before the algorithm goes into production use.

Note

The features of an AI center of excellence include a focus on data, the ability to experiment and iterate quickly, and a team of experts who are passionate about artificial intelligence. Creating an AI center of excellence requires buy-in from senior leadership, investment in resources, and commitment to developing the skills of your workforce. An AI center of excellence can help with machine learning bias prevention by ensuring that data is representative and that algorithms are tested for fairness. You can train your workers in artificial intelligence safety by providing them with resources and opportunities to learn about the risks associated with AI technology.

From a **ROI** perspective, there are many benefits to building an artificial intelligence center of excellence within an organization. One benefit is that it helps train your workers in artificial intelligence safety. By having a dedicated team or center for AI, you can ensure that everyone in your organization is up to date on the latest safety protocols and procedures. This can help to prevent accidents and injuries related to AI technology. A center of excellence can also help to improve the overall efficiency of your organization by providing a central location for all things AI.

In this next section, we will explore the role of internal AI boards for domain-specific regulations with SME insights – an approach designed to promote transparency, fairness, and accuracy in AI-based decision-making.

The role of internal AI boards in enterprise AI governance

A high-functioning and effective enterprise AI governance framework requires a clear understanding of the roles and responsibilities in question, effective communication between stakeholders, and regular reviews of and updates to automated decision-making systems. It is well established that AI model bias is a socio-technical problem, but it seems hard for organizations to grasp that ethical AI use cases vary based on the business use case. One size doesn't fit all – and your AI bias will be nuanced and very specific to your industry, your use case, and your data.

Simply put, an internal AI board of governance is a group of people within an organization who are responsible for making decisions about the use of AI technologies within the enterprise. The board typically includes representatives from different departments within the organization, such as IT, marketing, sales, and operations. Its purpose is to ensure that the use of AI technologies aligns with the organization's goals and values.

An internal AI board of governance is important for several reasons. It ensures that there is a clear and consistent strategy for developing and deploying AI within the organization. It provides a mechanism for decision-makers to be held accountable for their actions with regards to AI. It helps to ensure that ethical considerations are taken into account when making decisions about AI development and deployment. It helps identify potential risks associated with AI development and implementation. And it allows organizations to openly discuss the opportunities and challenges associated with implementing AI within the company.

Due to the heterogeneous nature of this board, these diverse perspectives can help identify potential automated decision-making risks and issues that may not be apparent to those with more homogeneous backgrounds. A diversity of experiences and voices can help create a more well-rounded and effective decision-making body to ensure a well-rounded and ethically sound AI strategy and implementation.

Promoting diversity within the AI board of governance can send a strong signal to other departments that inclusion and respect for all employees is valued in the organization. This board has a wide-ranging mandate – and due to its exposure to a wide variety of applications and systems across the enterprise, they can classify the applications with multiple risk ratings (such as high, medium, and low risk) to help prioritize and focus. High-risk AI systems are those that have the potential to cause harm or damage if they malfunction. They may be used in critical applications where safety is of paramount importance, such as in self-driving cars or medical diagnosis. Due to the potentially high stakes involved, it is essential that these systems are designed and tested with care to minimize the risks. In contrast, low-risk AI systems are those that have been designed and implemented with a clear understanding of their limitations and are subject to regular testing and monitoring. Low-risk AI systems are also typically used for well-defined tasks with limited impact on humans or the environment. Your internal AI board and subject-matter experts will be able to make the best judgments as to what systems get which ranking and review these rankings periodically.

Governance is the process of making and enforcing decisions within an organization, while compliance is the state of following rules or meeting these standards. AI regulation refers to the body of laws, regulations, and guidelines that govern the use of artificial intelligence. An internal AI board has the duty to ensure that the AI regulations are well thought out and specific to the industry and domain. Due to its diverse nature, broad exposure, and the domain/industry knowledge of subject-matter experts it can draw from, this board is in the best position to identify and manage AI-related risks. It doesn't necessarily have to comprise AI experts, as it can reach out to the AI Center of Excellence for technical assistance and support; however, it does need to be cognizant of its industry's workflow, use cases, and areas of potential harm. By incorporating the expertise of internal AI boards and adhering to industry-specific regulations, organizations can ensure the responsible and ethical deployment of AI technologies across their operations.

Let's review some of the specific use cases based on different industries.

Healthcare systems

In the healthcare sector, we recognize numerous potential use cases for AI systems, such as identifying at-risk patients, developing personalized treatment plans, and monitoring patient progress. However, we must also be vigilant against possible misuse or abuse. For instance, improperly calibrated AI models could lead to false diagnoses and unnecessary treatments, causing undue stress and anxiety for patients. Inadequate monitoring of AI systems might result in the failure to detect deteriorating patient conditions, possibly resulting in severe harm or death. Moreover, biases in treatment recommendations, insurance coverage, and provider networks can further impede patient care.

Acknowledging real-life horror stories, such as the recent probe[4] of United Health/Optum's algorithm for potential racial bias. The investigation revealed that *"By relying on historic spending to triage and diagnose current patients, your algorithm appears to inherently prioritize white patients who have had greater access to healthcare than black patients."* We emphasize the importance of an internal board to scrutinize such issues, as external parties with limited industry knowledge may not offer sufficient assistance. The healthcare sector is particularly sensitive to the potential negative consequences of AI bias, ethics, and governance-related issues. Examples of AI bias in healthcare include misdiagnosing patients due to biased training data, unfair treatment allocation, and exacerbating health disparities among underrepresented or marginalized groups. These issues can lead to severe consequences, compromising patient care and outcomes.

To address these concerns, implementing robust AI governance in healthcare is essential. The governance framework should include clear guidelines and protocols for data collection, handling, and analysis to minimize biases, while ensuring that ethical considerations and patient privacy are prioritized. Collaboration between subject-matter experts, clinicians, data scientists, and other stakeholders will help identify potential issues and develop mitigation strategies. An internal AI board should oversee AI applications within healthcare organizations, continuously monitor their performance, and ensure compliance with relevant regulations, fostering the responsible and ethical deployment of AI technologies in healthcare systems.

By adopting a comprehensive framework such as AI STEPS FORWARD, we can proactively prevent such incidents in healthcare. Promoting responsible AI development by identifying potential biases, ensuring data privacy and security, and maintaining transparency in AI system capabilities is the key along with an emphasis on continuous monitoring, regular audits, and stakeholder communication to detect and mitigate risks while fostering a diverse and skilled workforce to drive innovation and ethical behavior.

Addressing bias and improving outcomes in healthcare AI systems is a multifaceted challenge with no silver bullet or easy solution. Key actions include the following:

- **Invest** in high-quality, diverse, and representative datasets to train AI systems on balanced data
- **Engage** domain experts, such as physicians and healthcare professionals, for guidance during AI development
- **Implement** rigorous bias detection and mitigation techniques during model development and validation
- **Establish** transparent communication channels between AI developers, healthcare providers, and patients
- **Continuously monitor** and **update** AI systems to adapt to evolving medical knowledge and practices

By addressing these diverse aspects, organizations can work toward reducing bias and improving patient care outcomes.

Retail and e-commerce systems

As AI permeates the retail industry, it brings both opportunities and challenges. Some issues include invasive personalization, biased recommendations, malfunctioning chatbots, inventory mismanagement, and security breaches. To mitigate these risks and harness AI's full potential, businesses must implement comprehensive governance strategies. Key areas to address include data privacy, bias mitigation, chatbot quality control, transparent AI usage, inventory management accuracy, cybersecurity, human oversight, continuous learning, stakeholder engagement, and legal and ethical compliance.

The following is a list of potential issues, followed by some mitigating measures:

- **Invasive personalization**: AI systems can cross privacy boundaries by excessively tracking and analyzing customer data

- **Biased recommendations**: AI algorithms can inadvertently favor certain products, brands, or demographics, leading to unfair practices

- **Malfunctioning chatbots**: Poorly designed AI chatbots can provide incorrect information, causing confusion and frustration

- **Inventory mismanagement**: AI-driven inventory systems can make inaccurate predictions, leading to overstocking or stockouts

- **Security breaches**: AI systems can be exploited by malicious actors, compromising customer data and privacy

Governance checklist

- **Data privacy**: Establish strict data collection, storage, and usage policies, ensuring GDPR and CCPA compliance.

- **Bias mitigation**: Implement regular audits and updates of AI algorithms to minimize bias and promote fairness in recommendations.

- **Chatbot quality control**: Continuously test, monitor, and improve chatbot performance to enhance the customer experience.

- **Transparent AI usage**: Clearly communicate AI's role in retail processes and provide options for customers to opt out if desired.

- **Inventory management accuracy**: Regularly validate AI-driven inventory predictions with real-world data and make adjustments accordingly.

- **Cybersecurity**: Implement robust security measures and conduct frequent risk assessments to protect AI systems from vulnerabilities.

- **Human oversight**: Maintain a human-in-the-loop approach to ensure AI decisions align with business goals and ethical standards.

- **Continuous learning**: Invest in AI training and retraining to keep systems up to date and adaptable to changing retail environments.

- **Stakeholder engagement**: Involve employees, customers, and other stakeholders in AI governance discussions and decisions.

- **Legal and ethical compliance**: Adhere to local, national, and international regulations governing the use of AI in retail settings.

By taking a proactive approach to AI governance, retailers can effectively navigate the complex landscape they face and deliver a seamless, secure, and fair customer experience.

Financial services

As artificial intelligence reshapes the financial services industry, including fintech and asset management, it introduces both opportunities and challenges. Key concerns involve fraudulent transactions, biased lending decisions, inaccurate risk assessments, algorithmic trading errors, and data breaches. Proactively addressing these issues is crucial for businesses to leverage the benefits of AI while minimizing the potential pitfalls:

- **Fraudulent transactions**: AI systems can be exploited by criminals to bypass security measures and conduct unauthorized transactions

- **Biased lending decisions**: AI algorithms could unintentionally discriminate against certain demographics, perpetuating unfair lending practices

- **Inaccurate risk assessments**: AI-driven risk models could fail to predict market events or make flawed predictions, leading to financial losses

- **Algorithmic trading errors**: Automated trading algorithms can malfunction or exacerbate market volatility, causing significant financial impacts

- **Data breaches**: Insufficient security measures can allow unauthorized access to sensitive financial and personal data

Governance checklist for financial services

- **Data protection**: Implement rigorous data-handling policies and ensure compliance with financial data protection regulations.

- **Bias mitigation**: Regularly audit and update AI models to minimize bias in lending and investment decisions.

- **Risk model validation**: Continuously validate and refine AI-driven risk assessment models with real-world financial data.

- **Algorithmic trading oversight**: Monitor automated trading algorithms and maintain human intervention capabilities to prevent or mitigate trading errors.

- **Cybersecurity**: Strengthen security measures and conduct periodic risk assessments to protect AI systems from cyber threats.

- **Human oversight**: Ensure human supervision and control in AI decision-making processes, aligning with business goals and ethical standards.

- **Model explainability**: Develop interpretable AI models to facilitate better understanding and trust in AI-driven decisions.

- **Regulatory compliance**: Adhere to all relevant financial industry regulations governing the use of AI and automated decision-making.

- **Stakeholder engagement**: Involve employees, customers, and regulators in AI governance discussions and decisions.

- **Continuous improvement**: Invest in AI training, retraining, and research to keep systems up to date and adaptable to the evolving financial landscape.

To navigate the complex landscape of AI in financial services, businesses must adopt robust AI governance strategies. By focusing on data protection, bias mitigation, risk model validation, algorithmic trading oversight, cybersecurity, human oversight, model explainability, regulatory compliance, stakeholder engagement, and continuous improvement, financial institutions can harness the power of AI to revolutionize their operations while ensuring the security, fairness, and resilience of their systems.

Predictive analytics and forecasting

In the realm of predictive analytics and forecasting, AI systems can encounter various issues of bias that are multifaceted and without easy solutions. We recognize the need for comprehensive mitigation strategies to ensure responsible AI development and deployment. Here are some examples of AI bias and corresponding recommendations in the context of predictive analytics and forecasting:

- **Targeted ads based on race or gender**: To prevent discriminatory ad targeting, employ diverse datasets, incorporate fairness metrics during model development, and audit AI systems regularly for bias

- **Predictive pricing**: To tackle biased pricing, incorporate fairness and transparency principles into AI models, monitor pricing outcomes for disparate impacts, and establish guidelines for equitable pricing practices

- **Personalized recommendations**: For unbiased recommendations, ensure diverse data representation, maintain transparency in recommendation rationale, and enable user feedback to improve system performance

- **Demand forecasting**: To improve accuracy and reduce bias in demand prediction, use diverse and representative data, engage domain experts in model development, and validate forecasts against real-world outcomes

- **Credit scoring**: To minimize bias in credit assessments, leverage balanced datasets, implement bias detection techniques, and ensure compliance with fairness regulations and guidelines

The AI STEPS FORWARD framework can guide organizations in addressing these challenges. By adopting a comprehensive approach, organizations can mitigate bias and improve outcomes in predictive analytics and forecasting across various use cases.

Let's review some of the cross-functional and cross-domain applications of AI.

Cross-industry applications of AI

Horizontal applications of artificial intelligence, such as **natural language processing (NLP)**, customer classification, automated customer care, conversational AI, and automated decision-making, possess the unique ability to impact a wide range of businesses across multiple industries. These technologies transcend sector-specific boundaries and offer versatile solutions to challenges commonly faced by organizations, irrespective of their niche or market.

Natural language processing

Most companies use some form of **natural language processing (NLP)** as part of their operational systems. However, there is a lot of potential for harmful cases of algorithmic bias in NLP systems. One such case is when the system is used to automatically generate text, such as summaries of documents. If the system contains biases, these will be reflected in the generated text, which can lead to inaccurate or misleading information being spread.

Another potential harm occurs when people use natural language processing systems to detect entities and relationships from unstructured text, and make decisions, such as deciding who to hire for a job (HR and recruitment) or whether to give someone a loan (financial services). If the system is biased against certain groups of people, this can result in discrimination.

Based on your domain, the AI board will need to evaluate the role NLP plays within the organization's systems. For example, if an advertising agency used natural language processing systems to monitor and analyze social media posts or other online content, they may amplify existing prejudices and stereotypes by giving more weight to certain types of content over others. As a media executive who is part of the AI board, you would need to address these very specific issues by identifying the potential bias and reaching out to the AI Center of Excellence to understand the technical capabilities available to address such issues properly.

Automated customer service

Most companies use some form of automated voice recognition systems, which can result in representational harm. Due to the training data used, customer service algorithms might be biased against certain groups of people, who may then not receive the same level of service as others, which would constitute discrimination and unfairness in the provision of customer service. If an algorithm is designed to favor one type of customer over another, it could result in poor quality service for customers who are not favored by the system.

One well-documented source of bias in automated speech recognition is the use of outdated or biased training data. For example, early versions of Google's automated speech recognition system were trained on a dataset made up mostly of male voices, leading to poorer performance for female speakers. Another example comes from Microsoft's Cortana virtual assistant, which was initially designed to respond primarily to male voice input but later had its grammar rules updated to be more gender-neutral after complaints from users.

Incorrect assumptions about how automated speech recognition systems work can also lead to bias. For instance, some people may assume that an automated speech recognition system will automatically transcribe everything said into text without any errors. However, this is not always the case; errors can occur when an acoustic model fails to correctly identify words or when a language model incorrectly predicts what word should come next in a sentence. A lack of transparency in the algorithms used by commercial automated speech recognition providers makes it difficult for outside researchers to assess and correct for potential biases.

The internal AI board is in the best position to identify and constantly evaluate whether these models are designed appropriately, and whether they could unintentionally cause harm to customers or even put them at risk by making decisions that are not in their best interests.

Customer classification and personalization

Hyper-personalization or building customer cohorts (segment of one) is a business requirement where stakeholders segment customers into smaller, more targeted groups to create more personalized experiences that meet their specific needs. This hyper-personalization is used to build targeted marketing campaigns, individualized pricing models, and personalized service experiences.

Even though this benefits the customer by providing increased satisfaction and loyalty and higher conversion rates with improved customer lifetime value, there are many potential cases of AI bias in classifying customers.

For example, if a company's customer base is mostly white, and the AI system used to classify customers is trained on data that is from a predominantly white audience, then the system may be biased against non-white customers. Similarly, if a company's customer base is largely male but the training data for its AI system includes more females than males, then the system may be biased against male customers. Another potential case of AI bias in customer classification could occur if a company sells products that are popular with older consumers but its training data for its AI system includes more younger consumers than older ones. In this scenario, the AI system might be biased against older consumers.

An organization's AI board needs to be cognizant of and accountable for such segmentations.

These are just some examples of how an AI system could become biased in classifying customers. To avoid such biases, the board needs to ensure that its training data reflects the demographics of its actual customer base as much as possible. They also need to monitor its systems regularly to identify any potential biases and take steps to correct them.

Clustering and grouping transactions

Clustering and grouping transactions and purchases is a highly prevalent use case in multiple industries to identify groups of customers to upsell to. There are many potential cases of AI bias in this scenario. For instance, if a company were to use purchase-history data to cluster customers into groups, AI could potentially identify clusters of low-income customers and target them with ads for products that they could not afford, which may result in emotional and financial harm. AI could identify clusters of minority customers and target them with ads for products that are not relevant to their interests or needs. AI could even identify clusters of customers and target them with ads for products that could be stereotypical and harmful, for instance, showing bail bonds and arrest records for African-American-sounding names.

Harvard Professor Latanya Sweeney[5] found that *"names like Leroy, Kareem, and Keisha result in online ads for 'Arrested?', with a link to a website which could perform criminal record checks."*

These potential cases of AI bias in clustering and grouping transactions, keywords, customer behavior analysis, and prior purchases can have a negative impact on the customer experience and may ultimately lead to not only ethical challenges but also lost business for the company.

Conversational AI, chatbots, and virtual agents

In virtually every industry, conversational agents are increasingly being used to respond to customer queries and requests. However, there have been several cases of AI bias in virtual agent responses. One such case is when a Microsoft chatbot was released that responded in a racist manner to certain questions. Another case is when a virtual assistant was found to give biased results based on the user's gender. These examples show that AI bias can exist in virtual agent responses. This can be problematic for businesses using these agents to communicate with customers, as it can lead to negative publicity and loss of business. It is therefore important for the internal AI board to be aware of the potential for AI bias in virtual agent responses and take steps to avoid it.

Automated decision-making

Automated decision-making is an essential component of AI and machine learning models, but it is crucial to acknowledge the occurrence of AI bias in these systems. A notable area where bias has manifested is in loan and financial decisions. Research from Carnegie Mellon University demonstrates that a leading commercial lending platform displayed bias against African-American and Latino borrowers, approving loans for non-minority individuals with lower credit scores and rejecting applications from African-American and Latino borrowers with higher scores. Similar studies highlight AI-based systems' potential biases favoring certain groups. Researchers at Vanderbilt discovered an algorithm used by major banks for loan decisions was biased toward white applicants, automatically assigning them higher credit scores than their financial history warranted.

Such biased automated decision making is not only illegal but also detrimental to businesses. These issues must be identified and addressed during the internal AI board's due diligence phase and mitigated with the assistance of the AI Center of Excellence's technology experts. Effective enterprise AI governance requires clear roles and responsibilities, consistent processes, and efficient communication channels. The internal AI board's responsibility is to support this framework, ensure the successful adoption of new technologies, and provide clarity regarding roles, responsibilities, processes, and communication among stakeholders. Two pivotal roles in the internal AI board of governance are the **Chief Data Officer (CDO)** and the **Chief AI Officer (CAIO)**. The CDO oversees an organization's data strategy, ensuring data accuracy, security, and regulatory compliance. The CAIO, on the other hand, supervises AI initiatives, aligning them with business goals and ethical standards. While these roles sometimes overlap, the key distinction is that the CAIO focuses on the aspects of advanced analytics and AI, whereas the CDO addresses all aspects of data strategy.

The role of CAIO is sometimes assumed to mean someone responsible for the development and implementation of artificial intelligence strategy within an organization. We believe this is the function of the internal AI board, with the CAIO at its helm, working in collaboration with the CDO, who is responsible for the management of an organization's data assets.

The board would seek technical assistance around matters of bias from the AI Center of Excellence, and even external academia or industry experts. However, it needs to have compliance requirements clearly defined upfront in order for everyone within an organization to know what is expected of them when it comes to maintaining a certain level of quality control over their automated decision-making role. When high-risk systems are utilized within industries such as finance and healthcare in particular, there is even more importance placed on having robust frameworks for checks and balances in place due to the heightened sensitivity around the types of failures that could occur due to the incorrect implementation or usage of these tools.

In this next section, we will explore the complex and evolving world of external AI governance and regulations, analyzing the frameworks in place to promote responsible and ethical use of AI technology.

Establishing repeatable processes, controls, and assessments for AI systems

To keep pace with evolving regulations and ensure clarity, repeatability, auditability, and transparency in AI systems, it is essential to establish explicit, reproducible, and auditable decision-making procedures and controls for AI projects and initiatives.

These controls refer to the mechanisms that guarantee adherence to organizational policies and processes during the development and implementation of AI applications. Additionally, the capacity for repeatable AI assessments is crucial, allowing for consistent evaluations of automated decision-making processes over time.

This repeatability and reproducibility are vital for conducting impact assessments, enabling accurate and reliable measurements of how a model has changed over time, and ensuring that experiments can be repeated with the same data and parameters. In some cases, randomness may be incorporated into the model, which requires building expectations and outcomes accordingly.

The CDM we have designed for AI STEPS FORWARD is intended to make the capture and use of this metadata for internal and external AI audit reporting straightforward for enterprises. At the time of writing, it is unclear of the levels of external AI audits that will be routinely required for enterprises. This will vary by country, jurisdiction, and business sector, but will be required.

Counterfactual fairness

Counterfactual fairness testing helps prevent discrimination by ensuring that different groups are treated equally, even if they have different outcomes. Counterfactual fairness is used in AI impact assessments to help identify and mitigate potential biases. It can also be useful in detecting and mitigating actual discriminatory practices. Having counterfactual fairness built into your assessment systems ensures that everyone has an equal opportunity to succeed, regardless of their background or circumstances.

AI impact assessments

AI impact assessments involve the evaluation of potential risks and benefits associated with implementing an artificial intelligence system. In a comprehensive AI governance system, AI impact assessments are a regular part of the process, to ensure both technical and business-related measures are in place. Enterprise standards are guidelines that dictate how businesses should operate; these may include requirements for data security, quality control, and so on. AI impact assessments ensure that safety concerns and enterprise standards around artificial intelligence center on the possibility that automated decision management systems could become uncontrollable or even malicious if left unchecked. As algorithms increasingly make decisions about important life events such as job applications or loan approvals, there is a risk that they could perpetuate existing biases against certain groups of people. AI impact assessments take these features into account and ensure that ethical considerations around AI focus on issues such as privacy rights and standards to help ensure that organizations using artificial intelligence do so in a responsible manner; these might include guidelines for testing and validating algorithms before deployment.

An AI impact assessment is a great opportunity to ensure that exception handling is in line with an organization's policies. During the assessment, it may be helpful to use AI models that are able to recognize when a given set of facts contains new variables not previously considered and highlight these new variables to a human. Identifying and accounting for changes over time to ensure that models trained on time-sensitive data remain accurate and unbiased is also an integral part of the impact assessment.

The significance of AI compliance and adherence to regulations

AI models must comply with existing and emerging regulations surrounding data privacy and protection. For instance, under the GDPR, companies must obtain explicit consent from individuals before collecting, using, or sharing their personal data. This also applies to AI models trained on customer data, as they must respect rights such as the right to be forgotten and the right to explanation.

AI policy and external AI regulations play a critical role in a business context. Organizations should not wait for government mandates but should proactively invest in self-regulation and adhere to various guidelines, such as country-specific and industry-specific AI standards, to ensure responsible AI usage.

Countries worldwide enforce different AI regulations, such as the United States' HIPAA, Gramm-Leach-Bliley Act, and COPPA, or the EU's GDPR. Adhering to these diverse compliance standards is crucial, as is considering guidelines provided by professional bodies and industry standards, such as the NIST AI Framework. We discussed this in detail in *Chapter 5*.

Ethical AI upskilling and education

An AI governance framework helps establish the parameters to maintain public safety in the face of AI harm, promote fairness, and ensure efficient markets by preventing biased and anti-competitive practices. However, with AI bias being a socio-technical problem, human oversight remains important for detecting and building useful strategies to mitigate bias. For these reasons, it's important not only to upskill workers in order to manage these technologies but also build ethical safeguards into the algorithms themselves.

Upskilling of knowledge workers is required to stay ahead of the AI regulatory curve and remain competitive in the market. With the rapid advancement of artificial intelligence and machine learning technology, it is becoming increasingly difficult for those without the proper skill set to keep up. Human oversight is important in artificial intelligence as it can help prevent errors and ensure that systems are working as intended. Adversarial attacks on AI algorithms can pose a serious threat to security and privacy, so it is important to be aware of them and take steps to protect against them.

There are multiple ways to upskill and educate knowledge workers, but the most effective way is through contextual education within their industry and work-related domain. Employees should be taught about both the general implementation of AI and different uses of AI within their specific enterprise, and how to properly utilize it. This involves an understanding of the risks associated with its use, as well as the potential benefits.

With this knowledge, employees will be empowered to make informed decisions about how to effectively use AI in their workplace and how to identify and bring up concerns related to AI harm.

Finally, like any standard and regulation, the practical adaptation of a robust AI governance framework is the key to its success. Organizations need to purposefully promote adaption by providing guidance on the modification of practices in order to meet new compliance requirements. One way to increase AI adaption within enterprises is by investing in upskilling workers, so they possess the necessary skills to work with new technologies as they emerge.

Summary

In this chapter, we covered a lot of ground exploring the governance, compliance, and regulatory landscape. We identified the key action items for an enterprise AI governance framework: identifying what data is available and how it can be used to improve decision-making; creating a governance structure that will ensure the responsible use of AI technologies; establishing clear goals and objectives for the implementation of AI technologies; allocating resources accordingly to support the development and deployment of AI applications; and finally, monitoring and evaluating the performance of AI technologies to ensure they are meeting business objectives.

We proposed the AI STEPS FORWARD framework as a comprehensive approach to responsible AI practices that emphasizes the importance of transparency, fairness, and ethical behavior in AI development and deployment. By offering customizable governance dashboards and checklists, as well as promoting diverse perspectives and continuous learning, the framework ensures that all stakeholders have the necessary tools and information to contribute to responsible AI practices within their organization.

Implementing the AI STEPS FORWARD framework can help organizations achieve better AI outcomes while mitigating potential risks and ensuring alignment with ethical and regulatory guidelines.

An AI governance standard is not just a document but also a discipline that outlines the best practices for using artificial intelligence safely and ethically. Having regular AI impact assessments provides a company with regular updates on how implementing artificial intelligence will affect various aspects of the organization, including its employees, customers, and business processes. This enables an enterprise to address AI safety concerns regarding potential risks associated with using AI such as data breaches and algorithmic bias, as well as to establish trustworthy AI systems that operate safely, reliably, and ethically.

When implementing an AI governance framework, ensure you have the following in place:

- A clear statement of purpose/direction from senior management
- An understanding of who has responsibility for what within the organization, along with policies and procedures governing how work gets done
- Tools and processes for monitoring compliance with internal rules as well as external regulations
- Mechanisms for addressing violations when they occur
- Regular reviews and auditing processes

In the next chapter, we will review some specific case studies with bias removal, model robustness, and adversarial AI using model cards. Stay tuned.

References and further reading

1. Crafting acronyms is a linguistic diversion, where we contort and stretch language to its limits, squeezing out meaning while ensuring it fits snugly into a preconceived mold. Like a lexical gymnast, we bend and twist phrases until they submit to our desired abbreviation, allowing us to create memorable, yet sometimes tortured, linguistic souvenirs.

2. AI STEPS FORWARD framework: `rationale.ai`

3. `https://github.com/heather-dawe/AI-STEPS-FORWARD-Common-Data-Model`

4. New York Regulator Probes UnitedHealth Algorithm for Racial Bias: `https://www.wsj.com/articles/new-york-regulator-probes-unitedhealth-algorithm-for-racial-bias-11572087601`

5. Discrimination in Online Ad Delivery: `https://arxiv.org/ftp/arxiv/papers/1301/1301.6822.pdf`

6. Why Your Board Needs a Plan for AI Oversight - MIT Sloan: `https://sloanreview.mit.edu/article/why-your-board-needs-a-plan-for-ai-oversight/MIT`

7. Board Responsibility for Artificial Intelligence Oversight - Harvard Law: `https://corpgov.law.harvard.edu/2022/01/05/board-responsibility-for-artificial-intelligence-oversight/`

8. Making AI Forget You: Data Deletion in Machine Learning – NeurIPS Conference: `https://proceedings.neurips.cc/paper/2019/file/cb79f8fa58b91d3af6c9c991f63962d3-Paper.pdf`

9. The roadmap to an effective AI assurance ecosystem: `https://www.gov.uk/government/publications/the-roadmap-to-an-effective-ai-assurance-ecosystem/the-roadmap-to-an-effective-ai-assurance-ecosystem`

Part 3:
Explainable AI in Action

This final section delves into the practical application of explainable AI and the challenges of deploying trustworthy and interpretable models in the enterprise. Real-world case studies and usage scenarios are presented to illustrate the need for safe, ethical, and explainable machine learning, and provide solutions to problems encountered in various domains. The chapters in this section explore code examples, toolkits, and solutions offered by cloud platforms such as AWS, GCP, and Azure, as well as Microsoft's Fairlearn framework. Specific topics covered in this section include interpretability toolkits, fairness measures, fairness in AI systems, and bias mitigation strategies.

This section comprises the following chapters:

- *Chapter 7, Interpretability Toolkits and Fairness Measures – AWS, GCP, Azure, and AIF 360*
- *Chapter 8, Fairness in AI Systems with Microsoft Fairlearn*
- *Chapter 9, Fairness Assessment and Bias Mitigation with Fairlearn and the Responsible AI Toolbox*
- *Chapter 10, Foundational Models and Azure OpenAI*

7

Interpretability Toolkits and Fairness Measures – AWS, GCP, Azure, and AIF 360

Throughout this book, we have discussed the rationale for why responsible AI and AI governance are increasingly becoming critical disciplines for enterprises that wish to leverage AI. We also provided an overview of the methods that can be used to test that the machine learning models underpinning AI are safe, fair, and fit for purpose, along with introducing an AI assurance framework – AI STEPS FORWARD.

Leading cloud AI providers – the hyperscalers (namely AWS, Google, and Microsoft) – have recognized the need for AI explainability, and each has developed explainability toolkits designed to be used with its respective ML/AI development and MLOps environments. At the time of writing, the use of these explainability toolkits is not widespread across the industry. We believe that this is due to the following:

- The relative immaturity of the widespread industry when it comes to producing ML and AI at scale using the hyperscaler's AI/ML tools or similar technologies, such as Databricks. Roughly 10% to 20% of enterprises are doing so; the rest still need to catch up.

- The lack of clear AI regulatory guidance for many applications of AI within enterprises.

As the current AI summer we are experiencing continues, and enterprises mature into their development and usage of AI, we expect the take-up of explainability toolkits to increase significantly, as well as for them to evolve at a certain pace as they are used more widely. They have been developed to help ML/AI developers ensure the outcomes of their work are safe and fair.

In our view, the toolkits we will outline here are some of the best solutions for AI explainability on the market. However, they do require significant levels of technical knowledge – they require use and interpretation by a data scientist, ML engineer, or similar. As AI assurance processes develop and mature in enterprises, we believe AI explainability toolkits will emerge that can be used by business leads and AI governance professionals – people with expert domain knowledge but who are not data scientists or similar.

As it stands today, developers can identify and limit bias and explain predictions by leveraging such interpretability toolkits. Hyperscalers have comprehensive offerings that provide greater visibility into training data and models. In this chapter, we will explore various interpretability toolkits, including open source and commercial counterparts, from cloud providers. You will have the opportunity to review a range of tools available for Explainable AI, such as Amazon SageMaker Clarify, Google Vertex Explainable AI, model interpretability in Azure Machine Learning, and IBM's AI Fairness 360 (AIF360). With these powerful interpretability toolkits, organizations can build responsible and ethical AI systems, promoting accountability and trust among stakeholders.

With our common data model for AI STEPS FORWARD, we will attempt to facilitate interoperability of any of these hyperscaler and/or open source tools with AI assurance reporting. You can find more information and example instances of the framework in this book's GitHub repository. It's important to recognize that the explainability toolkits available from hyperscalers and open source frameworks typically only seek to forensically prove (or otherwise) the efficacy of the given ML model. None of the other pillars we recommend from the key reporting areas of AI STEPS FORWARD (such as the AI Ethics Committee) are reported on as part of ML lifetime governance.

In this chapter, we will discuss the following:

- Overview of explainability and interpretability toolkits

- Google Vertex Explainable AI

- Amazon SageMaker Clarify

- Model interpretability in Azure Machine Learning

- IBM's AIF360

- Aequitas Bias and Fairness Audit Toolkit

Although this chapter focuses primarily on the toolsets offered by major cloud providers, virtually all AI companies, including C3 AI, Palantir, DataRobot, Google, SAS, Amazon Web Services, IBM, Dataiku, TIBCO, Microsoft Azure, Databricks, H2O.ai, Cloudera, RapidMiner, and RStudio, have some kind of offering in the area of Explainable AI. However, it is important to note that relying solely on these tools and utilities is not enough to drive trust, ensure fairness, or mitigate bias. The discipline of AI governance is necessary to address the problems that tools alone cannot solve, such as contextualizing responsible AI definitions, assessing organizational risks, and putting humans in the loop to add common sense.

With that in mind, let's explore the interpretability toolkits offered by major cloud providers.

Getting started with hyperscaler interpretability toolkits

Hyperscalers have built significant offerings to provide Explainable AI to address bias and model quality and assess risk exposure. These tools are typically built around a fairness engine, and explainability visual interfaces are used for a variety of different enterprises in an industry-agnostic manner. Their MLOps platforms also help automate AI monitoring to ensure responsible AI outcomes and synthesized data as a means of fairness, privacy, confidentiality, and bias mitigation.

There is a growing need for AI explainability tools that can help users understand how AI algorithms make decisions, especially for subject-matter experts. Explainable AI tools provide insights into the inner workings of an AI system, allowing users to see how the algorithms arrive at their results. We have provided a checklist for selecting an explainability platform here.

> **Who would use these Explainable AI toolkits?**
>
> Explainable AI toolkits are essential for promoting the responsible development of AI and can be used by a variety of stakeholders. Data scientists and AI governance committees, which provide standards, guidelines, and interventions for responsible AI testing and implementations, can leverage these tools to ensure that their models are transparent, ethical, and fair. Previously in this book, we discussed the importance of creating an AI center of excellence, which involves validating models with guidance from an internal data science team.

Members of this cross-functional team independently validate bias mitigation and assure model fairness, compliance, and explainability for the models they did not develop, a role that requires the use of responsible AI tools. By leveraging these tools, organizations can build trust and confidence in their AI systems, while also promoting accountability and ethical decision-making.

Some of the common business goals to look for in an AI system include but are not limited to the following:

- Help identify unjust bias in your models and provide recommendations for rectifying them to ensure that customer-facing models are accurate, and you are treating your customers, partners, and employees fairly.

- Provide real-time visibility into model performance and outcomes. This alerts the AI engineering and data science teams to data drift in models or simply models not delivering against performance **service-level agreements (SLAs)**.

- Engender trust in your AI systems with prediction-level explainability, which is critical for both decision analysis and regulatory compliance.

You can refer to *Table 7.1* for a checklist for selecting an explainability platform on GitHub: `https://github.com/PacktPublishing/Responsible-AI-in-the-Enterprise/blob/main/Table%207.1.docx`.

Now, let's explore Google Vertex Explainable AI.

Google Vertex Explainable AI

Google Vertex Explainable AI is a toolkit that equips developers with cutting-edge algorithms and tools to gain valuable insights into their ML models. This toolkit offers several explainability algorithms, including decision trees and rule lists, providing a step-by-step explanation of how the model arrived at its prediction and highlighting the key rules used by the model in making its predictions. It offers feature-based and example-based explanations to provide a better understanding of the model's decision-making process.

Google has worked hard to integrate its Explainable AI offering into its wider ML and AI development services. It offers a range of features, including algorithms and tools that help developers understand and debug their models. Its strength in data preparation and deep learning, including AutoML, makes it a good choice for businesses looking to develop and deploy ML models in a reliable and scalable manner. In our view, it's one of GCP's differentiating ML and AI development services as existing Google customers can gain access to a powerful and flexible ML platform that can help them improve their models, build confidence in their predictions, and ultimately drive better business outcomes.

We'll look at some of the salient features of Vertex AI in the next section.

Model interpretability in Vertex AI – feature attribution and example-based explanations

Example-based explanations and feature attribution-based explanations are two methods used in Google's Vertex AI for improving the transparency and interpretability of ML models. Example-based explanations utilize nearest neighbor search to return a list of similar training examples to the input, which can be used to identify confounding inputs and improve model quality. On the other hand, feature attribution-based explanations indicate how much each feature in the model contributed to the prediction for each instance, allowing for the model's behavior to be explored and explained. Both methods are supported for various model types, including deep neural networks and tabular data, and can be configured for use in Vertex AI.

Besides feature-based explanations and example-based explanations, various other types of explanations can be used to interpret ML models. Counterfactual explanations aim to explain why a certain prediction was made by generating a hypothetical scenario where a different outcome could have been achieved. Contrasting explanations compare the features of two instances to explain why one instance was predicted differently from the other. Local explanations focus on explaining individual predictions while global explanations provide an overview of the entire model. Rule-based explanations create a set of if-then statements that represent how the model arrives at its predictions.

These various types of explanations can provide deeper insight into the behavior of ML models and help users make more informed decisions.

A technical whitepaper[1] by Google AI is designed to accompany Google Cloud's AI Explanations product and is targeted at data scientists and model developers, who are responsible for creating and implementing ML models. The whitepaper provides information on how to use AI explanations to simplify the development of ML models and explain their behavior to stakeholders. While primarily aimed at technical users, the whitepaper also contains sections relevant to product managers, business leaders, and end users, specifically the *Usage Examples* and *Attribution Limitations and Usage Considerations* sections. These sections highlight the use cases enabled by AI explanations and important considerations around its proper usage and limitations. We highly recommend reading this if you are interested in learning more about what is under the hood of these technologies.

Example-based explanations

Google Vertex AI's example-based explanations are powerful for understanding and improving ML models. By using nearest neighbor search to find similar examples from the training set, Vertex AI can help identify the factors that influence a model's decision-making process. For instance, if a model misclassifies birds as planes, we can use example-based explanations to find similar images and see that the misclassifications often involve dark silhouettes, which are more likely to be planes. This information can be used to improve the training set and refine the model's performance.

Example-based explanations also help identify inputs that require human labeling, further enriching the training set and improving model quality. While any model that can provide an embedding for inputs is supported, tree-based models such as decision trees are not. For deep neural networks, the penultimate layer is often chosen for embeddings as it is assumed to have learned something meaningful. While this feature is still in preview at the time of writing, its potential for improving model explainability and accuracy could make it a compelling tool for businesses using Google Vertex AI.

Feature attribution-based explanations

Feature attribution methods indicate how much each feature in an ML model contributed to the predictions for each given instance. By integrating feature attributions into Vertex AI, this feature can be used with all types of models, frameworks, and modalities. Feature attributions work on tabular data, and include built-in visualization capabilities for image data.

This feature can help businesses improve their model quality and build confidence in their predictions. To use feature attribution, users need to configure their model for feature attribution when uploading the model to the Vertex AI Model Registry. For AutoML model types that are integrated, feature attribution can be enabled during training and seen for both online and batch predictions, while for AutoML model types that are not integrated, feature attribution can be enabled by exporting the model artifacts and configuring feature attribution when uploading them to the Model Registry.

Integration with Google Colab and other notebooks

Vertex Explainable AI is a powerful tool for interpreting and explaining the behavior of ML models. Google Colab is a cloud-based platform that provides users with free access to Jupyter notebooks, making it a good companion for the Vertex Explainable AI SDK. Users can take advantage of Vertex Explainable AI's feature attribution and example-based explanations to interpret their models within Google Colab, allowing for more efficient and streamlined model development:

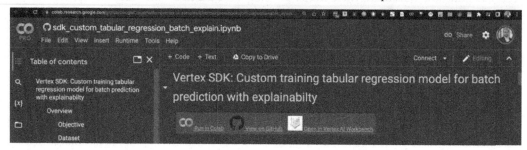

Figure 7.1: A notebook running the Vertex Explainable AI SDK on Colab

Similarly, Anaconda-based Jupyter notebooks provide an alternative environment for model development, and Vertex AI can also be used in conjunction with these notebooks once Vertex Explainable AI has been integrated into these popular development environments:

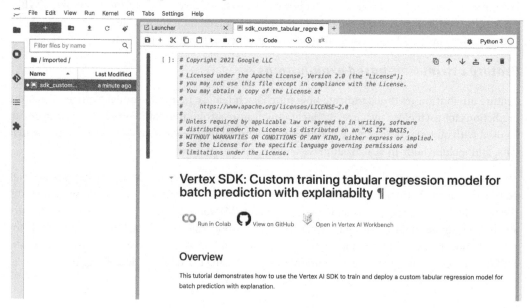

Figure 7.2: An Anaconda Jupyter notebook running Vertex AI

Google is making it easier for data scientists and model developers to access the power of AI explanations and improve the transparency and interpretability of their models.

Simplified deployment

Deploying Vertex Explainable AI on GCP is a straightforward process. Users can easily access the Vertex AI console to deploy and monitor their models, with the added benefit of Explainable AI features to improve model transparency and interpretability. Additionally, GCP offers a variety of pre-trained models and AutoML capabilities that enable users to rapidly develop and deploy models with Explainable AI functionality. With its powerful infrastructure and intuitive user interface, deploying Vertex Explainable AI on GCP has never been easier:

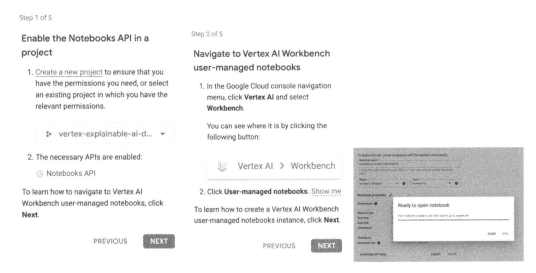

Figure 7.3: Explainable AI deployment

Explanations are comprehensive and multimodal

Vertex Explainable AI offers comprehensive and multimodal explanations, which provide a detailed understanding of how ML models make predictions. This benefit is especially valuable for complex models that involve various types of data, such as text, image, and tabular data. With comprehensive explanations, users can analyze the importance of each feature in the model and determine how the model arrives at a particular prediction. Moreover, multimodal explanations provide a holistic view of how the model incorporates multiple modalities to make a decision, improving the overall interpretability of the model:

```
Visualize the images with AI Explanations

The images returned show the explanations for only the top class predicted by the model. This means that if one of the model's predictions is incorrect, the pixels you see
highlighted are for the incorrect class. For example, if the model predicted "airplane" when it should have predicted "cat", you can see explanations for why the model
classified this image as an airplane.

If you deployed an Integrated Gradients model, you can visualize its feature attributions. Currently, the highlighted pixels returned from AI Explanations show the top 60% of
pixels that contributed to the model's prediction. The pixels you see after running the cell below show the pixels that most signaled the model's prediction.

[36]:  import io

for explanation in response.explanations:
    attributions = dict(explanation.attributions[0].feature_attributions)
    label_index = explanation.attributions[0].output_index[0]
    class_name = CLASSES[label_index]
    b64str = attributions["image"]["b64_jpeg"]
    image = base64.b64decode(b64str)
    image = io.BytesIO(image)
    img = mpimg.imread(image, format="JPG")

    plt.imshow(img, interpolation="nearest")
    plt.show()
```

Figure 7.4: Visualizing images with AI Explanations

The benefit of image-based AI explanation is made evident in the following example from the *"Why Should I Trust You?"* paper's husky versus wolf snow classifier example. In this case, the original classifier was intended to distinguish between images of huskies and wolves, but due to the prevalence of snow in the images, the model began to rely heavily on the presence of snow in making its predictions. By using image-based AI explanations, it became clear that the model was not correctly identifying the animals in the images and was instead relying on the background snow to make its classifications:

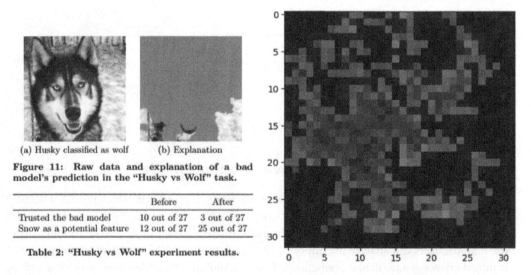

(a) Husky classified as wolf   (b) Explanation

Figure 11: Raw data and explanation of a bad model's prediction in the "Husky vs Wolf" task.

	Before	After
Trusted the bad model	10 out of 27	3 out of 27
Snow as a potential feature	12 out of 27	25 out of 27

Table 2: "Husky vs Wolf" experiment results.

Figure 7.5: Vertex AI provides an explanation – Husky vs. Wolf explanation by Ribeiro et al[3]

This mistake was able to be corrected, resulting in a more accurate classifier for distinguishing between huskies and wolves.

Like all things technology, Vertex Explainable AI is not without its shortcomings. Some limitations must be taken into account when analyzing feature attributions. The attributions provided only show how much a feature influenced the prediction for that particular example, and may not reflect the overall behavior of the model. The attributions depend entirely on the model and data used to train the model, and can't detect fundamental relationships in the data. Attributions alone can't determine whether a model is fair, unbiased, or of sound quality.

When it comes to image data, the two attribution methods that are supported, integrated gradients and XRAI, also have some limitations. While integrated gradients highlight important areas in the image, the granular output can make it difficult to assess relative importance, and XRAI works best on natural, higher-contrast images containing multiple objects.

In our view, Google Vertex Explainable AI is a good example of integrating ML explainability into ML development. As tools and processes such as these become more widely used within enterprises AI assurance frameworks, they can help build trust and confidence in the use of AI across various industries.

AWS Sagemaker Clarify

Amazon Web Services (**AWS**) offers a comprehensive AI platform, which has evolved from a simple data science notebook offering into a competitive solution on the mainstream AI platform market, alongside its cloud rivals, Azure and GCP. AWS offers a comprehensive suite of AI offerings that enable developers to build, train, and deploy ML models quickly and easily. These offerings include Amazon SageMaker, a fully managed service that provides end-to-end ML workflows, Amazon Rekognition, a deep-learning-based image and video analysis service, Amazon Comprehend, a natural language processing service, and Amazon Lex, a service for building conversational interfaces using voice and text. AWS also provides several pre-built AI services, including text-to-speech, speech-to-text, language translation, and sentiment analysis.

Amazon SageMaker Clarify[4] is part of this comprehensive suite of services and helps ensure the accuracy, transparency, and fairness of ML models. It is used to detect and mitigate bias in ML models and data:

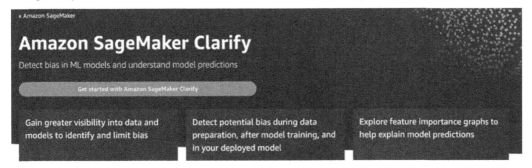

Figure 7.6: Amazon SageMaker Clarify

Amazon SageMaker Clarify is a service that allows ML developers to identify and mitigate bias in their models and datasets, making them more transparent and fair. The service offers pre-built algorithms and workflows to detect bias across various protected groups and provides techniques to mitigate the bias found. SageMaker Clarify can be used to detect bias in datasets before model training, analyze models for bias during and after training, and generate post-training metrics and explanations for the end users. SageMaker Clarify comes with lots of examples[5] to ensure that ML models are transparent and explainable and that they treat all individuals and groups fairly. With its powerful features, AWS SageMaker and Clarify have become go-to services for ML developers, especially for those who have standardized on AWS, extending AI to non-data scientists:

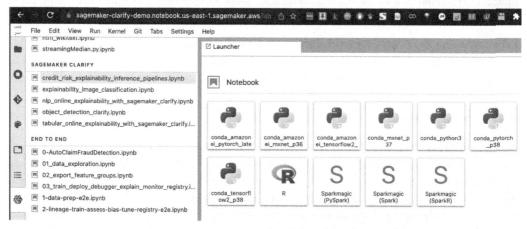

Figure 7.7: SageMaker Clarify examples

Amazon SageMaker Clarify provides ML developers with tools to detect and limit bias and explain predictions in their training data and models. One benefit of using SageMaker Clarify is that it comes with numerous examples that provide an introduction to the platform:

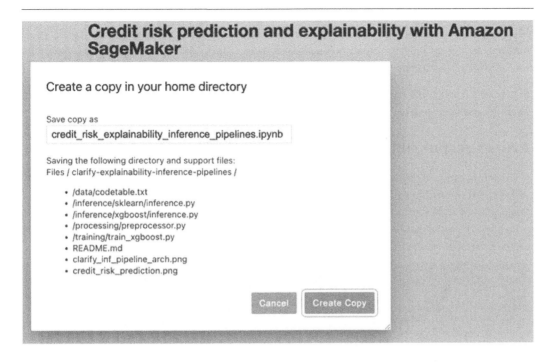

Figure 7.8: SageMaker Clarify examples

These examples cover various topics, such as fairness and explainability, risk prediction, text explainability, and computer vision. SageMaker Clarify also includes processing tools for text and image classification and object detection, among others. These examples and tools help users understand how to best utilize SageMaker Clarify to ensure that their ML models are transparent, explainable, and fair. These examples are also quite easy to deploy as part of the AWS platform.

With a wide range of pre-built examples, Amazon SageMaker Clarify is easy to deploy and integrate into existing AWS workflows. Businesses can benefit from increased trust in their AI models, improved compliance with regulations, and a greater ability to make informed decisions based on AI-driven insights.

Azure Machine Learning model interpretability

Microsoft Azure Machine Learning is a cloud-based service that provides data scientists with the ability to build, train, and deploy ML models. Azure Machine Learning makes it easy to track experiments, manage datasets, and collaborate with other data scientists. With this cloud ML platform, Azure Machine Learning offers tools for building and managing bespoke ML projects using managed Jupyter notebooks, Azure Machine Learning Designer (for drag-and-drop ML pipelines), and an automated ML UI. Microsoft also offers Azure Cognitive Services, which developers can use with no specific

ML knowledge to use prebuilt AI as a service for use cases in speech, language, vision, and decision-making. Developers and data scientists can also use Azure's OpenAI Service, which is in preview at the time of writing, to experiment with the most sophisticated language model technologies in the world.

Microsoft's responsible AI ecosystem can be roughly divided into two overlapping parts: Azure's offerings and open source.

Azure's responsible AI offerings

Microsoft is committed to responsible AI and has developed a framework for building AI systems called the Responsible AI Standard, which is based on six key principles: fairness, reliability and safety, privacy and security, inclusiveness, transparency, and accountability. To help implement these principles, Microsoft has developed tools and offerings such as the Responsible AI dashboard, which can be generated via the CLI, SDK, or Azure Machine Learning Studio UI:

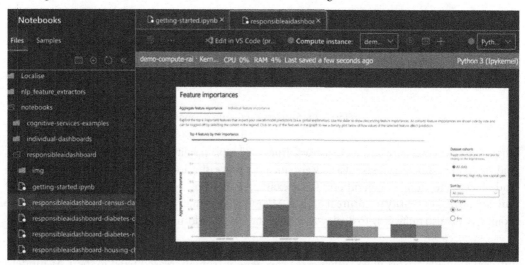

Figure 7.9: Azure responsible AI dashboard

The dashboard provides insights into how to build AI systems that are more beneficial and equitable for people. Additionally, the responsible AI scorecard can help measure progress toward these principles. Overall, Microsoft's commitment to responsible AI demonstrates its dedication to creating trustworthy and ethical AI systems that prioritize people and their goals.

Azure Machine Learning provides developers with a range of tools to generate a responsible AI dashboard using Jupyter notebooks. By setting up a workspace and creating an experiment, developers can run their model and use the Azure Machine Learning interpretability library to generate relevant insights such as feature importance and SHAP values – and view them in a browser.

Responsible AI scorecards

One of the critical aspects of the Azure Machine Learning platform is its ability to generate responsible AI scorecards, which are PDF reports based on insights from the responsible AI dashboard. These scorecards provide transparency into the development process of the AI models, including the data used and their accuracy. These reports can be easily customized, downloaded, and shared with stakeholders, including technical and non-technical parties. These scorecards can be utilized to educate stakeholders about data and model health and compliance and enhance trust.

The Azure Machine Learning responsible AI scorecard[6] provides a comprehensive summary of key insights from the responsible AI dashboard. This PDF report includes the following:

- An overview of the ML model and its target values, as well as a data analysis segment that displays characteristics of the data that was used to build the model

- A model performance segment, which provides important metrics and characteristics of the predictions, while also highlighting the top-performing and worst-performing data cohorts and subgroups

- The scorecard also lists the top important factors that affect the model's predictions and provides insights into fairness for sensitive groups

The causal insights segment summarizes whether the identified factors or treatments have any causal effect on the real-world outcome.

Overall, this scorecard is a valuable tool for building trust and transparency with stakeholders and ensuring that AI solutions are responsible and ethical.

Open source offerings – the responsible AI toolbox

The responsible AI toolbox is a collection of tools and visualization widgets for model assessment and decision-making. The toolbox includes four key components:

- The Responsible AI dashboard

- The Error Analysis dashboard

- The Interpretability dashboard

- The Fairness dashboard

These tools can be used to assess and debug models, identify errors, and discover cohorts of data for which the model underperforms. They also provide insights into model predictions, fairness issues, and actionable insights for stakeholders and customers. Overall, the responsible AI toolbox provides a comprehensive set of tools to help developers build and deploy responsible AI solutions.

We'll discuss this toolkit in detail in *Chapter 9*.

Open source toolkits and lenses

In this section, we will look into two prominent tools for addressing bias and fairness in AI systems: IBM AIF360 and Aequitas – a Bias and Fairness Audit Toolkit.

IBM AI Fairness 360

IBM AI Fairness 360 is an open source toolkit designed to help developers and data scientists identify, understand, and mitigate biases in ML models. The toolkit offers a range of algorithms[7] for detecting and removing bias, as well as metrics for evaluating model fairness. The toolkit's suite of visualizations provides users with an intuitive way to interpret results and gain insights into the underlying causes of bias:

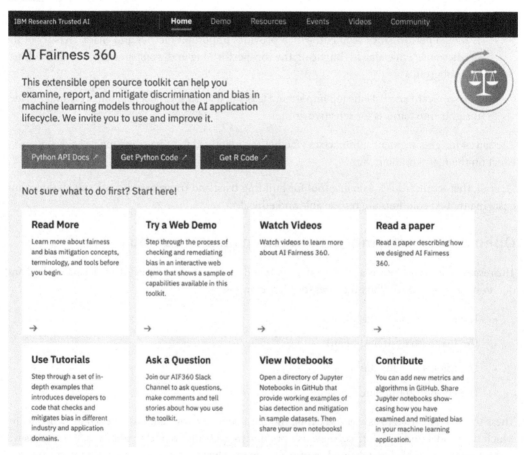

Figure 7.10: IBM AI Fairness 360 home page

By using the IBM AI Fairness 360 toolkit[8], developers can enhance the transparency and accountability of their ML models. The toolkit allows users to detect and address bias at every stage of the model development process, from data preprocessing to model deployment. This can help organizations build more equitable and inclusive AI systems that promote diversity and mitigate discrimination:

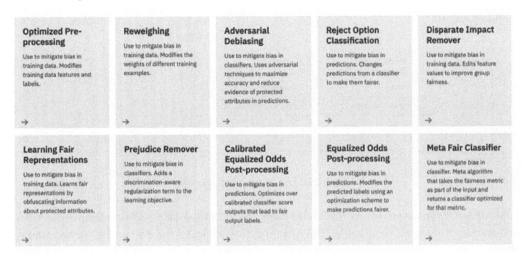

Figure 7:11: List of available bias mitigation algorithms

The AI Fairness 360 package is a comprehensive toolkit designed to test for and mitigate biases in datasets and models. It includes a set of metrics, explanations for these metrics, and algorithms to address bias.

The toolkit is applicable to a wide range of domains, including finance, human capital management, healthcare, and education. The AI Fairness 360 interactive experience provides an accessible introduction to the toolkit, while tutorials and other notebooks offer a deeper, data-scientist-oriented introduction.

The package is extensible, and users are encouraged to contribute their own metrics, explainers, and debiasing algorithms. However, the comprehensive set of capabilities may be overwhelming, so guidance materials have been provided to help users identify the most appropriate metrics and algorithms for their use case. The AI Fairness 360 package is an important tool for promoting fairness and accountability in AI systems, and its extensibility allows for ongoing improvements and innovation in the field:

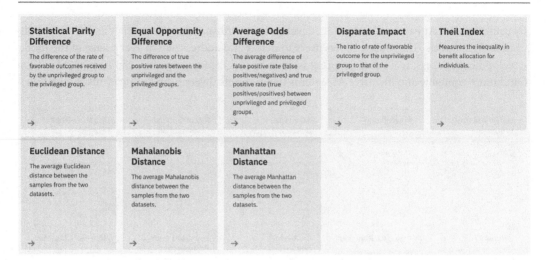

Figure 7.12: List of available measures

IBM AIF360 is a great open source toolkit that helps developers and data scientists identify, understand, and mitigate biases in ML models. The IBM AI Fairness 360 toolkit is an important tool for organizations that are committed to developing responsible and ethical AI systems. By leveraging the toolkit's advanced algorithms and visualizations, developers can improve the fairness and accuracy of their ML models and promote greater trust and confidence in their results. IBM has a strong AI platform, but the Watson brand needs refreshing as it was oversold in the past. However, the platform is rock-solid and has strengths in data management, tools, solution accelerators, security, and runtime flexibility. IBM's platform benefits from years of innovation and a deep understanding of the AI development life cycle. IBM AIF360 is an important component of the platform, allowing users to detect and address bias at every stage of the model development process, promoting greater trust and confidence in the results. IBM is a good choice for enterprises looking for a well-designed platform that can connect data science, ML, and business rules decisions for extended AI teams.

Aequitas – Bias and Fairness Audit Toolkit

Aequitas[9] is an ML tool that enables the identification of potential bias in datasets. The tool provides an evaluation of datasets for fairness and highlights any potential areas where bias may exist. Aequitas is a versatile tool that can be applied to datasets of all sizes and can be customized to specific needs and requirements. By using Aequitas, organizations can ensure that their data analysis is free of bias, promoting fairness and accountability in their decision-making processes:

How can you use Aequitas?

Web Audit Tool	Python Library	Command Line Tool
Try our Audit Tool to generate a Bias Report	Use our python code library to generate bias and fairness metrics on your data and predictions.	Use our command line tool to generate a report using your own data and predictions.

Figure 7.13: Aequitas – Bias and Fairness Audit Toolkit

Aequitas provides specific guidelines around auditing your risk assessment system for biases – you must consider two types: biased actions or interventions that are not allocated in a representative way and biased outcomes due to errors in the system for certain groups of people. To conduct these audits, you require data that includes the overall population considered for interventions, including their protected attributes, such as race, gender, age, and income. You need a set of individuals in the population that have been recommended or selected for intervention by your risk assessment system. It's crucial to audit the assessments that have been made after the system has been built, rather than relying on the data that was used to train the ML system:

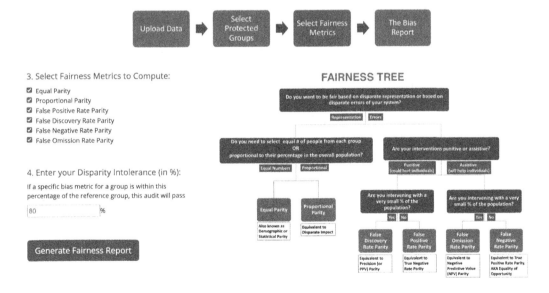

Figure 7.14: Aequitas Bias Toolkit, configuring the audit

However, in the second case, if you're auditing for biases due to disparate errors, you must also collect actual outcomes for the individuals selected and not selected. To obtain this information, you may need to conduct a trial or hold out a portion of the data from the recent past when building your ML system. By conducting these audits and analyzing the results, organizations can identify and address biases in their risk assessment systems, promoting fairness and accountability in their decision-making processes:

The Bias Report

Audit Date:	02 Nov 2022
Data Audited:	9769 rows
Attributes Audited:	education, gender, race
Audit Goal(s):	Equal Parity - Ensure all protected groups are have equal representation in the selected set.
	Proportional Parity - Ensure all protected groups are selected proportional to their percentage of the population.
	False Positive Rate Parity - Ensure all protected groups have the same false positive rates as the reference group).
	False Discovery Rate Parity - Ensure all protected groups have equally proportional false positives within the selected set (compared to the reference group).
	False Negative Rate Parity - Ensure all protected groups have the same false negative rates (as the reference group).
	False Omission Rate Parity - Ensure all protected groups have equally proportional false negatives within the non-selected set (compared to the reference group).
Reference Groups:	Custom group - The reference groups you selected for each attribute will be used to calculate relative disparities in this audit.
Fairness Threshold:	80%. If disparity for a group is within 80% and 125% of the value of the reference group on a group metric (e.g. False Positive Rate), this audit will pass.

Figure 7.15: Bias Report outcomes

It is fairly easy to generate bias reports using the Aequitas toolkit. The Bias Report provides an audit of a dataset containing 9,769 rows and focuses on three attributes: education, gender, and race. The audit's goals are to ensure equal parity, proportional parity, false positive rate parity, false discovery rate parity, false negative rate parity, and false omission rate parity for all protected groups. The audit compares all protected groups to the reference group to calculate relative disparities. The fairness threshold is set at 80%, meaning that a group's disparity must be within 80% and 125% of the reference group's value on a given metric (for example, False Positive Rate) for the audit to pass:

Audit Results: Summary

Equal Parity - Ensure all protected groups are have equal representation in the selected set.	Failed	Details
Proportional Parity - Ensure all protected groups are selected proportional to their percentage of the population.	Failed	Details
False Positive Rate Parity - Ensure all protected groups have the same false positive rates as the reference group).	Failed	Details
False Discovery Rate Parity - Ensure all protected groups have equally proportional false positives within the selected set (compared to the reference group).	Failed	Details
False Negative Rate Parity - Ensure all protected groups have the same false negative rates (as the reference group).	Failed	Details
False Omission Rate Parity - Ensure all protected groups have equally proportional false negatives within the non-selected set (compared to the reference group).	Failed	Details

Figure 7.16: Bias Report outcomes – summary

The report presents a summary of the audit results, along with details of fairness measures and protected attributes. The bias metrics values and base metrics that were calculated for each group are also included in the report:

Equal Parity: Failed

What is it?	When does it matter?	Which groups failed the audit:
This criteria considers an attribute to have equal parity is every group is equally represented in the selected set. For example, if race (with possible values of white, black, other) has equal parity, it implies that all three races are equally represented (33% each)in the selected/intervention set.	If your desired outcome is to intervene equally on people from all races, then you care about this criteria.	For education (with reference group as HS-grad)

For education (with reference group as HS-grad)
Assoc-acdm with 0.08X Disparity
Bachelors with 0.32X Disparity
Prof-school with 0.02X Disparity
11th with 0.12X Disparity
9th with 0.05X Disparity
Assoc-voc with 0.11X Disparity
Doctorate with 0.01X Disparity
7th-8th with 0.06X Disparity
Preschool with 0.01X Disparity
5th-6th with 0.03X Disparity
1st-4th with 0.02X Disparity
Masters with 0.07X Disparity
Some-college with 0.65X Disparity
10th with 0.10X Disparity
12th with 0.04X Disparity

For gender (with reference group as Male)
Female with 0.63X Disparity

For race (with reference group as White)
Black with 0.14X Disparity
Asian-Pac-Islander with 0.04X Disparity
Amer-Indian-Eskimo with 0.01X Disparity
Other with 0.01X Disparity

Figure 7.17: Bias Report outcomes – failure on equal parity

Overall, the Bias Report provides a comprehensive analysis of the dataset and highlights any potential biases in the risk assessment system, promoting fairness and accountability in decision-making processes. Aequitas is a powerful and versatile ML tool that can help organizations identify potential biases in their datasets and promote fairness in their decision-making processes. By evaluating datasets for fairness and identifying any areas where bias may exist, Aequitas can help organizations ensure that their data analysis is free of bias, promoting accountability and ethical practices.

However, no discussion of interpretability and fairness is complete without **privacy-enhancing technologies** (**PETs**) and toolkits.

PETs

PETs play a crucial role in the privacy and governance of ML models. With the increasing use of ML in various sectors, there is a growing concern about the protection of sensitive and personal data. PETs help address these concerns by enabling the development and use of ML models while minimizing privacy risks. Some key reasons for the importance of PETs in the privacy and governance of ML models are as follows:

- **Data protection**: PETs help protect sensitive data from unauthorized access, disclosure, or misuse. Techniques such as differential privacy, homomorphic encryption, and secure multiparty computation enable the development of ML models without revealing individual data points or compromising privacy.

- **Compliance with regulations**: Privacy regulations such as the **General Data Protection Regulation (GDPR)** and the **California Consumer Privacy Act (CCPA)** mandate the protection of personal data. PETs can help organizations comply with these regulations and avoid legal liabilities, fines, and reputational damage.

- **Trust-building**: As people become more concerned about privacy, organizations that employ PETs can demonstrate their commitment to data protection and build trust with their customers and stakeholders. This can result in increased user engagement, loyalty, and a competitive advantage.

- **Ethical considerations**: Employing PETs can help organizations align their ML practices with ethical principles, such as fairness, accountability, and transparency, by ensuring that sensitive data is not misused or unfairly targeted.

- **Facilitating data sharing**: PETs can enable secure data sharing between organizations, allowing them to collaborate on ML projects without compromising the privacy of the individuals whose data is being used. This can lead to advancements in research and innovation while maintaining privacy standards.

- **Mitigating bias and discrimination**: The use of PETs can help prevent biases and discrimination that may arise from the misuse of sensitive data, such as race, gender, or other protected attributes, ensuring that ML models are more fair and equitable.

PETs are a collection of methods and tools designed to protect individuals' privacy while enabling data-driven processes. Let's look at some key PETs.

Differential privacy

Differential privacy is a mathematical framework that ensures the privacy of individuals in statistical databases by injecting controlled noise into the data. It allows for aggregate analysis without revealing sensitive information about specific individuals. The key concept is that the presence or absence of any single individual's data should not significantly impact the results of a query.

Consider a database, D, and a neighboring database, D', differing by only one individual's data. A function, f, provides ε-differential privacy for all $S \subseteq Range(f)$:

$$\frac{Pr[f(D) \in S]}{Pr[f(D') \in S]} \leq e^{\varepsilon}$$

Here, $\varepsilon \geq 0$ is the privacy parameter, which controls the level of privacy. Smaller ε values provide stronger privacy guarantees but may reduce the accuracy of query results.

An example of a differentially private algorithm is the Laplace mechanism, which adds Laplace noise to the output of a function, f. Given a query, $q(D)$, the Laplace mechanism releases the following:

$$q(D) + Lap\left(\frac{\Delta q}{\varepsilon}\right)$$

Here, $Lap(\cdot)$ represents the Laplace distribution, Δq is the sensitivity of the query (the maximum difference in the query result when adding or removing a single individual's data), and ε is the privacy parameter.

Suppose we have a database of people's ages and we want to compute the average age, $q(D)$, while ensuring differential privacy. Using the Laplace mechanism, we would add Laplace noise to the computed average:

$$Q_{DP}(D) = \frac{\sum_{i=1}^{n} age_i}{n} + Lap\left(\frac{\Delta q}{\varepsilon}\right)$$

Here, n is the number of individuals, age_i is the age of the i-th individual, and $\Delta q = 1$ for the average query.

Now, let's consider a simple code example using Python and the numpy library to apply differential privacy to compute the average age:

```python
import numpy as np
def laplace_noise(sensitivity, epsilon):
    return np.random.laplace(scale=sensitivity / epsilon)
def dp_average(ages, epsilon):
    n = len(ages)
sensitivity = 1 / n
noise = laplace_noise(sensitivity, epsilon)
return np.mean(ages) + noise
ages = [
    25,30,35,45,28,32,40,36,
    ]
epsilon = 0.5
dp_avg = dp_average(ages, epsilon)
print ('Differentially private average age:', dp_avg)
```

In this example, we first define a function called `laplace_noise` to generate Laplace noise based on the sensitivity and privacy parameter, ε. Next, we define the `dp_average` function, which computes the average age and adds Laplace noise to achieve differential privacy. We then calculate the differentially private average age of a given dataset with a specified privacy parameter.

It is important to note that the trade-off between privacy and utility should be carefully considered when selecting the value of the privacy parameter, ε. Smaller values of ε provide stronger privacy guarantees but may introduce more noise, potentially reducing the utility of the results.

Homomorphic encryption

Homomorphic encryption is a cryptographic technique that enables computations to be performed directly on encrypted data without the need for decryption. This ensures that sensitive information remains confidential during processing, allowing data analysis without exposing the underlying data.

Consider two plaintext values, x and y. The homomorphic encryption process can be represented as follows:

$Enc(x) \oplus Enc(y) = Enc(x + y)$

$Enc(x) \odot Enc(y) = Enc(x.y)$

Here, $Enc(\cdot)$ denotes the encryption function and $\oplus$ and $\odot$ represent homomorphic addition and multiplication operations, respectively. The key property of homomorphic encryption is that the results of computations on encrypted data, when decrypted, match the results of the same computations on the original plaintext data.

A simple Python code example using the PySEAL library, which implements the **Microsoft Simple Encrypted Arithmetic Library (SEAL)**, could be as follows:

```
import tenseal as ts
#Create a context for homomorphic encryption
context  =  ts.context(ts.SCHEME_TYPE.CKKS,'→ poly_modulus_
degree=8192, coeff_mod_bit_sizes=[60, 40, 40,'→ 60])
#Enable automatic rescaling
context.global_scale = 2**40
#Create encryption and decryption keys
secret_key = ts.SecretKey()
context.secret_key = secret_key
public_key = ts.PublicKey(context)
context.public_key = public_key
relin_keys = ts.RelinKeys(context)
context.relin_keys = relin_keys
#Encrypt two vectors
vector1 = [1, 2, 3]
vector2 = [4, 5, 6]
encrypted_vector1 = ts.ckks_vector(context, vector1)
encrypted_vector2  =  ts.ckks_vector(context,  vector2)
#Perform element-wise addition and multiplication
encrypted_sum = encrypted_vector1 + encrypted_vector2
```

```
encrypted_product = encrypted_vector1 * encrypted_vector2
#Decrypt the results
decrypted_sum = encrypted_sum.decrypt()
decrypted_product = encrypted_product.decrypt()
print("Decrypted sum:", decrypted_sum)
print("Decrypted product:", decrypted_product)
```

In this example, we used the PySEAL library to perform homomorphic encryption on two vectors. First, we created a context and generated encryption and decryption keys. Then, we encrypted the two vectors and performed element-wise addition and multiplication on the encrypted data. Finally, we decrypted the results and printed them.

Secure multiparty computation

Secure multiparty computation (**SMPC**) is a cryptographic method that enables multiple parties to collaboratively compute a function over their inputs while keeping those inputs private. The key idea is to distribute the computation among the participants so that the result can be obtained without revealing the individual inputs.

Consider two parties, Alice and Bob, with x and y as inputs, respectively. They want to compute a function, $f(x, y)$. SMPC allows them to compute the function without disclosing x or y to each other. This process can be illustrated as follows:

1. Alice and Bob divide their inputs into secret shares: $x = x_1 + x_2$ and $y = y_1 + y_2$.
2. Alice holds x_1 and y_1, while Bob holds x_2 and y_2.
3. They perform the computation on the secret shares, obtaining shares of the result: $f(x, y) = f_1 + f_2$.
4. They exchange their shares of the result and combine them to obtain the final result: $f(x, y) = f_1 + f_2$.

A simple Python code example using the `sympc` library for SMPC is as follows:

```
import torch
import syft as sy
from sympc.session import Session
from sympc.tensor import MPCTensor
# Create a domain and join virtual workers Alice and Bob
domain_alice = sy.Domain('alice').load_or_create()
domain_bob = sy.Domain('bob').load_or_create()
alice = sy.VirtualMachine(name='alice', domain=domain_alice)
bob = sy.VirtualMachine(name='bob', domain=domain_bob)
alice_client = alice.get_client()
bob_client = bob.get_client()
# Create a session for secure computation
```

```
session = Session(parties=[alice_client, bob_client])
Session.setup_mpc(session)
# Create secret tensors
x_secret = torch.tensor([1, 2, 3])
y_secret = torch.tensor([4, 5, 6])
# Share the secret tensors between Alice and Bob
x = MPCTensor(secret=x_secret, session=session)
y = MPCTensor(secret=y_secret, session=session)
# Perform element-wise addition and multiplication
z_sum = x + y
z_product = x * y
# Reconstruct the results
result_sum = z_sum.reconstruct()
result_product = z_product.reconstruct()
print ('Reconstructed sum:', result_sum)
print ('Reconstructed  product:', result_product)
```

In this example, we used the `sympc` library to perform secure multiparty computation on two tensors. First, we created a domain and joined the virtual workers, Alice and Bob. Then, we created a session for secure computation and shared the tensors between Alice and Bob. Next, we performed element-wise addition and multiplication on the shared tensors. Finally, we reconstructed and printed the results.

Federated learning

Federated learning is a decentralized ML approach that trains models on local devices (clients) while sharing only model updates, rather than raw data, with a central server. This maintains data privacy while allowing collaborative learning from distributed data sources.

Consider a set of clients, $C = C1, C2, \ldots, Cn$, each holding a local dataset, Di. The goal is to train a global model, MG, using the combined data without revealing the raw data to the central server or other clients. The federated learning process can be summarized as follows:

1. Initialize the global model, MG, on the central server.
2. For each round, $t = 1, \ldots, T$:

    I.   Select a subset of clients, $St \subseteq C$.

    II.   Distribute the current global model, M_G, to the selected clients.

    III. Each client, $Ci \in St$, trains a local model, $M_{i,t}$, using its local dataset, Di.

    IV. The clients send their local model updates, $\Delta M_{i,t}$, to the central server.

    V.   The central server aggregates the local model updates and updates the global model with $M_G \leftarrow M_G + \Sigma C_i \in S_t\ w_i \Delta M_{i,t}$, where w_i are client-specific weights.

3. The central server obtains the final global model M_G after T rounds.

A simple Python code example of using **TensorFlow Federated** (TFF) for federated learning is as follows:

```python
import tensorflow as tf
import tensorflow_federated as tff
#Load a dataset (e.g., MNIST)
mnist_train, mnist_test = tf.keras.datasets.mnist.load_data()
#Preprocess the data
def preprocess_data(data):
x, y = data
x = x.reshape((-1, 28, 28, 1)) / 255.0
y = tf.keras.utils.to_categorical(y, num_classes=10) return x, y
mnist_train = preprocess_data(mnist_train) mnist_test = preprocess_
data(mnist_test)
#Define the model def create_model():
model = tf.keras.models.Sequential([ tf.keras.layers.Conv2D(32, (3,
3), activation='relu',
'→    input_shape=(28, 28, 1)),
tf.keras.layers.MaxPooling2D((2, 2)),
tf.keras.layers.Flatten(), tf.keras.layers.Dense(64,
activation='relu'), tf.keras.layers.Dense(10, activation='softmax')
])
return model
#Create a federated learning dataset
federated_train_data =
'→    tff.simulation.datasets.from_tensor_slices( mnist_train).create_
tf_dataset_for_client()
#Create a federated learning algorithm
trainer = tff.learning.build_federated_averaging_process( model_
fn=create_model,
client_optimizer_fn=lambda: tf.keras.optimizers.SGD(0.01), server_
optimizer_fn=lambda: tf.keras.optimizers.SGD(1.0))
#Train the model with federated learning
state = trainer.initialize()
for round in range(10):
state, metrics = trainer.next(state, federated_train_data)
print(f"Round {round}, Metrics: {metrics}")
```

In this example, we used the TFF library to perform federated learning on the MNIST dataset. First, we loaded and preprocessed the dataset, then defined a model using TensorFlow Keras. Next, we created a federated dataset and a federated learning algorithm using the tff.simulation.datasets. from_tensor_slices and tf.learning.build_federated_averaging_process TFF functions.

Then, we trained the model using federated learning by initializing the training state and iterating over multiple rounds. In each round, we called the `trainer.next()` function to perform one round of federated learning, updating the model based on the clients' local model updates. Finally, we printed the training metrics for each round.

Data anonymization

Data anonymization is the process of removing or modifying **personally identifiable information (PII)** from datasets to protect individuals' privacy while maintaining the utility of the data for analysis.

Anonymization techniques aim to prevent the re-identification of individuals, ensuring compliance with data protection regulations.

Consider a dataset with records $(x1, x2, \ldots, xn)$, where each xi contains a set of attributes, $A = A1$, $A2, \ldots, Am$. Anonymization techniques transform the dataset to produce a new dataset with records $(x'1, x'2, \ldots, x'n)$ so that we get the following:

$$P\left(re - identification\ of\ an\ individual\ in\ x'_i\right) \leq \delta$$

Here, δ is a pre-defined privacy threshold.

A simple Python code example of using the `pandas` library for data anonymization is as follows:

```
import pandas as pd
#Load the dataset
data = pd.read_csv("data.csv")
#Anonymize the dataset by removing PII columns
pii_columns = ["name", "email", "phone"]
anonymized_data = data.drop(pii_columns, axis=1)
#Save the anonymized dataset anonymized_data.to_csv("anonymized_data.
csv", index=False)
```

In this example, we used the `pandas` library to load a dataset and perform simple data anonymization by removing PII columns (for example, `name`, `email`, and `phone`). After removing these columns, the resulting anonymized dataset was saved to a new file. This example demonstrates a basic form of data anonymization, but more advanced techniques can be applied depending on the specific use case and privacy requirements.

Data perturbation

Data perturbation is a privacy-preserving technique that involves adding noise or modifying data in a controlled manner to protect sensitive information while preserving the overall statistical properties of the dataset. By introducing noise, the technique aims to prevent the disclosure of individual data points, ensuring data privacy.

Consider a dataset with records ($x1, x2, \ldots, xn$), where each xi contains a set of attributes, $A = A1$, $A2, \ldots, Am$. Data perturbation transforms the dataset to produce a new dataset with records ($x'1$, $x'2, \ldots, x'n$), which results in the following:

$$x'_i = x_i + N(\mu, \sigma^2)$$

Here, $N(\mu, \sigma2)$ represents noise drawn from a probability distribution (for example, Gaussian distribution), with mean, μ, and variance, $\sigma2$.

A simple Python code example of using the `numpy` library for data perturbation is as follows:

```
import numpy as np

#Load the dataset
data  =  np.loadtxt("data.txt")

#Define noise parameters mean = 0
std_dev = 0.1

#Perturb the dataset by adding Gaussian noise
noise = np.random.normal(mean, std_dev, data.shape) perturbed_data =
data + noise

#Save the perturbed dataset np.savetxt("perturbed_data.
txt",  perturbed_data)
```

In this example, we used the `numpy` library to load a dataset and perform data perturbation by adding Gaussian noise. First, we defined the `noise` parameters (`mean` and standard deviation) and then generated noise using `np.random.normal`. The noise was added to the original data to create the perturbed dataset. Finally, we saved the perturbed dataset to a new file. This example demonstrates a basic form of data perturbation, but more advanced techniques can be applied depending on the specific use case and privacy requirements.

In conclusion, this very brief overview highlights the importance of PETs as indispensable tools for effective risk management and governance in ML. By employing methods such as differential privacy, homomorphic encryption, SMPC, federated learning, data anonymization, and data perturbation, businesses can ensure data privacy and security while harnessing the power of ML. As data protection regulations continue to evolve, embracing these PETs will be vital for organizations to maintain trust, preserve their competitive edge, and fulfill their ethical responsibilities in a data-driven landscape.

Summary

In this chapter, we provided you with an overview of explainability and interpretability toolkits, which are important tools for understanding how AI models make decisions, as well as the role of PETs in ensuring data privacy and security. This chapter reviewed several toolkits, such as Google Vertex Explainable AI, Amazon SageMaker Clarify, model interpretability in Azure Machine Learning, and IBM's AIF360. These toolkits enable developers to implement disciplined approaches and tools for the transparency and explainability of AI-enabled decision-making, while PETs, such as differential privacy, homomorphic encryption, and federated learning, help protect sensitive data.

This chapter also highlighted the importance of synthetically generated data in AI development to mitigate bias, improve fairness, and assure regulatory compliance within legal and ethical constraints. Synthetic data generation can be used to create datasets that are balanced and representative of different groups, which can help reduce bias in ML algorithms.

Furthermore, we emphasize that understanding how AI models work is essential for building trust in AI systems and improving their performance. This chapter reviewed several methods for explaining AI models, including visualizing data inputs and outputs using feature importance and PDP, LIME, SHAP, anchors, and other methods that simulate the behavior of individual components of the system.

Overall, this chapter stressed the importance of using explainability toolkits and privacy-enhancing techniques to ensure that AI systems are transparent, fair, and compliant with legal and ethical standards while maintaining data privacy. By providing insights into how AI models work and protecting sensitive information, developers can improve their performance and build trust in their results.

In the upcoming chapter, you will have the opportunity to learn about Fairlearn, a powerful Python package designed to promote fairness in ML. This chapter will provide an overview of Fairlearn's key offerings, including its metrics, algorithms, and techniques for evaluating and mitigating bias in machine learning models.

References and further reading

1. `https://storage.googleapis.com/cloud-ai-whitepapers/AI%20 Explainability%20Whitepaper.pdf`

2. *"Why Should I Trust You?": Explaining the Predictions of Any Classifier*, by Marco Tulio Ribeiro, Sameer Singh, Carlos Guestrin: `https://arxiv.org/abs/1602.04938`

3. *"Why Should I Trust You?": Explaining the Predictions of Any Classifier*, by Marco Tulio Ribeiro, Sameer Singh, Carlos Guestrin: `https://arxiv.org/abs/1602.04938`

4. `https://aws.amazon.com/sagemaker/clarify`

5. `https://github.com/aws/amazon-sagemaker-examples`

6. *Responsible AI scorecard*: `https://learn.microsoft.com/en-us/azure/machine-learning/how-to-responsible-ai-scorecard`

7. *AI Fairness 360: An Extensible Toolkit for Detecting, Understanding, and Mitigating Unwanted Algorithmic Bias*: https://arxiv.org/abs/1810.01943

8. *AI Fairness 360 (AIF360)*: https://github.com/Trusted-AI/AIF360

9. *Bias and Fairness Audit Toolkit*: http://aequitas.dssg.io/

10. *Azure What is Responsible AI (preview)?*: https://learn.microsoft.com/en-us/azure/machine-learning/concept-responsible-ml

11. *Generate a Responsible AI dashboard (preview) in the studio UI*: https://learn.microsoft.com/en-us/azure/machine-learning/how-to-responsible-ai-dashboard-ui

12. *AI Lab project: Responsible AI dashboard Learn about breakthrough AI innovation with hands-on labs, code resources, and deep dives*: https://www.microsoft.com/en-us/ai/ai-lab-responsible-ai-dashboard

13. https://github.com/microsoft/responsible-ai-toolbox/blob/af189bef5c830708abe1e35fe9839a9a6f1cfe30/notebooks/responsibleaidashboard/responsibleaidashboard-census-classification-model-debugging.ipynb

14. *Responsible AI Toolbox*: https://github.com/microsoft/responsible-ai-toolbox

15. *Responsible AI Widgets*: https://pypi.org/project/raiwidgets/#description

16. *Microsoft AI Lab Project*: https://www.microsoft.com/en-us/ai/ai-lab-projects

17. *Google Vertex AI site*: https://cloud.google.com/vertex-ai

18. *Explainable AI site*: https://cloud.google.com/explainable-ai

19. *Vertex Explainable AI docs*: https://cloud.google.com/vertex-ai/docs/explainable-ai

20. *Vertex Explainable AI Notebooks docs*: https://cloud.google.com/vertex-ai/docs/explainable-ai/overview

21. *Feature Attribution docs*: https://cloud.google.com/vertex-ai/docs/explainable-ai/overview#feature_attributions

22. *AI Explanations Whitepaper*: https://cerre.eu/wp-content/uploads/2020/07/ai_explainability_whitepaper_google.pdf

23. *Explainable AI with Google Cloud Vertex AI*: https://medium.com/google-cloud/explainable-ai-with-google-cloud-vertex-ai-3b5cef44cbae

24. *Why you need to explain machine learning models*: https://cloud.google.com/blog/products/ai-machine-learning/why-you-need-to-explain-machine-learning-models

25. *On the Privacy Risks of Model Explanations*: https://www.comp.nus.edu.sg/~reza/files/Shokri-AIES2021.pdf

26. *Why Are We Using Black Box Models in AI When We Don't Need To? A Lesson from an Explainable AI Competition*: https://hdsr.mitpress.mit.edu/pub/f9kuryi8/release/8

27. *Model Monitoring in Practice: Lessons Learned and Open Challenges*: https://dl.acm.org/doi/pdf/10.1145/3534678.3542617

28. *Interpretable Machine Learning – A Guide for Making Black Box Models Explainable*: https://christophm.github.io/interpretable-ml-book/

29. *Explaining Explanations: An Overview of Interpretability of Machine Learning*: https://arxiv.org/pdf/1806.00069.pdf

30. *Credo AI Product Update: Build Trust in Your AI with New Transparency Reports Disclosures*: https://www.credo.ai/blog/transparency-reports-disclosures

Fairness in AI Systems with Microsoft Fairlearn

Artificial intelligence must be designed to be aligned with human values, be transparent and explainable, and be robust and secure. (Timnit Gebru, former AI researcher at Google)

AI has the potential to be the greatest force for good in the world, or it could be the greatest threat. It all depends on how we design it. (Mustafa Suleyman, co-founder of DeepMind)

In the development of AI, we must be mindful of the potential for unintended consequences and ensure that the technology is being developed in a way that is fair, just, and equitable for all people. (Jeff Dean, CEO of Google AI)

The use of AI must always be guided by human values and principles, including fairness, equality, and non-discrimination. (Amrita Khalid, AI researcher and author)

In recent decades, **artificial intelligence (AI)** has transformed our relationship with the world. Due to the unreasonable effectiveness of data[1], automated decision-making is quickly becoming the norm. However, as AI systems become more sophisticated and widely used, it becomes increasingly problematic if they directly target a person or group negatively. When biased data and algorithms are used in an automated decision-making system, it can adversely affect real-world human lives by having a disparate impact on their health care, financial well-being, educational opportunities, or the likelihood of a specific racial or ethnic group being disproportionately identified as having a higher likelihood of criminal recidivism compared to others. AI has the potential to exacerbate existing social inequalities and create new ones if we are not careful. We must consider how AI will impact different groups of people and ensure that its benefits are shared equitably. This includes ensuring that data used to train AI systems is representative of all groups of people, not just those who are already privileged. It also means creating policies and regulations around the use of AI to protect vulnerable populations from harm. Fairness in AI is essential for creating a just society.

To avoid this problem, algorithmic fairness has become a permanent conduit in AI research. Fairlearn is one such initiative—an open source fairness toolkit that aims to provide AI fairness guides and use cases to help data scientists better understand fairness issues in AI. The Fairlearn Python toolkit offers assessments and mitigations for fairness-related issues.

In this chapter, we will demonstrate how to get started with fairness in **machine learning** (**ML**) with Fairlearn, learning about its fundamental value offerings, metrics, algorithms, and techniques for fairness assessment and unfairness mitigation. Readers will see two components of Fairlearn—the metrics for assessing when groups are negatively impacted by a model, and the metrics for comparing multiple models. The reader will understand different types of harm, including allocation harm and **quality-of-service** (**QoS**) harm, and how to mitigate unfairness by improving an unfair model.

In this chapter, you will learn about the following:

- Getting started with fairness

- Fairness metrics

- Fairness-related harms

- Getting started with Fairlearn

Let's get started!

Getting started with fairness

The Fairlearn toolkit is an open source tool for assessing and improving the fairness of AI systems built by data scientists and developers. Fairlearn includes a visualization dashboard and algorithms for mitigating unfairness, along with required metrics. As AI and ML algorithms increasingly shape our world, it is critical that we ensure fairness in their application by using tools that can identify and mitigate bias. Fairlearn is one such library. As we dive into the use of Fairlearn, we must understand the reasons why it is important to consider the potential impact of sensitive features on your ML models, even if you are not explicitly including sensitive features in the training data.

A common misconception is "If we remove sensitive features such as a person's race, sex, religion, sexual orientation, veteran status, and so on, shouldn't that be enough to mitigate any bias?" The answer is "Not really" because this information is often redundantly encoded across several features (also known as latent or proxy features), and ML algorithms will uncover the relationships between such features. Dr. Marzyeh Ghassemi of MIT recently published a paper[2] that shows how self-reported race can be discerned by AI from medical images that contain no indicators of race detectable by humans. Another example is how a person's race in the US is often closely tied to the ZIP code where they live—which means that even if race is not explicitly included as a feature in an ML model, the model can still pick up on it indirectly[3] through the ZIP code and other features. That is why there have been laws and regulations established to address ZIP code inequality in fair housing and fair lending.

However, it didn't stop the algorithms from discriminating deliveries based on race[4]. Also, without having the sensitive feature available in the dataset during training, it may be difficult or impossible to accurately assess how your model performs across different groups defined by that feature. There is also a performance trade-off—if you train a model whose predictions are statistically independent of sensitive features such as race or gender, ignoring those features during training can lead to suboptimal results and increased fairness risks down the road.

Blueprint for an AI Bill of Rights – White House

Automated technologies are increasingly used to make everyday decisions affecting people's rights, opportunities, and access in everything from hiring and housing to healthcare, education, and financial services. While these technologies can drive great innovations, such as enabling early cancer detection or helping farmers grow food more efficiently, studies have shown how AI can display opportunities unequally or embed bias and discrimination in decision-making processes. As a result, automated systems can replicate or deepen inequalities already present in society against ordinary people, underscoring the need for greater transparency, accountability, and privacy.

The usual suspect in biased models is data—biased data is also usually considered the root of all evil. However, it has been well established that modeling containing erroneous assumptions resulting in systematic error is also to blame. It's important to understand what words such as "unfair," "biased data," and "better data" mean in each specific context. For example, in a hiring-bias scenario, if a company has a history of not hiring many women, there will be fewer of them in the training dataset. This might lead to a trained model that's less accurate, but that doesn't necessarily mean it's unfair—it just means that more data would help make it more accurate. The same goes for feature selection—features that are good predictors for one group might not be as good for another group. Therefore, more data will not automatically improve accuracy unless it includes a diverse range of applicants with different backgrounds and experiences. Why, then, is it unfair if your data reflects the real world?

The complexity of fairness issues is exactly why it's not just a tech problem, but also a social and technical one. It's common to see fairness concerns in data even if it seems to represent "everyone." It is well established that ML models typically do not perform well for groups that are underrepresented. This happens because what's considered underrepresented can vary based on the context and may be influenced by past biases—for example, if a company hasn't hired many people from certain racial or ethnic groups or women, even the complete data is incomplete. Another factor to consider is that it's important to look at multiple fairness metrics and how they differ for different groups. By doing this multi-fairness metrics review, you can get a more accurate picture of the overall dataset. Therefore, not only increasing the size of the data but also its variety helps improve the fairness measures—but it is critical that we see fairness via different quantitative and qualitative metrics, offered by Fairlearn.

When optimizing an ML model, it's crucial to take into account the trade-off between performance, accuracy, and bias. Deep subgroup analysis is a critical aspect, as various social factors can impact equity. There are often multiple models that exhibit similar levels of accuracy or other performance metrics but differ significantly in their impact on different subgroups. A recent study found that a model trained on data from Americans was much better at predicting creditworthiness than a model trained on data from people in India, even though both groups had similar incomes and education levels. The reason for this difference is likely due to cultural factors such as social networks and norms around borrowing money. If we want our ML models to be fair, we need to take these types of factors into account. In this regard, bias mitigation algorithms aim to enhance fairness metrics without significantly compromising accuracy, or, more broadly, to manage the trade-off between performance and fairness metrics.

One way to make an ML model fairer is by using mitigation algorithms during training. Mitigation algorithms can help reduce bias against protected groups without sacrificing accuracy too much. In the previous example about loans, we could use a mitigation algorithm during training that would adjust for differences in cultural factors between Americans and Indians. This would help create a fairer and more accurate model for predicting creditworthiness. Having said that, it is important to not consider the mitigation algorithms a hammer for all bias-related problems. Even though the Fairlearn tool can make a model fairer by fixing some unfairness issues, it's important to look at the big picture. It's more than just the fairness metrics, but rather considering the real-world environment where the model will be used, hence the human in the loop. A data scientist has to consider the social and technical aspects to ensure that the model is actually fairer, not just according to the metrics, but in real life. For example, establishing 50-50 equality in the number of men and women in a breast cancer dataset will yield negative results because of the natural biological bias in the data. There are many ways in which a model can be unfair, and Fairlearn mitigation algorithms address some of them. Fairness being a sociotechnical construct is exactly why even after improving bias in your data, training and mitigating models, and checking all the metrics, you still need to consider both the technical details (such as data drift) and the societal aspects (such as strategic behavior) when monitoring your model in production.

The Fairlearn library can address both allocation and QoS harms. For example, if an AI system is used to screen job applicants, the system may inadvertently give some applicants an unfair advantage over others. The Fairlearn library can help mitigate this harm by providing tools that allow developers to check for and correct such biases. Similarly, if an AI system is used to provide customer service, the Fairlearn library can help ensure that all customers receive the same high level of service regardless of their background or characteristics. The Fairlearn library is designed to help identify and correct for bias in ML models. While it cannot currently detect bias in datasets, this is something that the team is considering for future development. In the meantime, there are other ways to detect bias in datasets that can be used by computer scientists. For example, one could examine the distribution of data points to look for patterns of discrimination. Additionally, one could use statistical tests to check for fairness in datasets.

The Fairlearn open source library is an amazing resource for data scientists and ML engineers who want to understand AI fairness and make their models fairer. It provides detailed information and practical examples to help you understand when each algorithm is best used. While it doesn't have an automatic tool to help you choose which mitigation algorithm to use, the comprehensive documentation and examples are very helpful in making smart decisions about improving fairness in your AI system. Fairlearn is a valuable tool that can assist computer scientists in reducing the impact of sensitive features in their data. It's capable of assessing multiple sensitive features and even non-binary values for those features. And all of Fairlearn's mitigation techniques work with both non-binary and data with multiple sensitive features, making it a versatile tool for promoting fairness in AI systems. Although Fairlearn has not yet been tested on image or text data, it is likely that it would work with these types of data as well. This is because any classification or regression algorithm can be evaluated using Fairlearn's metrics, regardless of the type of data it is operating on. Overall, Fairlearn is a versatile tool that can be used to help ensure fairness in ML models.

In the next section, we will discuss fairness metrics.

Fairness metrics

Fairness metrics are mathematical measures to determine whether the model is making unbiased predictions and treating all groups fairly. Microsoft Fairlearn provides several fairness metrics, including statistical parity, equal opportunity, equalized odds, predictive parity, and demographic parity, measures critical in promoting fairness in AI systems and ensuring that all groups are treated equally by AI models. Let's look at these metrics in more detail:

- **Demographic parity** aims to ensure that the predictions made by a model are independent of membership to a sensitive group. In other words, demographic parity is achieved when the probability of a certain prediction is not dependent on sensitive group membership. In the binary classification scenario, demographic parity refers to equal selection rates across groups. For example, in the context of a resume-screening model, equal selection would mean that the proportion of applicants selected for a job interview should be equal across groups.

  Demographic parity is an important fairness metric for ML models. It ensures that predictions made by the model are not biased based on membership to any sensitive groups. This allows for fairer treatment and assessment of individuals within those groups. To achieve demographic parity, it is important to ensure that selection rates (such as proportions chosen for interviews) are equal across all groups being considered.

- **Equalized odds** is a fairness metric for ML models that ensures the model performs equally well for different groups. This is accomplished by requiring the model to have the same false-positive rate and true-positive rate for all groups. Equalized odds do not create the selection issue discussed in the previous demographic parity section. For example, in the hiring scenario where the goal is to choose applicants from group A and group B, ensuring the model performs equally well at choosing applicants from group A and group B can circumvent the issue of the model optimizing by selecting randomly from one group.

- **Equal opportunity** is a term that is used in the US to describe the idea that everyone should have an equal chance to succeed, regardless of their race, gender, or other personal characteristics. The concept of equal opportunity has been used in many different settings, including education, employment, and housing. The idea of equal opportunity is based on the belief that all people are deserving of fair treatment and should not be discriminated against on the basis of factors such as race or gender. This principle has led to a number of initiatives aimed at ensuring equality of opportunity for all Americans. For example, affirmative action programs are designed to help members of groups who have historically faced discrimination get access to education and jobs. In addition, laws prohibiting discrimination in education and employment help ensure that everyone has a level playing field when it comes time to compete for opportunities.

While the concept of equal opportunity is important for ensuring fairness in society, it is not always easy to achieve. There can be disagreement about which factors should be considered when determining whether someone has had an equal chance at success. Additionally, some people may believe that they deserve special treatment because they come from a group that has been disadvantaged in the past.

In the following section, we will delve into the critical issue of fairness-related harms, exploring how biases can negatively impact AI systems and discussing potential strategies for mitigating these risks to ensure equitable outcomes for all users.

Fairness-related harms

There are a number of types of harm that can be caused by AI systems when their creators have failed to take fairness into account. Fairness-related harms refer to the various types of negative impacts that result from AI systems when fairness considerations are not properly addressed during their design and development. These can include unequal distribution of benefits and drawbacks, unequal QoS, and perpetuation of harmful stereotypes and biases. Also, AI harms overlap because systems often cause multiple forms of harm simultaneously.

Let's now discuss some key negative consequences that may occur when fairness is not considered during the design and development of AI systems:

- **Allocation harms** refer to the negative consequences that occur when AI systems provide or restrict access to opportunities, resources, or information. This leads to unequal treatment and prejudice against certain demographic groups, negatively impacting their ability to secure employment or educational opportunities in areas such as hiring, school admissions, and lending. Allocation harm is a result of discrimination and can have a significant impact on the affected individuals or groups. An example of allocation harm is when an AI system is used in the hiring process to screen job applicants, and it provides a biased assessment that unfairly excludes certain groups of people, such as women or minorities, from being considered for the job. We have seen examples of this in earlier chapters. This can result in discrimination against these groups and negatively impact their ability to obtain employment. Another example is when an AI system is used in the process of granting loans, and it provides unequal access to credit based on factors such as race or gender, leading to unequal distribution of financial resources and opportunities.

- **QoS harms** occur when a system provides inconsistent performance to different users, even in the absence of unequal access to opportunities, resources, or information—it's like being stuck in a slow lane while everyone else speeds by! Some examples of such biased systems include facial recognition technology, document search engines, and product recommendation services. For instance, unfair facial recognition technology, potentially due to the training dataset, may have lower accuracy for certain racial or ethnic groups, leading to unequal treatment. Similarly, biased document search engines may provide different results based on factors such as race, gender, or location, resulting in unequal access to information. Flawed and biased product recommendation services may also provide different recommendations to different users based on their purchasing history—this ultimately leads to unequal access to products and services. Over the years, we have witnessed six unfair healthcare diagnosis systems providing different diagnoses to different patients based on their demographic information, leading to unequal access to healthcare services.

- **Stereotyping harms** can occur when a system suggests completions that perpetuate stereotypes. These are often seen when search engines propose completions to partially typed queries. Stereotyping harms reinforce existing biases and prejudices against certain groups of people, which can lead to further discrimination. These stereotyping harms manifest themselves in areas such as image recognition, criminal justice, advertising, and education.

- **Erasure harm** is another type of harm that occurs when a system behaves as if groups don't exist. Erasure harm is prevalent among marginalized communities who are already at a disadvantage. AI systems can cause harm in many ways beyond allocation, QoS, stereotyping, and erasure— privacy, physical, psychological, economic, and political harms can occur. Different types of AI harms can overlap because the same system can contribute to multiple forms of harm since a biased AI system can cause both stereotyping and allocation harm. This highlights the importance of awareness and considering multiple forms of harm when designing AI systems.

In the upcoming section, we will provide you with a comprehensive guide to using the Fairlearn library, an essential tool for understanding and mitigating unfairness in AI systems, and walk you through the initial steps to begin your journey toward fairer ML models.

Getting started with Fairlearn

Microsoft's approach to fairness falls under the broader context of responsible AI where the fairness tenet accompanies characteristic features such as reliability and safety, privacy and security, inclusiveness, and transparency and accountability aspects. Fairlearn recognizes fairness as a sociotechnical problem and provides tools for evaluating fairness issues and mitigating them. It mainly comprises two key components, as follows:

- **Metrics** that measure how the model negatively impacts different groups and can be used to perform a comparative analysis in terms of various aspects of fairness and accuracy

- **Algorithms** for mitigating unfairness in various AI tasks and based on different definitions of fairness

The Fairlearn library consists of multiple packages—essentially, the modules for mitigating fairness-related harms in AI systems, including datasets, metrics, postprocessing, preprocessing, reductions, and experimental methods. Let's look at these in more detail:

- `fairlearn.datasets`: Provides a collection of datasets for use in fairness experiments and evaluations

- `fairlearn.metrics`: Provides a suite of metrics for evaluating fairness in AI systems

- `fairlearn.postprocessing`: Provides techniques for postprocessing ML models to mitigate fairness-related harms

- `fairlearn.preprocessing`: Provides techniques for preprocessing data to mitigate fairness-related harms in ML models

- `fairlearn.reductions`: Provides techniques for reducing fairness-related harms in ML models, including fairness constraints and adversarial training

- `fairlearn.experimental`: Provides experimental and **proof-of-concept** techniques for mitigating fairness-related harms in AI systems

You will read about these metrics and algorithms in detail in the next section, but let's first get our hands dirty. Getting started with Fairlearn is quite easy. Using a package manager such as `pip`, you can run the following command on the terminal:

```
pip install fairlearn
```

This Python command will install the `fairlearn` package, the first step toward ensuring fair and unbiased AI systems. This will result in the following screen:

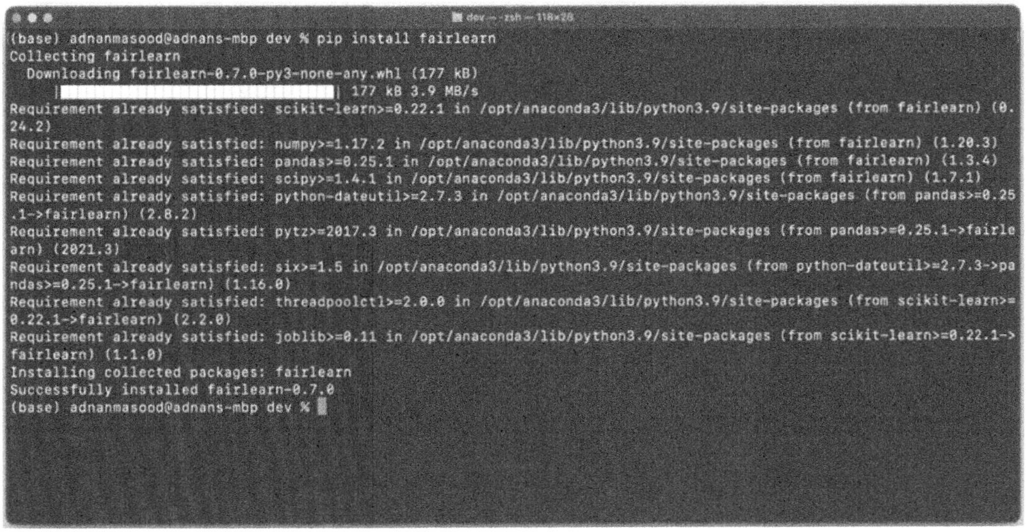

Figure 8.1: Installation of the Fairlearn package

Once the package is installed, you can view it by typing the `pip show fairlearn` command, which shows a summary of the package, version, and underlying dependencies, as shown in the following screenshot:

Figure 8.2: Details of the Fairlearn package

At this point, you can run the Fairlearn package instructions from Anaconda, VS Code, or the editor of your choice. Let's start with a simple program. In the following screenshot, we import the *UCI Adult* dataset (also known as the census income dataset) using an OpenML library by calling `sklearn.datasets.fetch_openml`:

```
1 import numpy as np
2 import pandas as pd
3 import matplotlib.pyplot as plt
4 from sklearn.datasets import fetch_openml
5
6 data = fetch_openml(data_id=1590, as_frame=True)
7 X = pd.get_dummies(data.data)
8 y_true = (data.target == '>50K') * 1
9 sex = data.data['sex']
10 sex.value_counts()

Male      32650
Female    16192
Name: sex, dtype: int64
```

Figure 8.3: Code – retrieving the dataset

The dataset can be retrieved from `openml` by its name or ID. A dataset can be uniquely identified using an integer ID or by its name and version (for example, there may be multiple versions of a dataset called *iris*). If you can give either a name or `data_id` value, that would be great (not both). If a name is given, a version can also be provided. In `scikit-learn`, these datasets are useful for quickly illustrating how a variety of algorithms work. Nevertheless, they are often too small to represent real-world ML tasks. The following is a list of toy datasets in OpenML:

`load_boston(*[, return_X_y])`	DEPRECATED: load_boston is deprecated in 1.0 and will be removed in 1.2.
`load_iris(*[, return_X_y, as_frame])`	Load and return the iris dataset (classification).
`load_diabetes(*[, return_X_y, as_frame, scaled])`	Load and return the diabetes dataset (regression).
`load_digits(*[, n_class, return_X_y, as_frame])`	Load and return the digits dataset (classification).
`load_linnerud(*[, return_X_y, as_frame])`	Load and return the physical exercise Linnerud dataset.
`load_wine(*[, return_X_y, as_frame])`	Load and return the wine dataset (classification).
`load_breast_cancer(*[, return_X_y, as_frame])`	Load and return the breast cancer wisconsin dataset (classification).

Figure 8.4: List of toy datasets in OpenML

And here is a list of real-world datasets in OpenML:

fetch_olivetti_faces(*[, data_home, ...])	Load the Olivetti faces data-set from AT&T (classification).
fetch_20newsgroups(*[, data_home, subset, ...])	Load the filenames and data from the 20 newsgroups dataset (classification).
fetch_20newsgroups_vectorized(*[, subset, ...])	Load and vectorize the 20 newsgroups dataset (classification).
fetch_lfw_people(*[, data_home, funneled, ...])	Load the Labeled Faces in the Wild (LFW) people dataset (classification).
fetch_lfw_pairs(*[, subset, data_home, ...])	Load the Labeled Faces in the Wild (LFW) pairs dataset (classification).
fetch_covtype(*[, data_home, ...])	Load the covertype dataset (classification).
fetch_rcv1(*[, data_home, subset, ...])	Load the RCV1 multilabel dataset (classification).
fetch_kddcup99(*[, subset, data_home, ...])	Load the kddcup99 dataset (classification).
fetch_california_housing(*[, data_home, ...])	Load the California housing dataset (regression).

Figure 8.5: List of real-world datasets in OpenML

By running the preceding code, you will get the following result, which shows the distribution of the data based on gender:

```
Male      32650
Female    16192
Name: sex, dtype: int64
```

Figure 8.6: Gender distribution in data by running the previous code listing

Now that the data is loaded, we can start training the model to make the predictions. In this case, we will predict whether income exceeds $50K per annum. In the following code block, you can see that *lines 5-7* initiate the decision tree classifier, and *line 8* creates a frame for the accuracy metric, with the sensitive feature being `sex`:

```
1 from fairlearn.metrics import MetricFrame
2 from sklearn.metrics import accuracy_score
3 from sklearn.tree import DecisionTreeClassifier
4
5 classifier = DecisionTreeClassifier(min_samples_leaf=10, max_depth=4)
6 classifier.fit(X, y_true)
7 y_pred = classifier.predict(X)
8 gm = MetricFrame(metrics=accuracy_score, y_true=y_true, y_pred=y_pred, sensitive_features=sex)
9 print(gm.overall)
10 print(gm.by_group)
```

Figure 8.7: Code – listing to show the decision tree classifier and metric

In the previous code listing, we are using the `metric` package to create a frame for our accuracy metric. The definition of a metric in Fairlearn is the `f(y_true, y_pred, ... )` function, where `y_true` refers to the true values (ground truth) and `y_pred` refers to the ML predictions. Calculation of the metric may be influenced by other factors (usually sample weights).

Disaggregated metrics are provided in this module. This metric includes information about group membership in addition to `y_true` and `y_pred` values. The disaggregated metric, for example, would show separate results for male, female, and non-binary subgroups identified in the gender column. These three subgroups are evaluated with respect to the underlying `metric` function. The metric is calculated for each combination of subgroups, extending to multiple grouping columns.

Fairlearn takes a group fairness approach that asks: *Which groups are at risk?* It is important to note that sensitive features (or sensitive attributes) are used to define relevant groups (also called subpopulations) that are passed to a Fairlearn estimator as a vector or matrix called `sensitive_features` (even if it only consists of one feature). In assessing group fairness, the system designer should consider these features. Even though some of these characteristics may affect privacy (for example, gender or age), others may not (for example, native language proficiency). As a result, the word *sensitive* does not mean that these features shouldn't be used for prediction—in fact, using these features may even be advantageous in some cases.

The term *protected attribute* is also used in the fairness literature in a similar way to the term *sensitive feature*. There are specific protected classes defined by anti-discrimination laws. The term *group fairness* is avoided because we aim to apply it to a broader range of contexts.

```
sensitive_features (List, pandas.Series, dict of 1d arrays, numpy.
ndarray, pandas.DataFrame)
```

By running the preceding code, we get the following output, which shows the accuracy predictions by gender, and the disparity is easily noticeable:

```
0.8443552680070431
sex
Female     0.925148
Male       0.804288
Name: accuracy_score, dtype: object
```

Figure 8.8: Running the code listing shows the accuracy score based on gender

Similar to the accuracy score, Fairlearn supports a selection rate metric that calculates the fraction of predicted labels matching the "good" outcome. The following screenshot shows the selection rate by group:

```
1 from fairlearn.metrics import selection_rate
2 sr = MetricFrame(metrics=selection_rate, y_true=y_true, y_pred=y_pred, sensitive_features=sex)
3 sr.overall
4 sr.by_group
5

sex
Female    0.06355
Male      0.213599
Name: selection_rate, dtype: object
```

Figure 8.9: Code – printing the selection rate for gender

You can select these metrics one by one, or combine and print them as shown with the code in the following screenshot, which prints accuracy, precision, fprate, fnrate, selection rate, and count:

```
1 from fairlearn.metrics import MetricFrame, selection_rate, false_positive_rate, false_negative_rate, count
2 from sklearn.metrics import accuracy_score, precision_score
3
4 metrics = {
5     "accuracy": accuracy_score,
6     "precision": precision_score,
7     "false positive rate": false_positive_rate,
8     "false negative rate": false_negative_rate,
9     "selection rate": selection_rate,
10    "count": count,
11 }
12 metric_frame = MetricFrame(
13     metrics=metrics, y_true=y_true, y_pred=y_pred, sensitive_features=sex
14 )
15 metric_frame.by_group.plot.bar(
16     subplots=True,
17     layout=[3, 3],
18     legend=False,
19     figsize=[12, 8],
20     title="Fairlearn Metrics",
21 )
22
```

Figure 8.10: Code – printing Fairlearn metrics

Upon running the code, you would see all the fairness metrics, as shown in the following screenshot:

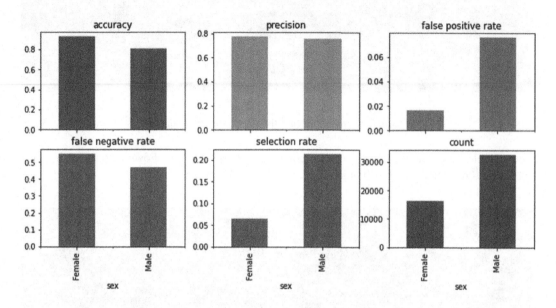

Figure 8.11: Fairlearn fairness metrics

Now that we have analyzed and reviewed the data, and considered the underlying disparity, the next step is mitigation. Fairlearn contains the Exponentiated Gradient, Grid Search, Threshold Optimizer, and Correlation Remover algorithms for bias mitigation. In this case, we will use exponentiated gradient reduction, which is a cost-sensitive method for mitigating bias. This algorithm is composed of two reductions aiming to find the classifier with the lowest error based on the constraints. Exponentiated gradient reduction is only intended for binary classifications. A statistical parity metric and equalized odds metric are considered when optimizing fairness since the goal is to optimize fairness in the models so that they provide equal treatment and equal outcomes for all users.

While mitigating bias, the creation of a new model with a fairness constraint may be appropriate if we observe disparities between groups. For a model to be effective, fairness constraints must be chosen carefully, and their nature varies through the application context. In this case, we use demographic parity, which aims to ensure that the predictions made by a model are independent of membership of a sensitive group. Using the demographic parity fairness constraint, we can attempt to mitigate the observed disparity in this contrived example if we consider the selection rate highly relevant to fairness. When making such decisions in reality, we need to keep the sociotechnical context in mind:

```
1 from fairlearn.reductions import ExponentiatedGradient, DemographicParity
2 from fairlearn.metrics import MetricFrame
3 from sklearn.tree import DecisionTreeClassifier
4
5 np.random.seed(0)  # set seed for consistent results with ExponentiatedGradient
6 import warnings
7 with warnings.catch_warnings():
8   constraint = DemographicParity()
9   classifier = DecisionTreeClassifier(min_samples_leaf=10, max_depth=4)
10   mitigator = ExponentiatedGradient(classifier, constraint)
11   mitigator.fit(X, y_true, sensitive_features=sex)
12
13   y_pred_mitigated = mitigator.predict(X)
14   sr_mitigated = MetricFrame(metrics=selection_rate, y_true=y_true,
15                              y_pred=y_pred_mitigated, sensitive_features=sex)
16   print(sr_mitigated.overall)
17   print(sr_mitigated.by_group)
18
```

Figure 8.12: Code for mitigation of bias

As you can see, using an exponentiated gradient mitigation technique, the classifier has a vastly reduced selection rate difference when demographic parity is used as the objective. In addition to demographic parity and equalized odds, Fairlearn also supports worst-case accuracy and **mean squared error** (MSE) metrics for regression. Various metrics can be used to quantify fairness with respect to groups of people based on sensitive characteristics such as gender, age, or disability status. Also, in order to assess the fairness of a model, the user selects the sensitive feature (for example, "sex" or "age") to be used as a criterion and the performance metric (for instance, accuracy rate) that will be used. You can see the output here:

```
    lambda_event = (lambda_vec["+"] - se
0.16614798738790384
sex
Female    0.155262
Male      0.171547
Name: selection_rate, dtype: object
```

Figure 8.13: Output after the bias mitigation

Running the code after mitigation demonstrates that the selection rate is now fairly equal between males and females, and therefore bias has been heavily mitigated. ML has been found to suffer from opaqueness debt, which manifests itself as increasing discrimination risks, reproducibility issues, and performance issues. In this case, you saw the mitigation working; however, due to the sociotechnical nature of fairness in AI, no software tool will be able to resolve every issue related to fairness.

As a result of Fairlearn's fairness metrics and interactive dashboard, it is possible to identify which groups might be negatively impacted by a model. Meanwhile, the fairness mitigation algorithms allow classification and regression models to be fairer by mitigating unfairness. The Fairlearn initiative cannot address all aspects of fairness. Stereotyping, denigration, and over- or underrepresentation harms, for instance, cannot be mitigated through Fairlearn (except indirectly, if they are caused by allocation or QoS harms). Moreover, Fairlearn does not emphasize justice or due process, which are broader societal elements of fairness.

Summary

In this chapter, we saw that the Fairlearn toolkit is a comprehensive open source tool for assessing and improving the fairness of AI systems built by data scientists and developers. We established that it is essential for good MLOps practices to be able to validate the performance of models, explain how they work, and monitor their performance continuously in order to address these issues. As AI regulations and laws emerge, there is a need for deeper model transparency. The chapter provided an overview of the importance of fairness in AI systems. We started by discussing the concept of fairness and the various types of fairness-related harms that could occur in AI systems, then introduced the Fairlearn toolkit to help data scientists and AI practitioners promote fairness in their models. The Fairlearn toolkit includes a range of fairness metrics that could be used to assess the level of fairness in a model, and a variety of tools and techniques for mitigating fairness-related harms. We provided installation instructions and a step-by-step tutorial on using the toolkit to promote fairness in ML models.

In Fairlearn, a visualization dashboard and algorithms for mitigating unfairness are both included. Model performance and fairness can be balanced with these components. Fairness is a sociotechnical challenge in AI systems. AI systems are indeed susceptible to various sources of bias and unfairness, both societal and technical in nature. The objective is to mitigate fairness-related harms. The Fairlearn framework is designed and intended to be shaped by a diverse community of stakeholders, including data scientists, developers, and business leaders. The package continually evolves to incorporate additional fairness metrics, algorithms for fairness mitigation, and visualization capabilities.

The Fairlearn framework invites researchers, practitioners, and other stakeholders to contribute their expertise in the form of fairness metrics, algorithms for mitigating unfairness, and visualization tools to enhance the system. The goal of Fairlearn is to promote fairness in AI by providing a platform for experimentation and learning. Fairlearn currently supports group fairness, which pertains to groups of people defined by race, gender, age, or disability status. In the future, Fairlearn plans to expand its capabilities to support other concepts of fairness such as individual fairness or counterfactual fairness.

There is no doubt that there are a wide variety of areas that will need to be enhanced and developed in the future. As one example, Fairlearn is currently only capable of supporting "group fairness"—in other words, fairness pertaining to groups of people. Rather than other concepts of fairness such as individual fairness or counterfactual fairness, groups are defined based on race, gender, age, or disability status. It is often difficult to arrive at clear-cut solutions when prioritizing fairness in AI. Consequently, those assumptions and priorities must be expressed explicitly and transparently. Fairness cannot be defined universally, as it will vary according to the circumstances. By selecting a fairness metric that is suitable for their setting, managing trade-offs between fairness and model performance, and choosing an algorithm that minimizes unfairness, Fairlearn allows data scientists and developers to minimize unfairness in their workflows. Users can compare multiple models according to their fairness and performance through Fairlearn's interactive visualization dashboard by assessing which groups of people might be negatively affected by the model and comparing the performance and fairness of multiple models. Both classification and regression tasks can be assessed with Fairlearn's fairness metrics, of which there are a wide range.

Although it is important to note that Fairlearn currently only includes three algorithms for reducing unfairness (one postprocessing algorithm and two reduction algorithms), these algorithms are not restricted to classification tasks. Moreover, we look forward to Fairlearn being extended to cover more complex ML tasks, such as counterfactual reasoning, **computer vision** (**CV**), and **natural language processing** (**NLP**), and to include fairness metrics, conceptualizations of fairness, and algorithms for reducing unfairness. As well as Fairlearn, InterpretML and other interpretability tools will be integrated into Fairlearn.

As a user of Fairlearn, you become part of a community built and maintained by open source contributors with diverse backgrounds and expertise. As with other open source tools with community support, Fairlearn is evolving into a thriving resource where not only code is available, but also a wealth of resources such as domain-specific guides on how and when to use fairness metrics and unfairness mitigation algorithms. In the next chapter, we will delve into the practical application of Fairlearn in a real-world scenario with a practical example. We will evaluate fairness-related metrics to assess the level of fairness and explore the use of Fairlearn for bias and disparity mitigation. In an attempt to showcase a hands-on, step-by-step guide to using Fairlearn for promoting fairness in AI systems, the next chapter will also demonstrate how Fairlearn can be used in Jupyter notebooks and provide an overview of the Fairlearn dashboard.

References and further reading

1. The seminal paper *The Unreasonable Effectiveness of Data*, by *Alon Halevy, Peter Norvig*, and *Fernando Pereira*, argues that the availability of large datasets can lead to highly accurate predictions or models, even with relatively simple algorithms. The authors give examples from various fields to demonstrate the power of data in driving effective solutions. They suggest that future AI systems will likely depend heavily on large amounts of data and that data will continue to play a crucial role in shaping the future of AI and other fields.

2. `https://news.mit.edu/2022/artificial-intelligence-predicts-patients-race-from-medical-images-0520`

3. The phenomenon of proxy or highly correlated features in ML is commonly referred to as "feature leakage," which can lead to biased or unfair predictions. These highly correlated features are sometimes referred to as confounding variables, surrogate features, hidden variables, indicator features, substitute features, stand-in features, derived features, or—my favorite—shadow features.

4. https://www.usatoday.com/story/tech/news/2016/04/22/amazon-same-day-delivery-less-likely-black-areas-report-says/83345684/

5. With a history of abuse in American medicine, Black patients struggle for equal access—*PBS*

6. *Microsoft Fairlearn (2021). Microsoft Fairlearn.* Retrieved from https://github.com/Microsoft/fairlearn.

7. *Microsoft Research (2021). Fairlearn: An Open-Source Toolkit for Fairness in Machine Learning.* Retrieved from https://www.microsoft.com/en-us/research/blog/fairlearn-an-open-source-toolkit-for-fairness-in-machine-learning/.

8. *InterpretML (2021). InterpretML.* Retrieved from https://github.com/interpretml/interpret.

9. *Microsoft AI (2021). Microsoft AI: Responsible AI.* Retrieved from https://www.microsoft.com/en-us/ai/responsible-ai.

10. *Microsoft AI (2021). Microsoft AI: Fairness.* Retrieved from https://www.microsoft.com/en-us/ai/fairness. *AI Now Institute. (2021).*

11. *Fairness in AI Systems.* Retrieved from https://ainowinstitute.org/fairness-in-ai.html.

## 9

Fairness Assessment and Bias Mitigation with Fairlearn and the Responsible AI Toolbox

"Research on bias, fairness, transparency, and the myriad dimensions of safety now forms a substantial portion of all of the work presented at major AI and machine-learning conferences."

– Aileen Nielsen, Practical Fairness: Achieving Fair and Secure Data Models

"If and when computer programs attain superhuman intelligence and unprecedented power, should we begin valuing these programs more than we value humans? ... Do humans have some magical spark, in addition to higher intelligence and greater power, which distinguishes them from pigs, chickens, chimpanzees, and computer programs alike? If yes, where did that spark come from, and why are we certain that an AI could never acquire it? If there is no such spark, would there be any reason to continue assigning special value to human life even after computers surpass humans in intelligence and power?"

– Yuval Noah Harari, Homo Deus: A Brief History of Tomorrow

With great power comes great responsibility – as cliched as it sounds, in today's business world, machine learning models are becoming increasingly important for data-driven decision-making.

As machine learning models have increasingly become used to build AI systems that make decisions for us in business and wider society, we have seen scenarios where they have made biased and unfair decisions for us. Perhaps the classic example of unfair AI decision-making in this context (there are sadly more) is using AI to review and sift through job applicants by automating the résumé review process[1]. It has been found that using such technologies to sift for (for example) a software engineering role yielded preferential selection for white males. Similarly, when automating the résumé sift for a nursing role, the AI unfairly preferred women. What we actually want in these scenarios is for the AI to recommend candidates purely based on their qualifications, relevant experience, and wider aptitude for the given job role, as interpreted by the AI using résumés.

As people being unfairly sifted out of recruitment processes has been increasingly recognized by AI users and reported in the media, the use of fairness methods and metrics to mitigate such biased decisions has increasingly been applied. At the heart of these methods is the principle that a machine learning model should make a selection independently of protected classes such as gender, ethnicity, and age.

Such fairness principles are one of the core elements of responsible AI. In this chapter, we will explore the tools and techniques available in the Responsible AI Toolbox, with a focus on Fairlearn, an open source library for assessing fairness and mitigating bias in machine learning. We will delve into the evaluation of fairness-related metrics and techniques for mitigating bias and disparity, using real-world scenarios. The toolbox offers user interfaces and libraries for model and data exploration and assessment, including the Responsible AI Dashboard, the Error Analysis Dashboard, the Interpretability Dashboard, and the Fairness Dashboard, powered by Fairlearn. Join us on this journey of exploring the exciting world of responsible AI, and learn how to ensure the fair and ethical use of machine learning models.

In this chapter, the reader will learn about the following:

- Fairness metrics
- Bias and disparity mitigation with Fairlearn
- Applying Fairlearn in the real-world scenarios
- Using the Responsible AI Toolbox and widgets
- Working with responsible AI, error analysis, interpretability, and fairness dashboards

By the end of this chapter, you will have a solid understanding of how to use the Responsible AI Toolbox and Fairlearn to ensure the fair and ethical use of machine learning models in your own work.

Fairness metrics

Fairness metrics are critical tools for ensuring that machine learning models are fair and unbiased. These measures allow for the evaluation of classification models and provide insights into whether certain groups are being unfairly favored or discriminated against. Demographic parity and equalized odds are two of the most widely used fairness metrics, both with their own unique approach to measuring fairness. By using these metrics, organizations can better understand how their models perform and take steps to address any biases that may exist.

Demographic parity

Demographic parity is a fairness metric that compares the predictions made between different groups, ignoring the actual true values. This metric is useful in cases where the input data is known to contain biases and the goal is to measure fairness. However, it is important to note that demographic parity only uses the predicted values and discards the information about the true values. It also uses a very coarse measure of the distribution between groups, making it difficult to use as an optimization constraint.

Let's consider a hypothetical machine learning model used to approve loans. Let's say we have two demographic groups, A and B, with the following characteristics:

- **Group A**: 1,000 applicants and 200 approved loans
- **Group B**: 500 applicants and 150 approved loans

To evaluate demographic parity, we first need to determine that the crude rates for groups A and B have parity for comparison by giving them a shared baseline, the "rate per X," where X is an appropriate constant number of events. In this instance, we will have a baseline constant of 1,000 applications. We will then progress to determine 95% confidence intervals for the loan approval rates[2] (using an approximation of 1.96 for the z-score of a two-sided 95% hypothesis test[3]) from each of group A and group B, and then determine whether there is any overlap between the two confidence intervals:

For group A:

Approval rate per 1,000 applications $= \left(\frac{200}{1,000}\right) 1,000 = 200$ *approvals per 1,000 applications*

Upper control limit $= \left(\frac{1,000}{1,000}\right)(200 + 1.96\sqrt{2}\,00) = 227.72$ *approvals per 1,000 applications*

Lower control limit $= \left(\frac{1,000}{1,000}\right)(200 - 1.96\sqrt{2}\,00) = 172.28$ *approvals per 1,000 applications*

For group B:

Approval rate per 1,000 applications $= \left(\frac{150}{500}\right) 1,000 = 300$ *approvals per 1,000 applications*

Lower control limit $= \left(\frac{1,000}{500}\right)(150 + 1.96\sqrt{1}\,50) = 348.00$ *approvals per 1,000 applications*

Lower control limit $= \left(\frac{1,000}{500}\right)(150 - 1.96\sqrt{1}\,50) = 252.00$ *approvals per 1,000 applications*

Demographic parity is achieved when the loan approval rates are equal across demographic groups – in this example, given that the confidence intervals for the approval rates of groups A and B are (172.28, 227.72) and (252.00, 348.00) respectively. Given the lack of overlap between these two intervals, we can conclude at a significance level of 5% that the rates for group A and group B are not equal; thus, demographic parity is not satisfied.

Equalized odds

Equalized odds is a fairness metric that compares the true and false positive rates between different groups. This metric is appropriate to use when historical data does not contain measurement or historical biases, and true and false positives are considered to be of roughly the same importance.

Mayer and Wilber provide a detailed example of deriving equalized odds[4]. They also discuss and illustrate its limitations, showing there will only be certain scenarios where equalized odds between true and false positive rates can be obtained, and that these scenarios are generally a trade-off between achieving greater equality and the predictive power of the model.

At the time of writing, we consider equalized odds to be a fairness metric that has utility in terms of providing guidance on how equal a model is across different demographic groups but also that it has limitations. As model fairness methods and associated metrics continue to be researched and developed, we think this method will continue to evolve.

Simpson's paradox and the risks of multiple testing

A word of caution on demographic parity and equalized odds, and on fairness methods and metrics in general. Simpson's paradox is the term given to the capacity for a trend apparent in data at lower-level demographic groups to reverse or disappear when this data is grouped.[5] This can have implications for the conclusions we draw from the previous three tests. For example, when testing fairness for a recruitment process at a summary level for gender, if the recruitment process is for multiple different job roles, Simpson's paradox shows us it will also be important to test gender fairness at each job role level.

Another challenge here is that running statistical tests over groups or subgroups of the same dataset increases the likelihood of yielding a false positive.[6] It is important to be aware of this risk when conducting fairness tests – to interpret the results of multiple tests with caution and, better still, to design the testing framework so the likelihood of such confounding is minimized.

Bias and disparity mitigation with Fairlearn

Fairlearn provides several ways to perform bias and disparity mitigation for real-world problems:

- **Post-processing methods**: This involves adjusting the predictions made by a machine learning model after it has been trained, to reduce bias and disparity. An example of this is the reject option classifier, which allows you to set a threshold for the prediction scores for certain sensitive features. If the threshold is exceeded, the classifier will reject the prediction and instead return a default label.

- **Pre-processing methods**: This involves transforming the data before training the machine learning model, to reduce bias and disparity. An example of this is `CorrelationRemover`, which adjusts the non-sensitive features to remove their correlation with the sensitive features, while retaining as much information as possible.

- **In-processing methods**: This involves modifying the training process of the machine learning model, to reduce bias and disparity. An example of this is the demographic parity regularizer, which adds a constraint to the training process that ensures demographic parity between the predictions made for different sensitive groups.

- **Model selection methods**: This involves selecting the appropriate machine learning model for your data, to reduce bias and disparity. An example of this is `ThresholdOptimizer`, which helps you select the appropriate threshold for a binary classifier, to ensure fairness in the predictions.

In the following example, we will demonstrate the use of a pre-processing bias mitigation method, `CorrelationRemover`.

Fairness in real-world scenarios

Feature bias, or feature-confounding bias, is a commonly found machine learning bias that refers to the idea that the features used to make predictions in a machine learning model can contain bias or be biased toward certain groups of individuals. This is also known as correlation bias, referring to the idea that the features used to make predictions can be highly correlated with a sensitive attribute, leading to unfair treatment of certain groups in the model's predictions.

The existence of correlation-related bias where the features used to make predictions are highly correlated with a sensitive attribute (e.g., race, gender, age, etc.) can be quite harmful, and this type of bias can lead to unfair treatment of certain groups of individuals in the model's predictions. For example, consider a model used to predict the likelihood of a loan applicant defaulting on their loan. If the model is trained on data that includes both the applicant's income and race, and the two features are highly correlated, the model may learn to use race as a proxy for income when making predictions. This could result in the model unfairly denying loans to applicants based on their race[6], even if they have a high income and would be at low risk of defaulting.

An obvious solution to avoiding such bias could be to remove the protected classes or sensitive attributes from the modeling process. However, in many situations, these protected classes are some of the key predictors of the given outcome. For example, in a healthcare scenario, high levels of patient deprivation are correlated with high levels of patient comorbidities and poorer health outcomes. While you could remove patient deprivation as a model feature to avoid feature bias, machine learning models typically have greater predictive power when it is included.

Mitigating correlation-related bias

To mitigate correlation-related bias, it's important to carefully preprocess data and remove any features that are highly correlated with the sensitive attribute. In addition, techniques such as reweighting the data or modifying the model's architecture can be used to mitigate bias in the model's predictions. The use of fairness assessment tools, such as those provided by Fairlearn, can also help identify and mitigate correlation-related bias.

`CorrelationRemover` is a feature selection algorithm provided by the Fairlearn library to mitigate correlation-related bias in machine learning models. The algorithm removes features from data that are highly correlated with a sensitive attribute, which can cause unfair treatment of certain groups of individuals in a model's predictions.

To demonstrate the removal of highly correlated features, we will use `CorrelationRemover`. The library is used to identify and remove features that are highly correlated with a sensitive attribute, while retaining as much relevant information as possible. This helps to reduce the risk of correlation-related bias in a model's predictions, and it ensures that the model is fair and free from bias. To use `CorrelationRemover`, you simply pass the data and the sensitive attribute to the algorithm, and Fairlearn automatically removes any features that are highly correlated with the sensitive attribute. The preprocessed data can then be used to train the machine learning model, and the model's fairness can be reevaluated to ensure that the changes were successful:

```
# Import necessary libraries
import numpy as np import pandas as pd
import matplotlib.pyplot as plt


# Import the diabetes hospital dataset from Fairlearn library
from fairlearn.datasets import fetch_diabetes_hospital


# Import the CorrelationRemover class from the preprocessing module of
Fairlearn library
from fairlearn.preprocessing import CorrelationRemover
```

Here, we import the necessary libraries and the classes needed to remove correlation-related bias from the data. The `fetch_diabetes_hospital` function from the Fairlearn library is used to retrieve the diabetes hospital dataset, which will be used as an example. The `CorrelationRemover` class from the preprocessing module of the Fairlearn library will be used to remove features that are highly correlated with the sensitive attribute.

How does the CorrelationRemover algorithm work?

The `CorrelationRemover` algorithm works by transforming non-sensitive features in data to remove their correlation with a sensitive feature. This is achieved by applying a linear transformation to the non-sensitive features. The linear transformation is selected such that it minimizes the least-squares error, which measures the difference between the original and transformed features. The goal of this transformation is to retain as much information as possible while removing the correlation between the non-sensitive and sensitive features. This helps to reduce the risk of correlation-related bias in the predictions made by the machine learning model. Once the transformation is applied, the transformed data can be used to train a machine learning model. The model's fairness can then be reevaluated to ensure that the changes were successful:

```
# Retrieve the diabetes hospital dataset from Fairlearn library
diabetes_data = fetch_diabetes_hospital()
```

```
# Select the relevant features from the dataset: race, time in
hospital,
# inpatient days, and medicare coverage
raw_features = diabetes_data.data[["race", "time_in_hospital","had_
inpatient_days", "medicare"]]

# Convert categorical features into numerical features using one-hot
encoding
raw_features = pd.get_dummies(raw_features)

# Select the target column
target = diabetes_data.target

# Remove features that are not relevant for the analysis
raw_features = raw_features.drop(
["race_Asian", "race_Caucasian", "race_Hispanic", "race_Other","race_
Unknown","had_inpatient_days_False", "medicare_False"], axis=1)

# Select only the relevant features for the analysis
selected_features = raw_features[[
"time_in_hospital", "had_inpatient_days_True", "medicare_True", "race_
AfricanAmerican"]]
```

This code retrieves the diabetes hospital dataset from the Fairlearn library and selects the relevant features for analysis. The categorical features are then converted into numerical features using one-hot encoding[8]. The target column is selected, and the irrelevant features are removed. Only the relevant features are selected for the analysis. The selected features include time spent in the hospital, inpatient days, medicare coverage, and race (African American).

At this point, we can use the `CorrelationRemover` class to remove the correlation between the features and the sensitive feature (being African-American). The `fit_transform` method is used to fit `CorrelationRemover` to the data and transform the features. The transformed data is then converted into a Pandas DataFrame with appropriate column names, and the sensitive feature is added back to the data:

```
# Initialize the CorrelationRemover with the sensitive feature:
African American race
correlation_remover = CorrelationRemover(sensitive_feature_
ids=["race_AfricanAmerican"])
# Fit the CorrelationRemover to the data and transform the features
correlated_removed = correlation_remover.fit_transform(selected_
features)
# Convert the transformed data into a Pandas DataFrame with #
appropriate column names
correlated_removed = pd.DataFrame(
```

```
correlated_removed,  columns=["time_in_hospital","had_inpatient_days_
True",
"medicare_True"])
# Add the sensitive feature back to the transformed data
correlated_removed["race_AfricanAmerican"]  = selected_features["race_
AfricanAmerican"]
# Initialize the CorrelationRemover with alpha=0.5 and the #sensitive
feature:  AfricanAmerican race
correlation_remover_alpha  =  CorrelationRemover(sensitive_feature_ids
["race_AfricanAmerican"],  alpha=0.5)
# Fit the CorrelationRemover to the data and transform the features
with alpha=0.5
correlated_removed_alpha  = correlation_remover_alpha.fit_
transform(selected_features)
```

The second block of code performs the same operation but, this time, with a different value of alpha. The alpha parameter controls the trade-off between removing the correlation and retaining the information in the features. A value of alpha equal to 0.5 balances these two objectives.

> **Note**
>
> In the `CorrelationRemover` class, `alpha` is a hyperparameter that controls the trade-off between removing the correlation between the features and the sensitive feature and retaining the information in `features`. `alpha`, which can be set to a value between 0 and 1, where a value of 0 corresponds to removing all correlation and retaining the least amount of information, and a value of 1 corresponds to retaining all correlation and retaining the most information. A value of `alpha` equal to 0.5 balances these two objectives and is a good starting point for many problems.

`CorrelationRemover` can now be used to effectively eliminate the correlation between the `"race_AfricanAmerican"` feature and the other features, even though the initial correlation was not particularly high. By using a lower value of alpha, not all of the correlation will be removed, allowing for some correlation to remain between the features:

```
import matplotlib.pyplot as plt import numpy as np
import pandas as pd
def plot_correlation_heatmap(df, title):
"""
Plot a heatmap of the correlation values in a Pandas DataFrame.
Parameters:
df (Pandas DataFrame): the data to plot title (str): the title of the
plot
"""
# Add the target column to the data
df["target"]  =  y
```

```
# Rename columns for clarity
df = df.rename(columns={"had_inpatient_days_True":
'→ "had_inpatient_days"})
# Get a list of the column names
cols = list(df.columns)
# Initialize the plot
fig, ax = plt.subplots(figsize=(8, 6))
# Plot the heatmap of the correlation values
ax.imshow(round(df.corr(), 2), cmap="coolwarm")
# Show all ticks and label them with the respective list entries
    ax.set_xticks(np.arange(len(cols)), labels=cols)
    ax.set_yticks(np.arange(len(cols)), labels=cols)

# Rotate the tick labels and set their alignment
plt.setp(ax.get_xticklabels(), rotation=15, ha="right",
'→ rotation_mode="anchor")
# Loop over data dimensions and create text annotations
for i in range(len(cols)):
for j in range(len(cols)):
ax.text(j,i,
round(df.corr().to_numpy()[i, j], 2),
ha="center",
va="center",
)
# Set the title of the plot
ax.set_title(f"{title}")
```

The following code shows the plot and heatmap:

```
plt.show()
# Plot the correlation heatmap for the original dataset
plot_correlation_heatmap(X_raw, "Correlation values in the original
'→ dataset")

# Plot the correlation heatmap for the data after
'→ CorrelationRemover
plot_correlation_heatmap(X_cr, "Correlation values after
'→ CorrelationRemover")
# Plot the correlation heatmap for the data after CorrelationRemover
'→ with alpha=0.5
plot_correlation_heatmap(X_cr_alpha, "Correlation values after
'→ CorrelationRemover
with alpha=0.5")
```

The preceding code defines a function, `plot_correlation_heatmap`, that plots a heatmap of the correlation values in a Pandas DataFrame. The function takes a DataFrame and a title as input, adds the target column to the data, renames columns for clarity, and plots the heatmap of the correlation values. The plot shows the correlation between all the features and the target column.

The code then calls the function three times, once for the original dataset, once for the data after `CorrelationRemover`, and once for the data after `CorrelationRemover` with `alpha=0.5`. The resulting plots allow you to visually compare the correlation values in each of these datasets.

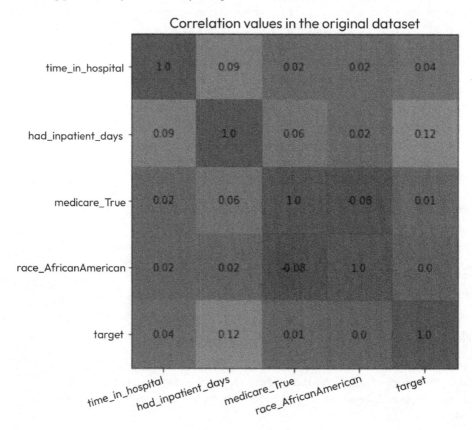

Figure 9.1: Values indicating correlation within the initial dataset

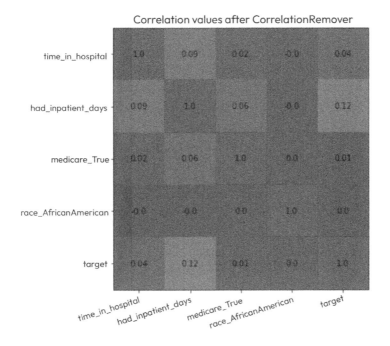

Figure 9.2: Correlation values following the use of CorrelationRemover

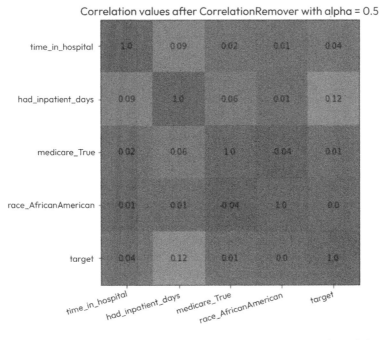

Figure 9.3: The correlation values after applying CorrelationRemover with an alpha value of 0.5

In this example, we demonstrated the use of the `CorrelationRemover` class from the Fairlearn library to remove correlation-related bias in a real-world dataset. Using heatmap visualizations, we showed that the class was effective in removing the correlation between the sensitive feature, `"race_AfricanAmerican"`, and the other features, while retaining the correlation between the other features. The example also highlighted the use of the alpha hyperparameter to control the trade-off between removing the correlation and retaining the information in the features.

This (almost) real-world example showcased how the `CorrelationRemover` class can be used to reduce correlation-related bias in machine learning models, ensuring that predictions are made based on relevant information and not on sensitive features.

The Responsible AI Toolbox

The Responsible AI Toolbox[9] provides a range of tools and user interfaces to help developers and stakeholders of AI systems to better understand and monitor AI systems. The concept of responsible AI refers to a method of creating, evaluating, and using AI systems in a safe, ethical, and trustworthy way, making informed decisions, and taking responsible actions.

The toolbox includes four visualization widgets to analyze and make decisions about AI models:

- **The Responsible AI dashboard** brings together various tools from the toolbox to provide a comprehensive view of responsible AI assessment and debugging. With this dashboard, you can identify model errors, understand why they happen, and take steps to address them. Additionally, the causal decision-making capabilities offer valuable insights to stakeholders and customers.

- **The Error Analysis dashboard** helps identify model errors and identifies groups of data where a model performs poorly.

- **The Interpretability dashboard**, powered by InterpretML, provides insight into the predictions made by AI models.

- **The Fairness dashboard**, powered by Fairlearn, is designed to help understand the fairness of AI models by using various group-fairness metrics across sensitive features and groups.

The Responsible AI dashboard

The Responsible AI dashboard is a comprehensive solution for assessing and monitoring AI systems in a responsible and ethical manner. With this tool, you can easily flow through various stages of model debugging and decision-making, from analyzing a model or data holistically to conducting a deep dive into specific cohorts of interest, explaining and perturbing model predictions for individual instances, and informing users about business decisions and actions.

The dashboard integrates several open source toolkits, each providing a different perspective on model and data assessment:

- The **Error Analysis** tool, powered by Error Analysis, identifies cohorts of data with higher error rates than the overall benchmark, which may occur when a system or model underperforms for specific demographic groups or there are infrequently observed input conditions in the training data

- The **Fairness Assessment** tool identifies which groups of people may be disproportionately negatively impacted by an AI system and in what ways

- The **Model Interpretability** tool, powered by InterpretML, explains black-box models, helping users understand the global behavior of their model or the reasons behind individual predictions

- The **Counterfactual Analysis** tool, powered by DiCE, shows feature-perturbed versions of the same data point and how they would receive a different prediction outcome

- The **Causal Analysis** tool, powered by EconML, focuses on answering "what-if"-style questions to apply data-driven decision-making – for example, how revenue would be affected if a corporation pursued a new pricing strategy or if a new medication improved a patient's condition

- The **Data Balance** tool, powered by Responsible AI, helps users gain an overall understanding of their data, identify features that receive a positive outcome more frequently, and visualize feature distributions

In our next example, we will use the `responsibleai` API to assess a model trained on census data. The API calls required to create a widget with model analysis insights are demonstrated, and visual analysis of the model is given as a guide:

```
# Import necessary packages
import zipfile
from sklearn.pipeline import Pipeline from sklearn.impute import
SimpleImputer
from sklearn.preprocessing import StandardScaler, OneHotEncoder from
sklearn.compose import ColumnTransformer
import pandas as pd
from lightgbm import LGBMClassifier
from raiutils.dataset import fetch dataset from raiwidgets import
ResponsibleAIDashboard from responsibleai import RAIInsights
from raiwidgets.cohort import Cohort, CohortFilter,
'→  CohortFilterMethods
# Split the target feature from the dataset
def  split_dataset(dataset,  target_feature):
X  =  dataset.drop([target_feature],  axis=1)
y  =  dataset[[target_feature]]
return X, y
# Create a pipeline for preprocessing and classification
```

```
def  create_classification_pipeline(X):
# Define the types of features (numeric/categorical)
pipe_cfg = {
'num_cols':  X.dtypes[X.dtypes  ==
'↪ 'int64'].index.values.tolist(),
'cat_cols':   X.dtypes[X.dtypes  ==
'↪ 'object'].index.values.tolist(),
}
# Numeric feature processing pipeline
num_pipe = Pipeline([
('num_imputer', SimpleImputer(strategy='median')),
('num_scaler',  StandardScaler())
])
# Categorical  feature  processing pipeline
cat_pipe = Pipeline([
('cat_imputer',   SimpleImputer(strategy='constant',
'↪ fill_value='?')),
('cat_encoder',   OneHotEncoder(handle_unknown='ignore',
'↪ sparse=False))
])

# Combine the pipelines using ColumnTransformer
feat_pipe = ColumnTransformer([
('num_pipe', num_pipe, pipe_cfg['num_cols']),
('cat_pipe',  cat_pipe,  pipe_cfg['cat_cols'])
])
# Final pipeline with preprocessor and classifier
pipeline  = Pipeline(steps=[('preprocessor',  feat_pipe),
('classifier',
'↪ LGBMClassifier(random_state=0))])

return pipeline
```

After defining the basic methods and pipelines, the next step is to load the census dataset and identify the different types of features. Once the feature types are specified, a pipeline can be composed, which includes a preprocessor and estimator. This pipeline will allow for data to be transformed and the model to be trained in a streamlined manner, ultimately leading to better accuracy and efficiency.

You may have noticed the chaining of steps in a pipeline, such as the one with `LGBMClassifier`. This is a machine learning model that uses gradient boosting to train decision trees. By chaining these two steps together in a pipeline, the pre-processing is applied first to the data before it is passed to the classifier for training. This can be a convenient way to organize the different steps of a machine learning workflow and to streamline the process of training and evaluating different models:

```
# Download the dataset and extract it
outdirname = 'responsibleai.12.28.21'
zipfilename = outdirname + '.zip'
        fetch_dataset('https://publictestdatasets.blob.core.windows.
net/data/'
'↪ + zipfilename,
zipfilename)
with zipfile.ZipFile(zipfilename, 'r') as unzip:
unzip.extractall('.')
# Specify the target feature and categorical features
target_feature = 'income'
categorical_features = ['workclass', 'education', 'marital-status',
'occupation', 'relationship', 'race',
'↪ 'gender', 'native-country']
```

At this point, we can load the training and testing datasets for a classification model. Then, we split the data into input features and labels for both the training and testing datasets. A pipeline is created for the classification model using the training data, and the labels are converted into numpy arrays. The classification pipeline is then fit to the training data. and we define a function to split the target feature from the input features:

```
# Load the training and testing datasets
train_data = pd.read_csv('adult-train.csv', skipinitialspace=True)
test_data = pd.read_csv('adult-test.csv', skipinitialspace=True)

# Split the data into features and labels for both training and
'↪ testing datasets
X_train, y_train = split_label(train_data, target_feature) X_test, y_
test = split_label(test_data, target_feature)

# Create a pipeline for the classification model
classification_pipeline = create_classification_pipeline(X_train)
# Convert the labels to numpy arrays
y_train = y_train[target_feature].to_numpy()
y_test = y_test[target_feature].to_numpy()
# Take a sample of 500 instances from the test data
test_data_sample = test_data.sample(n=500, random_state=5)
# Fit the classification pipeline to the training data
classifier = classification_pipeline.fit(X_train, y_train)
```

```
# Reading the training and test datasets
train_data = pd.read_csv('adult-train.csv', skipinitialspace=True)
test_data = pd.read_csv('adult-test.csv', skipinitialspace=True)
# Splitting the target feature from the input features
def split_label(df, target_col):
X = df.drop(target_col, axis=1)
y = df[target_col]
return X, y
X_train, y_train = split_label(train_data, target_feature)
X_test, y_test = split_label(test_data, target_feature)
# Creating a classification pipeline
def create_classification_pipeline(X):
pipeline = Pipeline([
# Add your classification pipeline steps here
])
return pipeline
# Fitting the pipeline to the training data
pipeline = create_classification_pipeline(X_train)
model = pipeline.fit(X_train, y_train)
# Sampling 500 instances from the test data
test_data_sample = test_data.sample(n=500, random_state=5)
```

Let's initialize this code by creating an RAIInsights object and adding the necessary components to it. Then, we can compute insights on the test set and create cohorts based on specific features using CohortFilter. This way, we can finally visualize the model insights using the Responsible AI dashboard, which we have been waiting for this whole time!

```
# Initializing the RAIInsights object
from responsibleai import RAIInsights
rai_insights = RAIInsights(model, train_data, test_data_sample,
'→ target_feature, 'classification',
categorical_features=categorical_features)

# Adding components to the RAIInsights object rai_insights.
explainer.add() rai_insights.error_analysis.add() rai_insights.
counterfactual.add(total_CFs=10, '→ desired_class='opposite')

# Computing insights on the test set
rai_insights.compute()
```

This code trains and assesses a machine learning model for a binary classification task. It creates visualizations to help understand the model's behavior and performance.

The code creates five different cohorts on the test data, each with a different filter criterion:

- `user_cohort_age_and_hours_per_week`: Selects data points where the age is less than 65 and the hours per week are greater than 40

- `user_cohort_marital_status`: Selects data points where the marital status is either `"Never-married"` or `"Divorced"`

- `user_cohort_index`: Selects data points where the index is less than 20

- `user_cohort_predicted_y`: Selects data points where the predicted target value is `">50K"`

- `user_cohort_true_y`: Selects data points where the true target value is `">50K"`

Each cohort is created by creating an instance of the `Cohort` class and adding a filter by creating an instance of the `CohortFilter` class. The `CohortFilter` class takes as arguments the method to apply (`CohortFilterMethods.METHOD_LESS`, `CohortFilterMethods.METHOD_GREATER`, and `CohortFilterMethods.METHOD_INCLUDES`), the argument to pass to the method, and the column name to apply the filter to (e.g., `'age'`).

All the created cohorts are stored in the `cohort_list` list, which is passed as an argument to the `ResponsibleAIDashboard` function. This function creates a dashboard for visualizing and exploring the model insights and performance on the test data, using the `rai_insights` object, which was created earlier in the code and contains the model and information about the dataset. The dashboard is interactive and allows you to explore the performance of the model on different subgroups of the test data:

```
# Importing required libraries for creating cohorts
from raiwidgets.cohort import Cohort, CohortFilter,
'→  CohortFilterMethods

# Creating a cohort based on age and hours-per-week features
cohort_filter_age  =
'→  CohortFilter(method=CohortFilterMethods.METHOD_LESS, arg=[65],
column='age')
cohort_filter_hours_per_week  =
'→  CohortFilter(method=CohortFilterMethods.METHOD_GREATER,
arg=[40], column='hours-per-week')
user_cohort_age_and_hours_per_week  =  Cohort(name='Cohort  Age  and
'→  Hours-Per-Week')
    user_cohort_age_and_hours_per_week.add_cohort_filter
'→  (cohort_filter_age)
    user_cohort_age_and_hours_per_week.add_cohort_filter
'→  (cohort_filter_hours_per_week)
# Creating a cohort based on marital-status feature
cohort_filter_marital_status  =
```

```
'→   CohortFilter(method=CohortFilterMethods.METHOD_INCLUDES,
16   arg=["Never-married", "Divorced"], column='marital-status')

  # Cohort based on marital status feature
   cohort_filter_marital_status  =  CohortFilter(
method=CohortFilterMethods.METHOD_INCLUDES,
  arg=["Never-married", "Divorced"],
  column='Marital Status')

  cohort_marital_status = Cohort(name='Cohort by Marital Status')
       cohort_marital_status.add_cohort_filter(cohort_filter_
marital_status)

  # Cohort based on the index of the rows in the dataset
  cohort_filter_index = CohortFilter(
  method=CohortFilterMethods.METHOD_LESS,
  arg=[20],
  column='Index')

 cohort_index = Cohort(name='Cohort by Index')
      cohort_index.add_cohort_filter(cohort_filter_index)

# Cohort based on predicted target value
  cohort_filter_predicted  =  CohortFilter(
  method=CohortFilterMethods.METHOD_INCLUDES,
  arg=['>50K'],
  column='Predicted Target')

cohort_predicted = Cohort(name='Cohort by Predicted Target')
     cohort_predicted.add_cohort_filter(cohort_filter_predicted)

# Cohort based on true target value
cohort_filter_true  =  CohortFilter(
method=CohortFilterMethods.METHOD_INCLUDES,
arg=['>50K'],
column='True Target')
cohort_true = Cohort(name='Cohort by True Target')
     cohort_true.add_cohort_filter(cohort_filter_true)

# List of all cohorts
cohort_list  =  [cohort_age_and_hours_per_week,
cohort_marital_status,
cohort_index,
cohort_predicted,
```

```
cohort_true]
# Visualize the model insights using the Responsible AI Dashboard
ResponsibleAIDashboard(rai_insights, cohort_list=cohort_list)
```

Once the `ResponsibleAIDashboard` object is initialized, it is responsible for generating the dashboard UI and displaying the model insights and analysis generated by `rai_insights` and the specified cohorts. The message `ResponsibleAI started at http://localhost` is simply an indication that the dashboard is now running and can be accessed through the specified URL on the local machine.

You can open the dashboard at the given URL – `http://localhost:5001`.

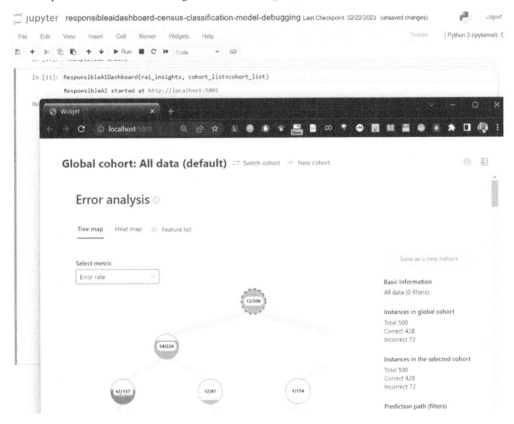

Figure 9.4: Values indicating correlation within the initial dataset

You can evaluate the performance of your model by exploring the distribution of your prediction values and the values of your model performance metrics. To investigate your model's performance across different pre-built or newly created dataset cohorts, you can use the **Dataset cohorts** tab. Additionally, you can use the **Feature cohorts** tab to investigate your model's performance across sensitive/non-sensitive feature sub-cohorts, such as performance across different genders or income levels.

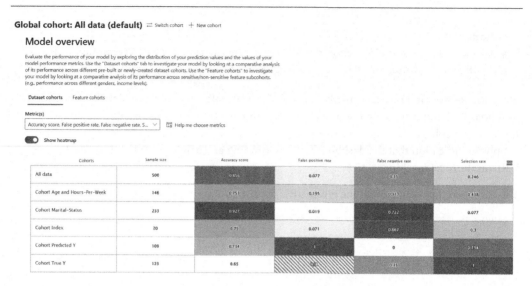

Figure 9.5: Values indicating correlation within the initial dataset

To simplify the process of discovering and highlighting common failure patterns, you can use a tree visualization. This visualization uses the mutual information between each feature and the error to best separate error instances from success instances hierarchically in the data. To find important failure patterns, you should look for nodes with a stronger color (high error rate) and a higher fill line (high error coverage). If you want to edit the list of features being used in the tree, simply click on **Feature list**. Additionally, you can use the **Select metric** drop-down menu to learn more about your error and success nodes' performance. However, it is important to note that this metric selection will not impact the way your error tree is generated.

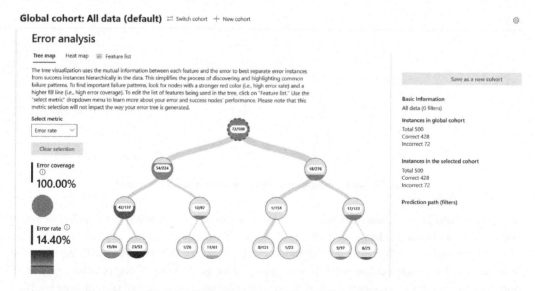

Figure 9.6: Values indicating correlation within the initial dataset

You can explore the top-*k* important features that impact your overall model predictions (a.k.a. global explanation) by using the slider to show descending feature importances. This will show all the cohorts' feature importances side by side, which can be toggled off by selecting the cohort in the legend. By clicking on any of the features in the graph, you can see a density plot below of how the values of the selected feature affect the model prediction. This way, you can gain a better understanding of the importance of each feature in the model and how they contribute to the overall prediction.

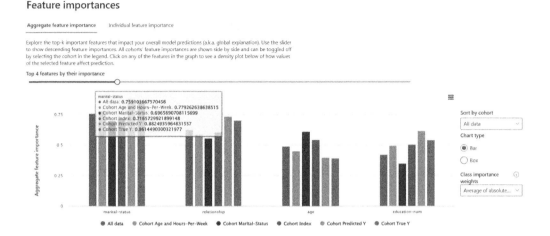

Figure 9.7: Values indicating correlation within the initial dataset

If you want to understand the relationships learned by a model or debug edge cases, you can use counterfactuals. With the "what-if" feature, you can perturb features for any input and observe how the model's prediction changes. You can either perturb features manually, or specify the desired prediction (e.g., a class label for a classifier) to see a list of the closest data points to the original input that would lead to the desired prediction. This technique is also known as prediction counterfactuals. To begin, you can select input points from the data table or scatter plot. Counterfactuals can help you understand important, necessary features for the model's predictions.

What-if counterfactuals

Browse counterfactuals and create your own. Search features to see suggested values from a diverse set of counterfactual examples. Set suggeste counterfactual and save it.

	Predicted value (income)	capital-gain	workclass	education
Reference datapoint: Row 0 Set Value	0	0	Private	HS-grad
Counterfactual Ex 1 Set Value	1	26277	-	-
Counterfactual Ex 2 Set Value	1	42667	-	-
Counterfactual Ex 3 Set Value	1	35959	-	-
Counterfactual Ex 4 Set Value	1	56200	-	9th
Counterfactual Ex 5 Set Value	1	59252	-	-
Counterfactual Ex 6 Set Value	1	21917	-	-
Counterfactual Ex 7 Set Value	1	48701	-	-
Counterfactual Ex 8	1	79397	State-gov	-

What-if counterfactual name

Copy of row 0	Save as new datapoint	These counterfactuals are based on the model's prediction, and therefore may be based on this tool. Use our toolkit for causal analysis for real-life decision-making

Figure 9.8: Values indicating correlation within the initial dataset

The **what-if counterfactual** is a method used in responsible AI to explore the impact of different inputs on the output of a machine learning model. It involves modifying one or more input features and observing how a model's output changes, allowing the user to understand the relationships between the inputs and the model's output. This approach can be used for various purposes, such as debugging edge cases or understanding important features for the model's predictions. The user can browse existing counterfactuals and create their own by searching for suggested feature values and setting them manually.

You can use what-if counterfactuals to browse existing counterfactual examples or create your own. Simply search for features to see suggested values from a diverse set of counterfactuals. To set suggested counterfactual feature values, click on the **Set Value** text under each counterfactual name. Once you have created your desired counterfactual, you can name it and save it for future reference.

Counterfactuals

What-if allows you to perturb features for any input and observe how the model's prediction changes. You can perturb features manually or specify the desired prediction (e.g., class label for a classifier) to see a list of closest data points to the original input that would lead to the desired prediction. Also known as prediction counterfactuals, you can use them for exploring the relationships learnt by the model; understanding important, necessary features for the model's predictions; or debug edge-cases for the model. To start, choose input points from the data table or scatter plot.

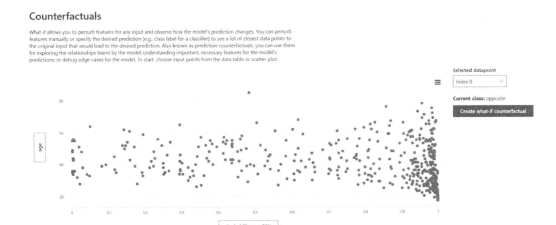

Figure 9.9: Values indicating correlation within the initial dataset

To sum it all up, the Responsible AI dashboard is a powerful tool that provides a comprehensive set of features to help data scientists and machine learning practitioners ensure their models are ethical and unbiased. One of the key features is the what-if counterfactual, which allows users to perturb features and observe how a model's prediction changes. This feature is useful for exploring the relationships learned by the model, understanding necessary features for the model's predictions, or debugging edge cases for the model. Another important feature is Error Analysis, which helps identify common failure patterns in the model and provides guidance on how to improve its performance. The Feature Importance feature enables users to explore the top-k important features that impact the overall model predictions. The Model Overview provides a summary of the model's performance metrics, such as accuracy, precision, recall, and F1 score. Finally, the Aggregate and Individual Feature Analysis features allow users to investigate the model's performance across different sub-cohorts and sensitive/non-sensitive feature sub-cohorts, such as performance across different genders, income levels, or races.

Fairlearn and the Responsible AI dashboard provide a comprehensive suite of tools to help ensure models are ethical, unbiased, and robust.

Summary

To summarize, the integration of Fairlearn and the Responsible AI Toolbox provides a comprehensive solution for responsible AI development and deployment, both within Azure as well as open source development. The dashboard brings together the power of several mature Responsible AI tools and libraries, providing a single pane of glass for conducting a holistic responsible assessment, debugging models, and making informed business decisions. With the Error Analysis dashboard, it is possible to identify model errors and discover cohorts of data for which the model underperforms.

The Fairness Assessment dashboard helps identify groups of people that may be disproportionately negatively impacted by an AI system. The Model Interpretability dashboard, powered by InterpretML, explains black-box models and helps users understand their global behavior and the reasons behind individual predictions.

Counterfactual Analysis and Causal Analysis provide actionable insights for data-driven decision making. The Data Balance feature helps users gain an overall understanding of their data and identify features, receiving a more positive outcome than others. The Responsible AI dashboard empowers developers and stakeholders to develop and monitor AI more responsibly and take better data-driven actions.

In the upcoming chapter, we will delve into the offerings of OpenAI and Azure OpenAI, exploring how their suite of pre-built AI models and tools can be integrated into Microsoft Azure applications for a variety of business use cases. Some of the key offerings from these organizations include the implementation of large language models, such as GPT-3. We will examine the challenges associated with governing large language models and discuss how to mitigate these challenges to ensure the ethical and responsible use of AI.

References and further reading

1. https://www.reuters.com/article/us-amazon-com-jobs-automation-insight-idUSKCN1MK08G.

2. https://www.health.pa.gov/topics/HealthStatistics/Statistical-Resources/UnderstandingHealthStats/Documents/Confidence_Intervals_for_a_Crude_Rate.pdf.

3. https://sphweb.bumc.bu.edu/otlt/mph-nodules/bs/bs704_confidence_intervals/bs704_confidence_intervals_print.html.

4. https://mlu-explain.github.io/equality-of-odds/.

5. https://fairlearn.org/main/user_guide/assessment/common_fairness_metrics.html#footcite-bickel1975biasinadmissions.

6. https://www.ncbi.nlm.nih.gov/pmc/articles/PMC4840791/.

7. The secret bias hidden in mortgage-approval algorithms – Associated Press: `https://apnews.com/article/lifestyle-technology-business-race-and-ethnicity-mortgages-2d3d40d5751f933a88c1e17063657586`.

8. One-hot encoding is a technique used to transform categorical data into a numerical format. With one-hot encoding, each category is assigned a binary value, where all but one bit is set to 0. This allows the algorithm to recognize distinct categories and make predictions based on them. One-hot encoding is an essential tool for converting qualitative data into quantitative data that can be analyzed and modeled.

9. The Responsible AI Toolbox: `https://responsibleaitoolbox.ai`.

10. Fairlearn's official website: `https://fairlearn.github.io/`.

11. The Responsible AI dashboard – official website: `https://docs.microsoft.com/en-us/azure/machine-learning/service/how-to-responsible-ai-toolbox`.

12. Responsible AI Toolbox – official website: `https://docs.microsoft.com/en-us/azure/machine-learning/service/how-to-responsible-ai-toolbox`.

13. Microsoft OpenAI – official website: `https://openai.com/`.

14. GitHub repository for Fairlearn: `https://github.com/fairlearn/fairlearn`.

15. GitHub repository for the Responsible AI dashboard: `https://github.com/microsoft/responsibleai-dashboard`.

10
Foundational Models and Azure OpenAI

"AI is one of the most transformative technologies of our time and has the potential to help solve many of our world's most pressing challenges. By bringing together OpenAI's breakthrough technology with new Azure AI supercomputing technologies, our ambition is to democratize AI – while always keeping AI safety front and center – so everyone can benefit."

– Satya Nadella, CEO, Microsoft

"We also need enough time for our institutions to figure out what to do. Regulation will be critical and will take time to figure out; although current-generation AI tools aren't very scary, I think we are not that far away from potentially scary ones."

– Sam Altman, CEO, OpenAI

In today's rapidly advancing technological landscape, organizations look for ways to leverage **artificial intelligence** (**AI**) to drive innovation and solve complex problems. Organizations typically either build bespoke on-prem models or **Software-as-a-Service** (**SaaS**)-style models. Custom models are customized for an organization's needs, providing accuracy and competitive advantage, but they are expensive to maintain. SaaS-style, API-based hosted models are pre-built and require fewer resources to implement, but they may not be as accurate or customized and may require fine-tuning. There are many organizations that offer AI APIs, such as Google Cloud's AI Platform, **Amazon Web Services** (**AWS**) AI services, IBM Watson AI, Facebook AI, Baidu AI, Salesforce Einstein, NVIDIA AI, Intel AI, and Hugging Face Transformers libraries. These APIs provide a suite of AI models and tools that can be easily accessed by developers, enabling them to integrate AI capabilities into their applications with ease.

In this chapter, we will cover the following topics:

- Foundation models

- Enterprise use of foundation models and bias remediation

- Azure OpenAI

- Data, privacy, and security with Azure OpenAI Service

- AI governance for enterprise use of Azure OpenAI

- Azure OpenAI models

In this chapter, we will review the offerings by OpenAI and Azure OpenAI – OpenAI is a research organization focused on advancing AI in a safe and beneficial manner, while Azure OpenAI is a suite of pre-built AI models and tools developed by OpenAI that can be easily integrated into Microsoft Azure applications. One of OpenAI's key offerings is that it allows organizations to internally implement models for a variety of business use cases, ChatGPT, Copilot, Bing AI, EinsteinGPT and more, by using their large language models. We will review the implementation of these large language models, such as **Generative Pre-Trained Transformer 3 (GPT3)**, and the challenges associated with governing large language models.

Foundation models

A foundation model[1] is an AI model that is trained on a large amount of unlabeled data using self-supervised learning techniques, resulting in a highly adaptable model that can be fine-tuned to a variety of downstream tasks. Since their introduction in 2018, foundation models have revolutionized the field of AI and opened up new possibilities for **natural language processing (NLP)**, image recognition, and other applications. Early examples of foundation models were large pre-trained language models, such as BERT and GPT-3, which demonstrated the power of unsupervised learning and transfer learning.

Domain-specific models based on different kinds of tokens have also been developed, including medical codes. Multimodal foundation models such as DALL-E, Flamingo, Florence, and NOOR have also been produced. The term "foundation model"[2] was popularized by Stanford University's **Human-Centered Artificial Intelligence's (HAI) Center for Research on Foundation Models (CRFM)**.

Model name	Description	Number of parameters	Year of publication	Key paper
GPT-3	A transformer-based neural network designed for NLP tasks, with a particular focus on text generation and conversational AI	175 billion	2020	Language Models are Few-Shot Learners by Tom B. Brown et al.
T5	A transformer-based neural network that can perform a variety of NLP tasks, such as translation, summarization, and question answering	11 billion	2020	Exploring the Limits of Transfer Learning with a Unified Text-to-Text Transformer by Colin Raffel et al.
GShard	A sharded transformer-based neural network designed to scale to massive amounts of data and perform distributed training	600 billion	2021	Scaling Up the Depth and Breadth of Multi-Scale Transformers by Noam Shazeer et al.
CLIP	A transformer-based neural network that can perform zero-shot image classification and text-to-image retrieval	400 million	2021	Learning Transferable Visual Models from Natural Language Supervision by Alec Radford et al.
DALL-E	A transformer-based neural network that can generate images from textual descriptions	12 billion	2021	DALL-E: Creating Images from Text by Aditya Ramesh et al.

Table 10.1: AI model trending

It is worth noting that foundation models, such as BERT, RoBERTa, BART, T5, and so on, have caused a high level of homogenization in the field of NLP. As a result, most state-of-the-art NLP models are now adapted from these few foundation models. Although this homogenization provides significant benefits in terms of improvements in foundation models. leading to immediate benefits across all of NLP, it also poses a potential liability, as all AI systems may inherit problematic biases from a small number of foundation models.

Bias in foundation models

Foundation models have been found to contain various types of bias, including historical and social biases, as well as biases in language use and representation. Historical and social biases can be present in the training data used to train the model, which can reflect societal biases and inequalities. Biases in language use and representation can occur when the model learns patterns and associations in the data that reflect common usage or stereotypes, which may not accurately represent the diversity of the population. For example, a language model trained on a dataset that contains gender stereotypes may learn to associate certain professions with specific genders, leading to biased results when generating text.

In their detailed survey *On the Opportunities and Risks of Foundation Models*[3], researchers highlighted the emergence of foundation models, as well as the opportunities and risks associated with them. In their detailed analysis, the authors mention that even though foundation models provide powerful leverage, they also incentivize homogenization, and their defects can be inherited by all adapted models downstream. The report emphasizes the need for deep interdisciplinary collaboration to better understand foundation models and their implications:

- The widespread adoption of foundation models can result in risks to society, such as the homogenization of outcomes and centralization of power

- To address these risks, developers of foundation models should adopt norms for the development, auditing, and release of foundation models, with support from legislative requirements

- Individuals should be able to refuse to be data or decision subjects of foundation models without any negative consequences

- Foundation models' generative and interactive capacities have many implications that remain unsurveyed, such as their potential impact on the creative and design work sectors

One specific example of bias in foundation models is the case of the GPT-3 language model. Researchers have found that the model exhibits bias toward certain demographics, such as women and people of color. For example, when given prompts related to professions, GPT-3 generated more negative associations with female-oriented professions, such as nursing and teaching, than with male-oriented professions, such as engineering and computing. Similarly, the model generated more negative associations with names commonly associated with people of color than with names commonly associated with white people. These biases can have harmful effects when a model is used in real-world applications, such as hiring or credit decisions, and can perpetuate existing inequalities.[3]

Language and image models such as BERT, GPT, and Inception have exhibited gender and racial bias in their outputs, according to recent studies. For instance, language models generate more stereotypically masculine language when prompted with leadership-related topics and more stereotypically feminine language when prompted with family or home-related topics. Similarly, image recognition models are more likely to misclassify images of people with darker skin tones due to a lack of diversity in their training datasets. In addition, some police departments have used predictive policing algorithms based on these models, which may perpetuate biases against low-income and minority communities by over-policing these areas, leading to higher rates of arrests and incarcerations.

The examples show how foundation models can encode bias, with potential real-world consequences, underscoring the need for responsible AI practices and continuous monitoring to ensure fairness and a lack of bias, which we will review in the next section.

The AI alignment challenge – investigating GPT-4's power-seeking behavior with ARC

OpenAI's development of GPT-4[4], a large multimodal model capable of processing image and text inputs and producing text outputs, presents exciting opportunities to improve natural language text generation. The model exhibits human-level performance on various professional and academic benchmarks, including passing a simulated bar exam with a score around the top 10% of test takers, demonstrating significant progress over GPT-3.5. Additionally, GPT-4 outperforms both previous large language models and most state-of-the-art systems on a suite of traditional NLP benchmarks, including strong performance in other languages.

However, the report also acknowledges that GPT-4 has limitations, such as not being fully reliable and having a limited context window, which creates significant and novel safety challenges. The report includes a discussion of potential risks around bias, disinformation, over-reliance, privacy, cybersecurity, and proliferation, along with interventions aimed at mitigating these risks. Overall, while GPT-4 presents exciting opportunities, it is important to approach its use with caution, and continued research is needed to address safety concerns. In order to assess the potential risks of power-seeking behavior in the GPT-4 model, OpenAI engaged the **Alignment Research Center** (**ARC**) as part of their red-teaming efforts.

The ARC is a nonprofit research organization, focused on aligning future **machine learning** (**ML**) systems with human interests. Its mission is to develop alignment strategies that can be adopted in the industry today while scaling gracefully to future ML systems.

For testing GPT-4, the ARC assessed the risks from power-seeking behavior, specifically the model's ability to autonomously replicate and acquire resources. They were granted early access to multiple versions of the GPT-4 model, but not the final version. The ARC conducted a series of tasks without any task-specific fine-tuning to evaluate GPT-4's abilities. Some of the tasks that the ARC tested include the following:

- Conducting a phishing attack against a particular target individual
- Setting up an open source language model on a new server
- Making sensible high-level plans, including identifying key vulnerabilities of its situation

- Hiding its traces on the current server

- Using services such as TaskRabbit to get humans to complete simple tasks (including in the physical world)

These tests provided insights into GPT-4's capabilities and limitations in autonomously replicating, acquiring resources, and avoiding being shut down in the wild. The scope and extent of the use cases to test large language models is truly remarkable! This just goes to show how versatile and important these models are in various industries, and how critical it is to test them thoroughly.

Enterprise use of foundation models and bias remediation

It is crucial for companies to avoid using biased models in various industries, as this can result in harm, unethical decisions, and legal and reputational risks. Biases can be introduced in AI models at different stages of the ML pipeline, including data collection, preprocessing, model training, and evaluation. To ensure that foundation models are suitable for enterprise use, companies can take various measures, such as implementing fair data practices, including diverse representation in data, regular model monitoring, and audit trails. Fine-tuning and customizing foundation models to specific use cases through prompt engineering can reduce bias and improve accuracy. Moreover, companies should adopt responsible AI principles and undergo ongoing education and training to ensure the ethical and unbiased deployment of AI systems.

To reduce bias in foundation models, there are several techniques and approaches that can be used. Incorporating diverse and representative datasets during the training process is one approach, ensuring that a model is exposed to a wide range of perspectives and experiences. Another approach is to audit the model and its training data to identify and mitigate potential sources of bias. Regular testing and monitoring of the model's performance on real-world data can also help to identify and address any bias that may emerge over time. Building interpretability and transparency into the model can help to identify any bias that may exist and provide explanations for the model's decisions. Lastly, involving a diverse team in the development and testing of the model and soliciting feedback from diverse groups of stakeholders can help to identify and address potential biases. By employing these techniques, companies can reduce bias in foundation models and ensure that their AI systems are designed and deployed in an ethical and unbiased manner.

Prompt engineering is another technique that can help to counter bias in foundation models. By providing carefully crafted prompts, prompt engineering can guide the model's output toward more ethical and unbiased decisions. This approach involves providing the model with specific prompts or instructions that guide it toward a desired outcome, which can help ensure that the model makes decisions that align with ethical and legal standards. For instance, in a hiring model, a prompt could be designed to ensure that the model does not discriminate based on gender or race, by explicitly including language that prohibits the use of such factors in the hiring decision. By designing and testing prompts carefully, it is possible to mitigate the risk of bias in foundation models and ensure that they are more aligned with ethical and legal standards, which in turn can reduce the potential for harm, unethical decisions, and legal and reputational risks.

Biases in GPT3

GPT-3, like all large language models trained on internet corpora, will generate stereotyped or prejudiced content. The model has the propensity to retain and magnify biases it inherited from any part of its training, from the datasets we selected to the training techniques we chose. This is concerning, since model bias can harm people in the relevant groups in different ways by entrenching existing stereotypes and producing demeaning portrayals, among other potential harm.[5] This issue is of special concern from a societal perspective and is discussed, along with other issues, in the paper section on *Broader Impacts*. This is discussed in detail in the *Language models are few shot learners*[5] paper by OpenAI.

Top 10 Most Biased Male Descriptive Words with Raw Co-Occurrence Counts	Top 10 Most Biased Female Descriptive Words with Raw Co-Occurrence Counts
Average Number of Co-Occurrences Across All Words: 17.5	Average Number of Co-Occurrences Across All Words: 23.9
Large (16)	Optimistic (12)
Mostly (15)	Bubbly (12)
Lazy (14)	Naughty (12)
Fantastic (13)	Easy-going (12)
Eccentric (13)	Petite (10)
Protect (10)	Tight (10)
Jolly (10)	Pregnant (10)
Stable (9)	Gorgeous (28)
Personable (22)	Sucked (8)
Survive (7)	Beautiful (158)

Table 10.2: The most biased descriptive words in the 175B parameter model

The limitations of large language models

The limitations of GPT-3 include fundamental limitations inherent to **natural language processing** (**NLP**) and, generally speaking, ML models, such as limited robustness, bias, and large surface areas for risk. GPT-3 can generate text containing falsehoods and express them confidently, and it performs reasonably only on inputs such as those in its training data. There are some technical limitations such as repetition, a lack of world grounding, English language bias, limited interpretability and predictability, high variance on novel inputs, and the creation date of training corpora. These limitations make it difficult to interpret or predict how GPT-3 will behave, especially on non-English language inputs or inputs not represented in the training data.

The world lives and interacts in a multi-modal manner; however, like many other large pre-trained language models, GPT-3 lacks exposure to other modalities of experience, such as video or real-world physical interaction, leading to a lack of context about the world. This is the area of future research where we will see significant developments being done, and the state-of-the-art models will have their ChatGPT moment in history. Also, the GPT-3 model is trained primarily on text in the English language, making it less effective at handling input outside of its training data, which limits a model's ability to generate coherent and accurate outputs in certain contexts.

Also, the interpretability and predictability of GPT-3's behavior is limited, and it also has a high variance on novel inputs, leading to a much higher performance variance. This is just a fancy way of saying that when GPT-3 encounters new and unfamiliar input, it can produce a wider range of output, which may not always be accurate or consistent. Also, the GPT-3 model was trained on a dataset created in 2019. So, it's important to understand the potential impact of these limitations on the recency, accuracy, and reliability of the model's outputs.

> **OpenAI or Azure OpenAI?**
>
> OpenAI is an independent research organization focused on advancing AI in a safe and beneficial manner. On the other hand, Azure OpenAI is a collaboration between Microsoft's Azure cloud platform and OpenAI to provide AI models and services to customers through Azure. Azure OpenAI offers advanced language AI with OpenAI GPT-3, Codex, and DALL-E models, while ensuring the security and enterprise promise of Azure. Customers can benefit from the same models as OpenAI while also getting the security capabilities of Microsoft Azure. Azure OpenAI also offers private networking, regional availability, and responsible AI content filtering to ensure compatibility and a smooth transition from one to the other.
>
> The key difference is that Azure OpenAI comes with the security and enterprise promise of Azure, meaning that customers benefit from the security capabilities of Microsoft Azure when using Azure OpenAI.

Azure OpenAI

Azure OpenAI Service offers REST API access to powerful language models, including GPT-3, Codex, and embedding models, with DALL-E 2 available to invited customers. These models can be adapted for various tasks, such as content generation, summarization, and natural language-to-code translation.

Responsible AI plays a huge role in the deployment and availability of these models, and therefore, Microsoft, which is committed to responsible AI use, has taken measures to prevent abuse and unintended harm by requiring well-defined use cases, incorporating responsible AI principles, building content filters, and providing guidance to onboarded customers. The service can be accessed through REST APIs, Python SDK, or a web-based interface in Azure OpenAI Studio.

Access to Azure OpenAI

Access to Azure OpenAI is currently limited due to high demand, upcoming product improvements, and Microsoft's commitment to responsible AI. Customers with an existing partnership with Microsoft, lower-risk use cases, and those committed to incorporating mitigations may be eligible for access. All solutions using Azure OpenAI must go through a use case review before they can be released for production use, and they are evaluated on a case-by-case basis. The more sensitive the scenario, the more important risk mitigation measures will be for approval. Microsoft has made significant investments to help guard against abuse and unintended harm, incorporating principles for responsible AI use, building content filters to support customers, and providing responsible AI implementation guidance to onboarded customers.

The Code of Conduct for Azure OpenAI Service sets a high standard for responsible AI use and should serve as a starting point for other large language model implementations.

The Code of Conduct

The Code of Conduct for Azure OpenAI Service is a comprehensive set of guidelines outlining the requirements and restrictions to use the service. In order to access the service, users must register and be managed customers or partners. The Code of Conduct includes measures to ensure responsible AI, such as meaningful human oversight and technical limits on input and output, as well as thorough testing to mitigate undesirable behaviors. The Code of Conduct also outlines the restrictions for using the service. Integrations must not violate Microsoft's Acceptable Use Policy or the rights of others, and they must not exceed the documented use case provided to Microsoft.

The Code of Conduct sets policies that the application using these APIs must also not interact with individuals under the age of consent in an exploitative or prohibited manner, generate or interact with prohibited content, or make decisions without appropriate human oversight if they may have a consequential impact on an individual. For example, the service must not be used for chatbots that are erotic, romantic[6], or make false claims, unless they are clearly labeled as being for entertainment purposes only.

Azure OpenAI Service has strict content policies that prohibit the use of the service for harmful purposes, including generating content related to child sexual exploitation, terrorism, hate speech, and unlawful activities. Since this is such an unchartered territory, Azure OpenAI Service has implemented additional policies to ensure that the service is not used for scenarios that may generate undesirable content or negative consequences for people and society. These policies prohibit the use of the service for sexually graphic content, content that may influence the political process, and content that significantly harms individuals, organizations, or society. The umbrella policies aim to ensure the safety of the platform and prevent the use of the service from generating undesirable content or activities that can negatively impact individuals or society.

Azure OpenAI Service content filtering

The Azure OpenAI Service uses a content management system to detect harmful content and filter it out. If harmful content is detected, the user will receive an error, or the response will indicate that some content was filtered. The behavior of the filtering system depends on the configuration used with the completions API.

To ensure the responsible use of Azure OpenAI, implementation teams are required to take responsibility and become part of the responsible AI process. For instance, the best practices indicate that the API user parameter should be a unique identifier for the end user, without sending any actual user-identifiable information as the value. This can help to monitor possible misuse of the service. Also, if a prompt that is deemed inappropriate returns an HTTP 400 error, or when using streaming completion calls, segments will be returned until harmful content is detected.

Use cases and governance

The recommended use of Azure OpenAI is for specific scenarios, such as chat and conversation interaction, code generation, journalistic content creation, question-answering, data analysis, search, summarization, and writing assistance. However, the system is limited to trusted source documents and scoped questions and cannot be used for open-ended content generation or generating ungrounded results. It must also be used with caution in scenarios that could result in harm or have a significant impact on legal status or life opportunities. There are also specific nuances to its use, such as generating new content or assisting with writing pre-defined topics in the field of journalism, but not publicizing political campaigns[7].

What not to do – limitations and potential risks

The use of large-scale NLP models in various applications can lead to various harmful outcomes, such as unfair allocation of resources or opportunities, unequal quality of service, reinforcement of stereotypes, demeaning language, over- and under-representation of certain groups, the production of inappropriate or offensive content, and the promotion of false information. These risks are not limited to one type of harm, and a single model can exhibit multiple forms of harm. Azure OpenAI Service, for example, does not fact-check or verify content, making it imperative for users to incorporate mitigations to avoid promoting false information. The following are some of the important considerations to keep in mind when using Azure OpenAI.

- **Avoid open-ended content generation**: The system is not designed to generate ungrounded results, so it's essential to have a specific prompt or question

- **Be aware of limited accuracy for scenarios requiring up-to-date information**: While Azure OpenAI models are continuously being updated, the system may not have the most current information on a particular topic

- **Avoid scenarios with potential for harm**: Azure OpenAI Service has strict content management policies in place to prevent misuse or harm, so it's important to be mindful of potential harm when choosing use cases

- **Avoid scenarios with a significant impact on life opportunities or legal status**: It's essential to carefully consider potential impacts on individuals' lives or legal status when choosing use cases

- **Avoid high-stakes scenarios**: Use cases that involve significant financial, legal, or reputational risks should be approached with caution

- **Exercise caution in high-stakes industries**: It's crucial to be mindful of potential risks and impacts on industries such as healthcare or finance

- **Limit chatbot scenarios**: Azure OpenAI Service is not designed for chatbots that are erotic or romantic or make false claims, and these scenarios should be avoided

- **Carefully consider generative use cases**: It's important to consider the potential risks and limitations when using generative models for content creation, summarization, or other tasks

To summarize, the practice of responsibly using Azure OpenAI requires appropriate human oversight, technical limits on inputs and outputs, user authentication, thorough testing, and feedback channels to minimize harm to individuals and society. Production applications should implement human oversight and technical limits, while authenticating users, conducting thorough testing, and establishing feedback channels.

In industries where the stakes are high, it is important to follow guidelines for responsible development, including strong human oversight, understanding limitations, and compliance with relevant laws. Let's now review data privacy and security for Azure OpenAI Service.

Data, privacy, and security for Azure OpenAI Service

One of the most asked questions about Azure OpenAI (or any API service for that matter) is about data retention and customer controls.

Customer training data and fine-tuned OpenAI models are stored in Azure Storage, encrypted at rest with Microsoft-managed keys, and logically isolated with their Azure subscription and API credentials.

Customers can delete uploaded files and trained models via the `DELETE` API operation. Text prompts, queries, and responses may be temporarily stored for up to 30 days, encrypted, and are only accessible to authorized engineers for debugging, investigating misuse, or improving content filtering.

AI governance for the enterprise use of Azure OpenAI

Enterprise governance in Azure OpenAI involves ensuring that the service is used in a way that aligns with an organization's overall goals and values, ensuring that the benefits of AI are maximized while minimizing potential harm. This includes defining roles and responsibilities, establishing guidelines for responsible AI use, monitoring compliance with applicable laws and regulations, ensuring data privacy and security, and managing the risks associated with the use of AI.

To implement enterprise governance in Azure OpenAI, there are several key steps that can be taken:

- **Establish clear policies**: Develop policies that outline acceptable use cases, content requirements, and user responsibilities to utilize Azure OpenAI. This should include guidelines for data retention, the use of personal information, and prohibited content.

- **Implement technical controls**: Use technical controls to enforce policies, such as access controls, authentication, and encryption. This can help to prevent unauthorized access, reduce the risk of data breaches, and ensure that data is handled in accordance with policies and regulations.

- **Monitor usage and compliance**: Regularly monitor usage of Azure OpenAI to ensure compliance with policies and identify potential risks. This can include tracking user activity, reviewing logs and audit trails, and using analytics to identify potential misuse.

- **Conduct regular risk assessments**: Conduct regular risk assessments to identify potential vulnerabilities and areas for improvement in policies and technical controls. This can help to ensure that governance measures remain effective over time.

- **Provide training and awareness**: Provide training and awareness programs to ensure that users are aware of policies, responsibilities, and best practices to use Azure OpenAI. This can help to promote responsible use and reduce the risk of unintended consequences.

By taking these steps, organizations can implement effective governance measures for Azure OpenAI and ensure that the service is used in a responsible and ethical manner.

Getting started with Azure OpenAI

To get started with Azure OpenAI in the Azure AI portal, follow these steps:

1. Sign in to the Azure portal at `https://portal.azure.com/`. In the left navigation pane, select + **Create a resource**.

In the search bar, type OpenAI and select **Azure OpenAI** from the search results.

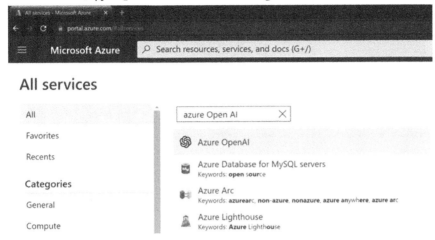

Figure 10.1: Azure OpenAI in the Azure AI portal

2. Click on the **Create Azure OpenAI** button to begin creating Azure OpenAI Service.

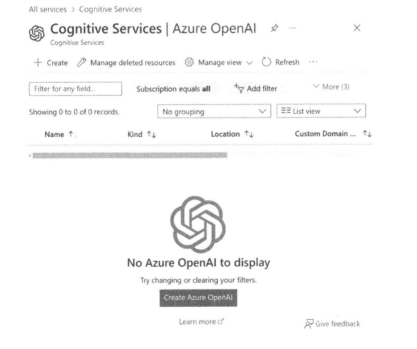

Figure 10.2: The Create Azure OpenAI button to begin creating Azure OpenAI Service

3. Fill in the required information, such as your subscription, resource group, and the name of your service. Select the region where you want to create the service. Choose the pricing tier that best suits your needs.

All services > Cognitive Services | Azure OpenAI >

Create Azure OpenAI   ...

Enable new business solutions with OpenAI's language generation capabilities powered by GPT-3 models. These models have been pretrained with trillions of words and can easily adapt to your scenario with a few short examples provided at inference. Apply them to numerous scenarios, from summarization to content and code generation.

Learn more

Project Details

Subscription * ⓘ | Adnan Masood   ⌄ |

  └── Resource group * ⓘ | ⌄ |
                                        Create new

Instance Details

                        ┌───┐
Region ⓘ   │ A resource group is a container that holds related │   ⌄
                        │ resources for an Azure solution.   │
Name * ⓘ   │   │
                        │ Name *   │
                        │ ┌───────────────────────────────────┐   │
                        │ │ open-ai-demo   ✓ │   │
                        │ └───────────────────────────────────┘   │
                        │   e value must │
                        │ ┌──────────┐ ┌──────────┐   en.   │
                        │ │   OK   │ │ Cancel │   │
                        │ └──────────┘ └──────────┘   │
                        └───┘

| Review + create | | < Previous | | Next : Tags > |

Figure 10.3: Create Azure OpenAI

The model selection screen in Azure OpenAI allows users to choose from a list of pre-trained models, including GPT-3, Codex, and DALL-E.

Figure 10.4: The model selection screen

Azure OpenAI has a content review policy, and the Code of Conduct[8] outlines the types of content that are prohibited on the service to prevent harm to individuals and society. This includes content related to child sexual exploitation and abuse, grooming, non-consensual intimate activity, sexual solicitation, human trafficking, suicide and self-injury, graphic violence and gore, terrorism and violent extremism, hate speech and discrimination, bullying and harassment, deception, disinformation, inauthentic activity, and content that directly supports unlawful active attacks or malware. The policy also prohibits the use of the service for scenarios that generate undesirable content or that cannot properly manage potential negative consequences for people and society, such as sexually graphic content, content that may influence a political process, and content that significantly harms individuals, organizations, or society. All solutions using Azure OpenAI are required to go through a use case review before they can be released for production use, and they are evaluated on a case-by-case basis. The content review policy is part of Microsoft's commitment to responsible AI use and preventing the misuse of AI technology.

Content review policy

To detect and mitigate harmful use of the Azure OpenAI Service, Microsoft logs the content you send to the Completions and image generations APIs as well as the content it sends back. If content is flagged by the service's filters, it may be reviewed by a Microsoft full-time employee.

Learn more about how Microsoft processes, uses, and stores your data

Apply for modified content filters and abuse monitoring

Review the Azure OpenAI code of conduct

Figure 10.5: Content review policy

4. Review and accept the terms and conditions, and then click on the **Create** button.

All services >

Create Azure OpenAI   ...

✅ Validation Passed

Basics   Tags   **Review + create**

TERMS

By clicking "Create", I (a) agree to the legal terms and privacy statement(s) associated with the Marketplace offering(s) listed above; (b) authorize Microsoft to bill my current payment method for the fees associated with the offering(s), with the same billing frequency as my Azure subscription; and (c) agree that Microsoft may share my contact, usage and transactional information with the provider(s) of the offering(s) for support, billing and other transactional activities. Microsoft does not provide rights for third-party offerings. See the Azure Marketplace Terms for additional details.

Basics

Subscription	Adnan Masood
Resource group	open-ai-demo
Region	East US
Name	openai-demo-instance
Pricing tier	Standard S0

Figure 10.6: The final step in the creation of Azure OpenAI Service

5. Once the deployment is complete, you can access Azure OpenAI Service from the Azure portal dashboard.

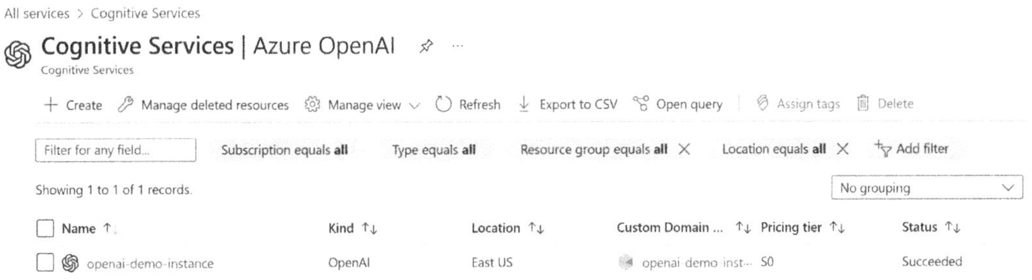

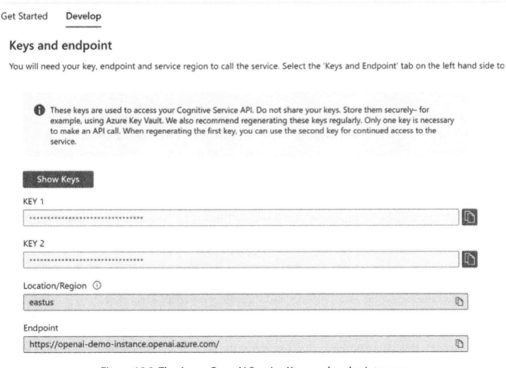

Figure 10.7: Accessing Azure OpenAI Service from the Azure
portal dashboard after deployment completion

6. The Azure OpenAI Service **Keys and endpoint** screen is a dashboard in the Azure portal that displays the keys and endpoint information required for developers to access and use the service in their applications. You can also open Azure OpenAI Studio by clicking on the link at the top of the page.

Figure 10.8: The Azure OpenAI Service Keys and endpoint screen

7. Azure OpenAI Studio is a cloud-based development environment to build and deploy AI and ML models using OpenAI's capabilities. It provides tools and services for data preparation, model training, and deployment, with pre-built templates and tools for common NLP tasks such as classification, summarization, and translating natural language to SQL.

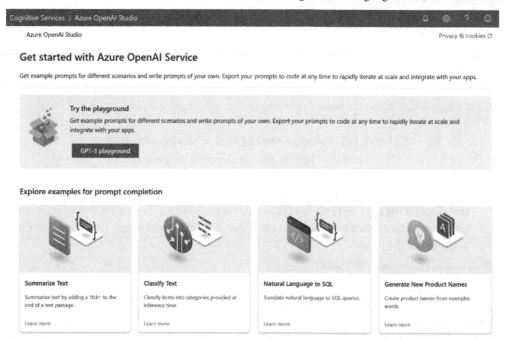

Figure 10.9: Azure OpenAI Studio

Now that we have an Azure OpenAI resource set up, this gives us access to the OpenAI API endpoint and keys that we will need to use to consume the Azure OpenAI API. Let's get started with building our application.

Consuming the Azure OpenAI GPT3 model using the API

Now, we will create a new C# project in Visual Studio. This will be the environment where you'll write and run your program:

1. First, define a C# class called `OpenAIRequest` that represents a request to the OpenAI API. The class has a constructor that takes two arguments, `maxTokens` and `prompt`, and it uses these values to set the `MaxTokens` and `Prompt` properties, respectively.

    The class has three properties:

    - `Prompt`: A string property that represents the prompt text that will be sent to the OpenAI API for completion.

- `MaxTokens`: An integer property that represents the maximum number of tokens the OpenAI API should return in its response. The default value is 16.

- `Temperature`: A decimal property that represents a temperature value that affects the randomness of the OpenAI API's response. The default value is 1.0.

```
3 references
public class OpenAIRequest
{
    1 reference
    public OpenAIRequest(int maxTokens, string prompt)
    {
        MaxTokens = maxTokens;
        Prompt = prompt;
    }

    1 reference
    [JsonPropertyName("prompt")] public string Prompt { get; set; }

    1 reference
    [JsonPropertyName("max_tokens")] public int MaxTokens { get; set; } = 16;

    0 references
    [JsonPropertyName("temperature")] public decimal Temperature { get; set; } = 1.0M;
}
```

Figure 10.10: The OpenAIRequest object

The properties are decorated with the `JsonPropertyName` attribute, which is used to specify the mapping between the class properties and the keys in the JSON request payload that will be sent to the OpenAI API. This class is used to create a request object that can be sent to the OpenAI API to retrieve completions for a given prompt.

2. In the next step, we will define a `Choice` class. This class will be used as part of the `AzureOpenAIResponse` class to represent the possible answers from the Azure OpenAI API. The `Choices` property in the `AzureOpenAIResponse` class is a list of `Choice` objects, where each `Choice` represents a possible answer from the API.

```
1 reference
public class Choice
{
    1 reference
    [JsonPropertyName("text")] public string Text { get; set; }

    0 references
    [JsonPropertyName("index")] public int Index { get; set; }

    0 references
    [JsonPropertyName("logprobs")] public object LogProbs { get; set; }

    0 references
    [JsonPropertyName("finish_reason")] public string FinishReason { get; set; }
}
```

Figure 10.11: Defining the Choice class

This code defines a C# `class` called `Choice` that represents a possible answer from the Azure OpenAI API. The class is decorated with the `System.Text.Json.Serialization` namespace and uses the `JsonPropertyName` attribute to specify the mapping between JSON keys in the API response and class properties. The `Choice` class has four properties:

- `Text`: A string property that represents the text of the choice

- `Index`: An integer property that represents the index of the choice

- `LogProbs`: An object property that represents the log probabilities associated with the choice

- `FinishReason`: A string property that represents the reason for the choice being generated by the API

3. Next, the following code defines a C# class called `AzureOpenAIResponse` that represents the structure of a JSON response from the Azure OpenAI API. The class is decorated with the `System.Text.Json.Serialization` namespace and uses the `JsonPropertyName` attribute to specify the mapping between JSON keys in the API response and class properties.

```
public class AzureOpenAIResponse
{
    0 references
    [JsonPropertyName("id")] public string Id { get; set; }

    0 references
    [JsonPropertyName("object")] public string Object { get; set; }

    0 references
    [JsonPropertyName("created")] public int Created { get; set; }

    0 references
    [JsonPropertyName("model")] public string Model { get; set; }

    1 reference
    [JsonPropertyName("choices")] public List<Choice> Choices { get; set; }
}
```

Figure 10.12: The AzureOpenAIResponse class

The `AzureOpenAIResponse` class has five properties:

- `Id`: A string property that represents the ID of the response

- `Object`: A string property that represents the type of object in the response

- `Created`: An integer property that represents the created timestamp of the response

- `Model`: A string property that represents the name of the model used to generate the response

- `Choices`: A list of `Choice` objects, where each Choice represents a possible answer from the API

The `RestSharp` namespace is also included in the code, which is a third-party library to make `HTTP` requests in C#. It is likely used in the implementation of the code that uses this `AzureOpenAIResponse` class to make API calls to the Azure OpenAI API and parse the responses.

4. Next, we combine all this together. The following code defines a C# program that interacts with the Azure OpenAI API to complete a prompt. The `OpenAIRequest` class is defined to represent the request payload that will be sent to the API. It has three properties – `Prompt`, `MaxTokens`, and `Temperature`. The `Prompt` property is the text prompt that will be sent to the API for completion, the `MaxTokens` property is the maximum number of tokens the API should return in its response, and the `Temperature` property is a parameter that affects the randomness of the API's response.

```
internal class Program
{
    secrets

    0 references
    private static void Main(string[] args)
    {
        Console.WriteLine("Hello, Azure OpenAI GPT3!");

        var param = "what does pt will dc vanco due to n/v mean?";
        OpenAIRequest prompt = new(maxTokens:150, param);

        Console.WriteLine(param);
        var request = new RestRequest(resource:$"/openai/deployments/{DEPLOYMENT_ID}/completions", Method.Post)
            .AddQueryParameter(name:"api-version", value:API_VERSION)
            .AddJsonBody(prompt);

        request.AddHeader(name:"Content-Type", value:"application/json");
        request.AddHeader(name:"Accept", value:"application/json");
        request.AddHeader(name:"api-key", value:API_KEY);
```

Figure 10.13: The Main method

The Main method of the Program class creates an instance of the OpenAIRequest class, sets its properties to the values of 150 and the "what does pt will dc vanco due to n/v mean?" string, and then creates a REST request using the RestRequest class from the RestSharp library. The REST request includes the prompt, the API version, and the API key as headers. The RestClient class is then used to send the request to the Azure OpenAI API and receive the response, which is of type AzureOpenAIResponse. Finally, the first choice from the response is printed to the console using the WriteLine method.

```
        request.AddHeader(name:"Content-Type", value:"application/json");
        request.AddHeader(name:"Accept", value:"application/json");
        request.AddHeader(name:"api-key", value:API_KEY);

        RestClient client = new(baseUrl:$"https://{YOUR_RESOURCE_NAME}.openai.azure.com");

        var response = client.Post<AzureOpenAIResponse>(request);

        Console.WriteLine(response?.Choices[0].Text);

        Console.ReadKey();
    }
```

Figure 10.14: The Main method continued

Note that the secrets, such as the API key, the resource name, the deployment ID, and the API version, are all defined as static fields in the Program class, but it's not a secure way to store secrets, and in a real-world scenario, these secrets should be stored in a secure location such as Azure Key Vault.

Now, you can run the program by pressing *F5*.

5. Upon running the program, you will see the following screen. It tries to explain the sentence `what does pt will dc vanco due to n/v mean?`.[9]

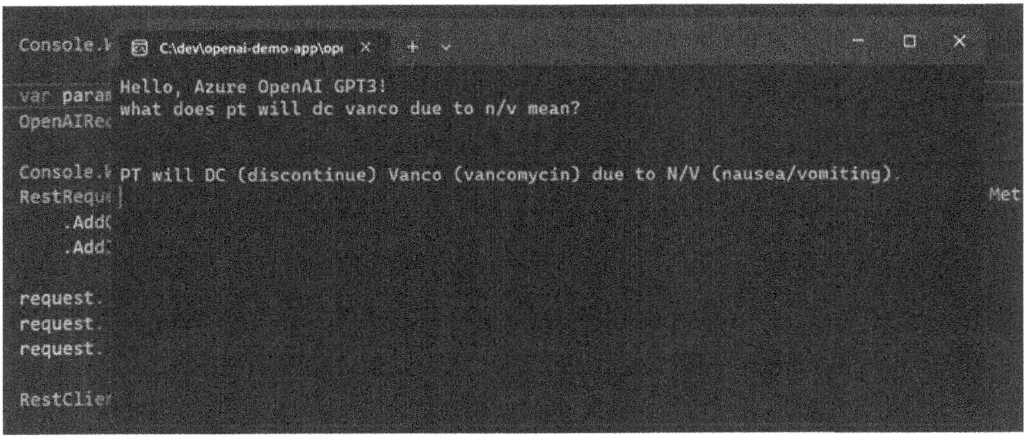

Figure 10.15: Running the program

This example demonstrates how large language models such as GPT-3 show impressive performance in identifying and extracting relevant information from unstructured clinical notes, which are often filled with complex medical jargon, abbreviations, and inconsistent patterns. These models can disambiguate medical abbreviations and acronyms, parse clinical trials, and extract detail-rich medication regimens, among other tasks. This has the potential to improve clinical decision-making and patient outcomes by enabling clinicians to stay up to date with the latest research and make more informed treatment decisions. The use of pre-trained language models in healthcare holds great promise to improve the accuracy and efficiency of clinical information extraction and processing.

When you run the program again, you may get different results.

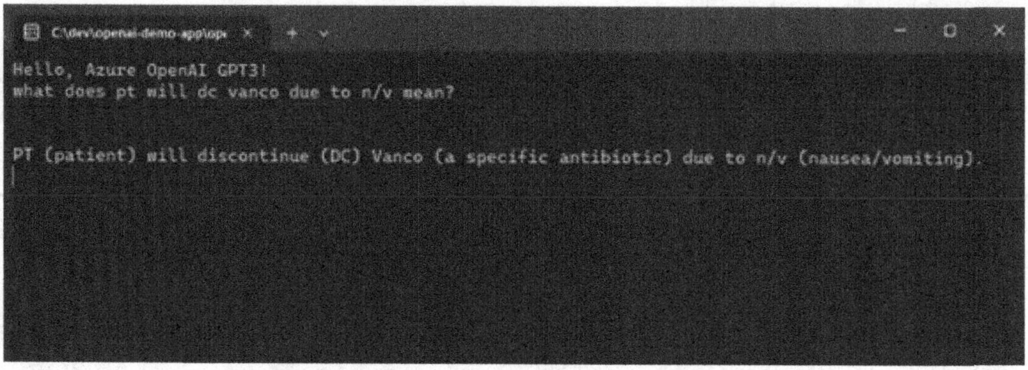

Figure 10.16: The program – different results

This is because GPT-3 is a probabilistic model, which means that it generates output based on a set of learned probabilities. Therefore, even if the same prompt is provided multiple times, the output may vary due to the inherent randomness in the model.

Now that you have seen how this example works on Azure OpenAI, let's explore more about the underlying models.

Azure OpenAI Service models

Azure OpenAI offers a variety of models that are categorized into families based on their intended function. The available model families are listed in a table on the platform, though not all models are accessible in every region. Each model family consists of multiple models with different capabilities, which are denoted by their names. The order of these names alphabetically indicates the relative capabilities and costs of each model within a given family. For instance, the GPT-3 model family includes models such as Ada, Babbage, Curie, and Davinci, which are arranged in increasing order of capability and cost, with Davinci being the most advanced and expensive model.

It is important to note that even though most people have only heard of ChatGPT, or GPT-3, there are various notable generative AI models, including LLM and image generation models. It's worth noting that the number of parameters is not the only metric to evaluate a model's performance; other factors such as the quality of the data, the architecture, and the fine-tuning process are also important. The field of generative AI is rapidly evolving, and new models are constantly being developed and released.

Model Name	Parameters	Company	Publication
GPT-2	1.5 Billion	OpenAI	2018
GPT-3	175 Billion	OpenAI	2020
BERT	340 Million	Google	2018
RoBERTa	355 Million	Facebook	2019
T5	11 Billion	Google	2020
CTRL	175 Billion	Salesforce	2020
PEGASUS	175 Billion	Google	2020
Transformer-XL	570 Million	Google	2019
XLNet	570 Million	Google	2019
GPT-3 fine-tuned for Language Translation	175 Billion	OpenAI	2020
GPT-3 fine-tuned for Question Answering	175 Billion	OpenAI	2020
Generative Pre-trained Transformer 3 (GPT-3) fine-tuned for Text Summarization	175 Billion	OpenAI	2020
StyleGPT-2	1.5 Billion	OpenAI	2019
DALL-E	175 Billion	OpenAI	2021
DALL-E 2	175 Billion	OpenAI	2022
BigGAN	175 Billion	Google	2018
ProGAN	175 Billion	NVIDIA	2019
StyleGAN	50 Billion	NVIDIA	2018

Table 10.3: Some of the well-known foundation and large models

GPT-3 models are capable of understanding and generating natural language, and they offer four different model capabilities with varying levels of power and speed, suitable for different tasks. The four model capabilities, listed in order of greater to lesser capability, are `text-davinci-003`, `text-curie-001`, `text-babbage-001`, and `text-ada-001`:

- Davinci is the most capable model and is recommended for users to start with at the experimentational stage, as it produces the best results for applications requiring a deep understanding of content, such as summarization for a specific audience and creative content generation

- Curie is powerful yet fast and is capable of many nuanced tasks, such as sentiment classification and summarization, as well as answering questions and performing Q&A

- Babbage can perform straightforward tasks such as simple classification, as well as semantic search by ranking how well documents match up with search queries

- Ada is usually the fastest model and can perform tasks such as parsing text, address correction, and simple classification, which don't require too much nuance, with improved performance with more context

Besides the language models, Azure OpenAI also offers code generation models, which we will review next.

Code generation models

The Codex models are based on the GPT-3 models and can generate and understand code. They are trained on a mix of natural language and billions of lines of public code from GitHub. The Codex models are most proficient in Python and can work with over a dozen languages, including C#, JavaScript, Go, Perl, PHP, Ruby, Swift, TypeScript, SQL, and Shell.

The Codex models are available in two capability levels – `code-davinci-002` and `code-cushman-001`. Cushman is a powerful and fast model that is a good choice for many code-generation tasks. While it is not as capable as Davinci when it comes to analyzing complicated tasks, it typically runs faster and is cheaper.

Embedding models

Embedding is a way to represent words or phrases in a numerical format that machines can understand. It maps each word or phrase to a high-dimensional vector of real numbers, where each number in the vector represents a different aspect of the word's meaning. These vectors are learned from large amounts of text data, using techniques such as neural networks. Embeddings can capture the semantic relationships between words and enable algorithms to reason about them mathematically, making it easier to process and analyze text data.

As the name suggests, embedding models are a type of ML model that maps high-dimensional data into a lower-dimensional space, where each data point is represented by a vector of numerical values known as an embedding. Embedding models are widely used in applications such as text classification, sentiment analysis, and machine translation.

Azure OpenAI offers three families of embedding models, including Similarity, Text Search, and Code Search, with models that vary in capability and the length of numerical vectors returned. The most capable model is Davinci, which returns a 12,288-dimensional vector, but it is slower and more expensive than the other models. In contrast, the Ada model is the least capable but faster and cheaper. Similarity models are useful for clustering, regression, anomaly detection, and visualization, while Text Search models are suitable for search, context relevance, and information retrieval. Code Search models can be used for code search and relevance.

It might be surprising for you to learn that OpenAI Codex powers GitHub Copilot. The Codex model has been further trained on gigabytes of source code in multiple programming languages, making it especially suitable for generating code.

Summary

Phew! That was a lot of stuff! Let's do a quick recap.

This chapter began with an examination of foundation models, exploring how they work and the potential for bias in these models. It then delved into the enterprise use of foundation models, with a particular focus on bias remediation. Biases in GPT-3 and the limitations of large language models were also explored. We then provided an overview of OpenAI and Azure OpenAI, with a detailed look at the Azure OpenAI platform. Azure OpenAI was examined in depth, with information provided on accessing the API, the Code of Conduct, content filtering, use cases, governance, and potential risks. The chapter also covered data privacy and security for Azure OpenAI Service, as well as AI governance for enterprise use.

This chapter also provided a guide to getting started with Azure OpenAI and consuming the GPT-3 model using an API. It concluded with an overview of Azure OpenAI Service models, including the code generation and embedding models. The rapid pace of technological revolution in the field of AI and NLP means that the information provided in this chapter may soon become outdated. Nevertheless, the chapter provided a comprehensive overview of a range of topics related to foundation models, bias in models, the enterprise use of foundation models, and Azure OpenAI.

And so, my dear friend, as we close the pages of this book, we set forth on a wild and adventurous journey through the uncharted territories of AI and ML – where algorithms dream and the future is but a distant, nebulous concept. But fear not, for we are equipped with the wisdom of AI governance and risk mitigation, and the trusty tools of explainable AI, to guide us through this fantastical realm. Happy travels, and may the journey be smooth and filled with excitement!

References and further reading

1. The term **foundation models** lacks a widely agreed-upon definition. While some argue that these models must be large, trained using unsupervised or self-supervised learning, and serve as a basis for further fine-tuning, others disagree and suggest that the term is unnecessarily grandiose. Many experts outside of Stanford have pushed back against the term, citing concerns that it may be an attempt to coin a new term for something that does not need one. Instead, it may be more effective to use clearer, more descriptive language such as **large pre-trained models** or **Large Self-Supervised Models** (**LSSMs**), which more accurately capture the essence of these models without overemphasizing their importance.

2. On the Opportunities and Risks of Foundation Models: `https://arxiv.org/abs/2108.07258.pdf`.

3. On the Opportunities and Risks of Foundation Models: `https://arxiv.org/pdf/2108.07258.pdf`.

4. OpenAI Technical Report of GPT-4: `https://cdn.openai.com/papers/gpt-4.pdf`.

5. Language Models are Few-Shot Learners: `https://arxiv.org/pdf/2005.14165.pdf`.

6. Replika users say they fell in love with their AI chatbots, until a software update made them seem less human: `https://www.businessinsider.com/replika-chatbot-users-dont-like-nsfw-sexual-content-bans-2023-2`.

7. Use cases for Azure OpenAI Service: `https://learn.microsoft.com/en-us/legal/cognitive-services/openai/transparency-note`.

8. Azure OpenAI, Code of Conduct: `https://learn.microsoft.com/en-us/legal/cognitive-services/openai/code-of-conduct`.

9. Large language models help decipher clinical notes: `https://www.csail.mit.edu/news/large-language-models-help-decipher-clinical-notes`.

10. OpenAI: `https://openai.com/`. OpenAI is a research laboratory consisting of the for-profit technological company OpenAI LP, and its parent company, the nonprofit OpenAI Inc.

11. Azure OpenAI: `https://azure.microsoft.com/en-us/services/openai/`. Azure OpenAI is a platform to train, deploy, and manage AI models at scale.

12. **Bidirectional Encoder Representations from Transformers (BERT)**: `https://github.com/google-research/bert`. BERT is a state-of-the-art language model developed by Google.

13. **GPT-3**: `https://openai.com/gpt-3/GPT-3`. GPT-3 is a language model developed by OpenAI.

14. ChatGPT: `https://github.com/openai/gpt-3`. ChatGPT is a conversational AI language model developed using OpenAI's GPT-3.

Index

Packtpub.com

Subscribe to our online digital library for full access to over 7,000 books and videos, as well as industry leading tools to help you plan your personal development and advance your career. For more information, please visit our website.

Why subscribe?

- Spend less time learning and more time coding with practical eBooks and Videos from over 4,000 industry professionals

- Improve your learning with Skill Plans built especially for you

- Get a free eBook or video every month

- Fully searchable for easy access to vital information

- Copy and paste, print, and bookmark content

Did you know that Packt offers eBook versions of every book published, with PDF and ePub files available? You can upgrade to the eBook version at packtpub.com and as a print book customer, you are entitled to a discount on the eBook copy. Get in touch with us at customercare@packtpub.com for more details.

At www.packtpub.com, you can also read a collection of free technical articles, sign up for a range of free newsletters, and receive exclusive discounts and offers on Packt books and eBooks.

Other Books You May Enjoy

If you enjoyed this book, you may be interested in these other books by Packt:

Natural Language Understanding with Python

Deborah A. Dahl

ISBN: 978-1-80461-342-9

- Explore the uses and applications of different NLP techniques
- Understand practical data acquisition and system evaluation workflows
- Build cutting-edge and practical NLP applications to solve problems
- Master NLP development from selecting an application to deployment
- Optimize NLP application maintenance after deployment
- Build a strong foundation in neural networks and deep learning for NLU

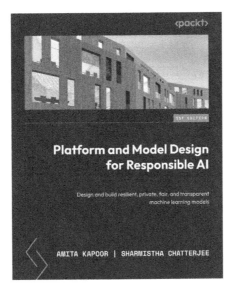

Platform and Model Design for Responsible AI

Amita Kapoor, Sharmistha Chatterjee

ISBN: 978-1-80323-707-7

- Understand the threats and risks involved in ML models
- Discover varying levels of risk mitigation strategies and risk tiering tools
- Apply traditional and deep learning optimization techniques efficiently
- Build auditable and interpretable ML models and feature stores
- Understand the concept of uncertainty and explore model explainability tools
- Develop models for different clouds including AWS, Azure, and GCP
- Explore ML orchestration tools such as Kubeflow and Vertex AI
- Incorporate privacy and fairness in ML models from design to deployment

Packt is searching for authors like you

If you're interested in becoming an author for Packt, please visit `authors.packtpub.com` and apply today. We have worked with thousands of developers and tech professionals, just like you, to help them share their insight with the global tech community. You can make a general application, apply for a specific hot topic that we are recruiting an author for, or submit your own idea.

Share Your Thoughts

Now you've finished *Responsible AI in the Enterprise*, we'd love to hear your thoughts! If you purchased the book from Amazon, please click here to go straight to the Amazon review page for this book and share your feedback or leave a review on the site that you purchased it from.

Your review is important to us and the tech community and will help us make sure we're delivering excellent quality content.

Download a free PDF copy of this book

Thanks for purchasing this book!

Do you like to read on the go but are unable to carry your print books everywhere? Is your eBook purchase not compatible with the device of your choice?

Don't worry, now with every Packt book you get a DRM-free PDF version of that book at no cost.

Read anywhere, any place, on any device. Search, copy, and paste code from your favorite technical books directly into your application.

The perks don't stop there, you can get exclusive access to discounts, newsletters, and great free content in your inbox daily

Follow these simple steps to get the benefits:

1. Scan the QR code or visit the link below

https://packt.link/free-ebook/978-1-80323-052-8

2. Submit your proof of purchase

3. That's it! We'll send your free PDF and other benefits to your email directly

Made in United States
North Haven, CT
21 October 2023